THE ULTIMATE
DIGITAL SAT
MASTERCLASS

Break Through the SAT Barrier: 5 Full Tests, 10 Online Exams, 500 Flashcards, and a 98% Pass Rate Guaranteed!

To get the 500 Flashcards, and 10 Online Practice Tests to Excel on Your Exams, just go to page 247 and scan the code

By
Roman Row

GET YOUR 8 DIGITAL SAT BONUSES

SCAN HERE TO DOWNLOAD THEM

Disclaimer

The questions and reading passages presented in this book, The Ultimate Digital SAT Masterclass, have been meticulously crafted by the author using a variety of online resources, including official SAT practice tests. These materials have been adapted, modified, and created anew to suit the instructional purposes of this masterclass.

It is important to note that while every effort has been made to ensure the quality and accuracy of the questions and passages, they are not endorsed by the College Board, the organization responsible for the SAT exam. Additionally, the questions and passages in this masterclass are not indicative of actual SAT exam questions, and no guarantee is made regarding their resemblance to questions that may appear on the official SAT exam.

Furthermore, any similarities between the questions and passages in this masterclass and those found on official SAT exams are purely coincidental. The primary goal of this masterclass is to provide students with comprehensive practice and instruction to aid in their preparation for the SAT exam.

By using this masterclass, readers acknowledge and understand that the questions and passages are for educational purposes only and are not intended to replicate the exact content of the SAT exam. The author and publisher assume no responsibility for any consequences resulting from the use or misuse of the materials presented herein

Table of Contents

Practice Test 3 with Detailed Answers and Explanations   130

Practice Test 4 with Detailed Answers and Explanations   168

Practice Test 4 Answers   193

Introduction

WELCOME TO 21-DAY DIGITAL SAT PREP, WHICH AIMS TO GUIDE HIGH SCHOOL STUDENTS THROUGH A COMPREHENSIVE PREPARATION PROGRAM FOR THE REDESIGNED DIGITAL SAT.

As an experienced SAT instructor and tutor, I have worked with thousands of students over the past decade to help maximize their SAT scores and gain admission to top colleges. Throughout my career, I have witnessed firsthand the evolving landscape of standardized testing as the SAT transitioned to a digital format in 2023. This new digital SAT presents both challenges and opportunities for test-takers that differ considerably from the prior paper-based version of the exam.

It is my goal with this book to thoroughly prepare students for the specific skills and strategies required to excel on the digital SAT. Unlike other SAT prep books currently on the market, this resource is uniquely designed around the digital testing modality with targeted lessons, drills, and practice tailored for success in the contemporary digital testing environment. Over the course of 21 days, readers will embark on an intensive SAT prep journey addressing every major aspect of the redesigned exam. They will gain a comprehensive understanding of the digital SAT structure and format, master core reading, writing, and math skills, and learn invaluable test-taking techniques optimized for the digital testing experience. Additionally, readers will benefit from 5 full-length practice tests modeled after the actual digital SAT to gain extensive practice navigating the digital platform and familiarity with adaptive testing.

In part one of this book, students are introduced to the evolution of the SAT and an overview of the digital testing format. Here, they will learn about the transition from paper-based testing to computer-based adaptive assessments. Students will gain insider knowledge about the structure and flow of the digital SAT, with detailed explanations of the Reading, Writing and Language, Math, and Essay (optional) modules. Most importantly, part one equips students to confidently navigate the digital testing environment through comprehensive guidance on the ins and outs of the online testing platform.

Part two delves into the Reading and Writing portions of the exam with a focus first on core comprehension, vocabulary, and writing strategies. Students will learn how to analyze texts, identify main ideas and supporting details, integrate textual evidence, and determine the meaning of words in context. Techniques for efficiently answering passage-based multiple-choice and selected-response questions are provided in-depth. Part two also offers extensive lessons and drills targeting the grammar, punctuation, and language conventions assessed in the Writing module. Advanced reading skills, such as making inferences and determining central ideas and relationships, are then covered along with comprehensive reviews and full-length practice tests.

The mathematics content and strategies for excelling are addressed at length in part three. Students learn essential algebra, geometry, trigonometry, and statistics skills assessed on the digital SAT through targeted lessons and practice questions. Calculator functionality in the Desmos digital calculator applet is explored, and useful shortcuts are taught. Students gain mastery over all SAT Math question types, including multiple-choice, grid-in, and multi-step word problems. Carefully designed in-depth reviews prepare students to tackle even the most challenging math concepts and questions confidently on test day.

In part four, all-important digital SAT strategies and full-length practice tests are provided. Students learn valuable time-saving techniques, approach methods for question types, and techniques for managing stress and mental stamina. Five complete digital practice tests then allow for realistic practice applying strategies within the digital testing interface. Detailed explanations of answers provide insights to maximize learning.

By the end, you will exit armed not only with content mastery but enhanced test-taking abilities tailored for the digital platform. The lessons, drills, and strategies shared will empower you to feel ownership over your performance and walk into the test center confidently and in command of the adaptive computerized testing process. Most importantly, you will gain an advantage over other test-takers merely relying on paper guides by being fully equipped to thrive with the new digital tools, protocols, and uncertainties.

This book promises to be your one-stop resource for fully preparing for all aspects of the computer-based SAT. It offers the tailored preparation approach critical to ensuring top performance. Let's get started on your individualized program for digital SAT success!

Understanding the Digital SAT

The Evolution of the SAT: Transition to Digital

IN A SIGNIFICANT SHIFT TOWARDS MODERNIZING THE COLLEGE ADMISSIONS PROCESS, THE COLLEGE BOARD HAS ANNOUNCED THAT THE SAT WILL TRANSITION TO A FULLY DIGITAL FORMAT STARTING IN 2023 FOR INTERNATIONAL TEST-TAKERS AND 2024 FOR U.S.-BASED STUDENTS.

This move marks a new era in the history of the SAT, which has been a pivotal factor in college admissions since its inception in 1926.

The decision to adopt a digital format for the SAT comes as a response to the changing needs of students, educators, and colleges in an increasingly technology-driven world. The digital SAT aims to provide a more secure, flexible, and student-friendly testing experience while maintaining the rigor and fairness that colleges rely on for admissions decisions.

One of the primary motivations behind the transition to digital is to address concerns about test security and cheating. With the digital format, each student will receive a unique test form, making it virtually impossible to share answers or benefit from leaked questions. Additionally, the digital SAT will enable more efficient and reliable administration, reducing the risk of human error and logistical challenges associated with paper-based testing.

The shift to digital technology also presents an opportunity to enhance students' testing experience. The digital SAT will feature a more intuitive and user-friendly interface, with built-in tools such as a timer, calculator, and reference information. Students will have the ability to flag questions for review, navigate easily between questions, and track their progress throughout the test.

Moreover, the transition to digital allows for a more personalized and adaptive testing experience. The digital SAT will employ adaptive testing technology, which adjusts the difficulty of questions based on a student's performance. This approach enables a more precise measurement of a student's skills and knowledge while reducing the potential for "guessing" strategies.

Overview of the Digital SAT Structure

FIRST STEP SIGN-IN FOR EXAM

The SAT is administered several times a year at designated high schools and testing centers across the United States and at English-speaking schools abroad. This section outlines the registration process for the exam, including when to register and the approved payment methods.

DECIDING ON THE TIMING FOR TAKING AND RETAKING THE SAT

The SAT is available about seven times annually, and you are free to sit for the exam multiple times. It is recommended to attempt the SAT two or three times, though more attempts are allowed if needed. This is a common approach among high school students.

- Begin in your sophomore fall: Engage with the PSAT/NMSQT, also known as the Preliminary SAT/National Merit Scholarship Qualifying Test. As a 10th grader, this serves mainly as a preparatory and introductory test to the upcoming series of examinations.

- Continue in your junior fall: Take the PSAT/NMSQT once more, but this time, it counts towards scholarship eligibility and special programs if you perform well.

- In your junior spring: Sit for the SAT primarily as a practice opportunity, although you can choose to submit your scores if they are satisfactory. Note that an unscored practice test is also an option, though it doesn't mimic the actual exam environment as closely. It's not uncommon for some juniors to take the SAT twice during this period.

- In your senior fall: Attempt the SAT seriously, as these scores will likely be used in your college applications. If applying for an early decision, aim to take the exam in October or November.

- In your senior winter: You get another opportunity to enhance your score, or, if you've already achieved well, another chance to secure a scholarship. At this stage, you should be well-prepared to succeed, as this may be your final attempt.

The SAT is generally scheduled on a Saturday, but alternate arrangements are available for those who cannot test on this day due to religious obligations. If this applies to you, your SAT could be scheduled on a Sunday or the following Wednesday. Ensure to provide a letter from your religious leader along with your registration. It's advisable to register early to secure your preferred testing location. You can request a specific test site during registration, but if it's full, an alternate will be provided. Therefore, it's best to register as soon as possible, preferably at a familiar location like your own high school.

TEST REGISTRATION OPTIONS

You have several methods to register for the SAT: online, by mail, or by phone if you are a returning test taker.

For online registration, visit *www.sat.collegeboard.org/register*. The process involves creating an account and selecting a test center and date. You'll need a credit card or PayPal to make the payment and a digital photo to upload. Ensure your photo is a clear headshot, showing your full face, with no others in the picture. Religious head coverings are permitted.

Mail registration is necessary if you are under 13 or over 21 years old or if you need a Sunday test date for religious reasons.

You can obtain a registration form from your school guidance counselor. Homeschoolers should contact the nearest public or private high school or reach out to the College Board Customer Service for assistance. When registering by mail, attach a photo and include your payment details (credit card, U.S. bank check, or bank draft).

The College Board Customer Service can be reached at 866-756-7346 within the U.S. and at 212-713-7789 internationally. For those with hearing impairments, the TTY number is 888-857-2477 within the U.S. and 609-882-4118 internationally. You can also write to the College Board at: College Board SSD Program, P.O. Box 8060, Mount Vernon, IL 62864-0060.

Regardless of your registration method, you'll be prompted to join the Student Search Service. Agreeing to participate allows colleges, universities, and scholarship organizations to learn about you. While the influx of communications can be overwhelming, it's an opportunity to connect with educational institutions and discover potential scholarships or programs ideally suited to your needs.

SECURING FINANCIAL ASSISTANCE FOR FEES

If you're in need of financial support, consider applying for a fee waiver, which is offered to economically disadvantaged high school juniors and seniors residing in the United States, Puerto Rico, and other U.S. territories. (U.S. citizens living abroad may also qualify for these waivers.) Additionally, the College Board provides four free score reports and four college application fee waiver requests. The College Board strives to assist where possible.

Consult your school counselor for applications for fee waivers. (For homeschoolers, obtaining a form from a local high school is advised.) Be mindful to sidestep any unnecessary fees. Extra charges may apply for late registration, modifications to your registration, expedited score delivery, detailed score analysis, and similar services.

STRUCTURE OF SAT

The digital SAT spans 2 hours and 14 minutes and comprises 98 questions, divided into two main sections: Reading and Writing and Math. Both sections are evenly split into two modules.

Here's a breakdown of the test structure:

COMPONENT	TIME ALLOTTED (minutes)	NUMBER OF QUESTIONS/TASKS
Reading and Writing	64 (two 32-minute mod-ules)	54
Math	70 (two 35-minute mod-ules)	44
TOTAL	134	98

Most questions are multiple-choice, though some math questions require entering the answer directly. There's no penalty for guessing, so it's better to guess than to leave a response blank.

SCORING SYSTEM

The scoring system for the digital SAT is designed to be on par with the traditional paper format, with a total possible score of 1600. In this structure, each of the two main sections - Reading and Writing and Math - is graded on a scale from 200 to 800. The scores from these sections are then combined, resulting in a cumulative score ranging from 400 to 1600.

To maintain consistency and fairness between the digital and paper versions of the SAT, extensive statistical analyses have been conducted. This ensures that a particular score, say 1250, reflects the same level of proficiency and achievement on both the digital and paper formats of the exam.

Passing Score for the SAT

The SAT doesn't have a specific "passing" score. Instead, the College Board offers benchmarks that reflect a student's preparedness for college and career:

· SAT Math: Scoring 530+ means a 75% likelihood of achieving at least a C in introductory college math courses.

· SAT Reading and Writing: Scoring 480+ indicates a 75% probability of earning a C or better in entry-level college classes related to literature, writing, social sciences, or history.

Good SAT Score Overall

A strong SAT score is one that enables you to secure admission to your desired colleges, including your safety schools. To set a target score, investigate the middle 50% of admitted students' test scores for each school you're considering. This data is available in the Common Data Set (CDS) of each institution.

Average SAT Score

The College Board reports an average SAT score of 1050. Scores exceeding this are deemed above average, while scoring 1350 or higher places you in the 90th percentile, increasing your chances at more competitive universities.

Colleges employ various score-use policies when assessing SAT results:

· Superscoring: Some colleges consider your top score from each section, even if they're from separate test administrations.

· Score Choice: This allows you to decide which scores to share with colleges.

- Highest Total Score: Certain colleges look at your best overall score, irrespective of test date.

- Requiring All Scores: A few schools ask for scores from every SAT attempt.

Many universities now offer test-optional admissions. If you're applying to such a school and are dissatisfied with your SAT performance, prioritize strengthening other aspects of your application.

SAT SCORE EXPECTATIONS FOR WELL-KNOWN U.S. COLLEGES:

The table below presents the middle 50% SAT score ranges for the Class of 2026 at several prominent U.S. universities:

COLLEGE/UNIVERSITY	MIDDLE 50% SCORE RANGE
Boston University	1370-1480
Bowdoin College	1340-1520
Brown University	1500-1560
Columbia University	1500-1560
Cornell University	1470-1550
Emory University	1450-1530
Georgetown University	1410-1540
Harvard University	1490-1580
Massachusetts Institute of Technology	1520-1570
New York University	1470-1560
Northeastern University	1450-1535
Northwestern University	1500-1560
Pomona College	1480-1540
Princeton University	1510-1570
Rice University	1500-1560
Stanford University	1500-1570
Tufts University	1460-1540
Tulane University	1400-1500
University of Southern California	1460-1540
Vanderbilt University	1490-1570
Vassar College	1440-1510
Washington and Lee University	1410-1533
Washington University in St. Louis	1500-1570
Wesleyan University	1310-1505
Yale University	1470-1560

READING AND WRITING COMPONENT

The Reading and Writing Section

The Reading and Writing section comprise short passages or passage pairs followed by a single multiple-choice question. Questions represent four content domains: Craft and Structure, Information and Ideas, Standard English Conventions, and Expression of Ideas. Questions testing similar skills are grouped together and arranged from easiest to hardest.

What the Reading and Writing Passages Are Like

Passages range from 25 to 150 words and cover subjects such as literature, history/social studies, the humanities, and science.

What the Reading and Writing Questions Are Like

Questions fall into four content domains:

1.   Information and Ideas

· Tests comprehension, analysis, and reasoning skills.

· Requires locating, interpreting, evaluating, and integrating information from texts and informational graphics (tables, bar graphs, and line graphs).

2.   Craft and Structure

· Measures comprehension, vocabulary, analysis, synthesis, and reasoning.

· Involves understanding and using high-utility words in context, evaluating texts rhetorically, and making connections between related texts.

3.   Expression of Ideas

· Assesses the ability to revise texts to improve written expression and meet specific rhetorical goals.

4.   Standard English Conventions

· Focuses on editing text to conform to core conventions of sentence structure, usage, and punctuation.

The Math Section

The Math section emphasizes areas crucial for college and career success: Algebra, Advanced Math, Problem-Solving and Data Analysis, and Geometry and Trigonometry. The section is divided into two modules, featuring multiple-choice and student-produced response questions. These questions measure fluency, understanding, and application of essential math concepts and skills.

Approximately 30% of Math questions are set in real-world contexts, requiring you to apply math skills to science, social studies, or real-world scenarios.

In the Math section, which is 70 minutes long with 44 questions, the questions are evenly divided into two 35-minute modules. Each module contains a mix of upto 75% multiple-choice questions and upto 25% student-produced responses. The Math section covers a broad spectrum of mathematical domains, including:

1. Algebra (approximately 35% of the section): This domain covers fundamental algebraic concepts such as linear equations and inequalities, systems of equations, and function properties.

2. Advanced Math (also around 35% of the section): This area delves into more complex topics, such as nonlinear equations and functions, including quadratic, polynomial, and exponential functions.

3. Problem-Solving and Data Analysis (about 15% of the section): Questions in this domain test ability in statistical analysis, including understanding distributions, probability, and evaluating statistical claims.

4. Geometry and Trigonometry (roughly 15% of the section): This domain assesses knowledge in geometry, including concepts related to area, volume, and trigonometry.

Like the Reading and Writing section, the Math section's questions are organized by difficulty, starting with simpler questions and progressively moving towards more challenging ones.

Navigating the Digital Testing Environment

The digital SAT will be administered on a secure testing application that students can access on school-owned devices or their personal computers. The testing application will provide a consistent and user-friendly interface across various devices, ensuring that all students have a comparable testing experience.

One of the key features of the digital testing environment is the built-in tools and resources available to students during the test. These tools are designed to enhance the testing experience and provide students with the necessary support to demonstrate their skills and knowledge effectively.

1. Timer: The digital SAT will include a countdown timer that displays the remaining time for each section. This timer will help students pace themselves and manage their time effectively throughout the test. Students can use the timer to allocate their time strategically, ensuring that they have sufficient time to answer all questions and review their work.

2. Calculator: For the Math with Calculator section, students will have access to a built-in digital calculator. The digital calculator will include standard functions such as basic arithmetic, square roots, and trigonometric functions. Students should familiarize themselves with the digital calculator's interface and functionality so that they can use it efficiently during the test.

3. Reference Information: The digital SAT will provide relevant reference information, such as formulas and definitions, within the testing application. This reference information will be easily accessible to students during the test, reducing the need to memorize formulas and allowing them to focus on applying their knowledge to solve problems.

4. Flagging and Reviewing Questions: Students will have the ability to flag questions they want to review later during the test. This feature allows students to manage their time effectively by focusing on answering questions they are more confident about first and returning to flagged questions if time permits. Students can easily navigate between flagged questions and track their progress throughout the test.

In addition to these built-in tools, the digital testing environment offers several advantages over the traditional paper-based format. For example, students can easily navigate between questions, zoom in on passages or figures, and highlight text within the testing application. These features enhance the readability and accessibility of the test content, making it easier for students to engage with the material and demonstrate their understanding.

REQUESTING ACCOMMODATIONS FOR THE SAT

The SAT aims to ensure fairness and accessibility for all examinees, including those with disabilities. Even if you don't initially think you qualify for accommodations, it's worth reviewing this information as you might find a beneficial option.

Accommodations for Learning Disabilities

If you have a learning disability, you might be eligible to take the SAT under modified conditions. Start by obtaining an Eligibility Form from your school counselor. If you are homeschooled, contact a nearby high school to acquire this form. Additionally, you can request the College Board Services for Students with Disabilities brochure from your school's college counseling office. If unavailable, reach out directly to the College Board or visit their website at the College Board accommodations page.

Once approved for accommodations on any College Board exam (including AP tests, SAT Subject Tests, or the PSAT/NMSQT), the certification applies across all College Board exams unless the accommodations are required due to a temporary condition.

Submit your Eligibility Form well before your expected test date. Approved accommodations might include additional time—up to 50% more per test section. For instance, if a typical test section allows 32 minutes, you would receive 48 minutes.

Accommodations for Physical Disabilities

The SAT also offers various physical accommodations at no extra cost, such as wheelchair access, large-print exams, and more. To arrange these, submit your Eligibility Form promptly so that the College Board can review any necessary documentation and organize your accommodations. Documentation can be submitted on paper or online. For more information, visit the College Board accommodations page.

If you encounter a physical issue like a broken arm close to your exam date and cannot reschedule easily, contact the College Board Customer Service. You'll need to explain your situation and have your physician complete the necessary forms to request the required accommodations.

Adaptive Testing

Adaptive testing can be broadly categorized into two forms. In the type known as question-level adaptive testing, exemplified by Smarter Balanced or MAP assessments, the next question you face is determined by your response to the previous one. Contrastingly, multistage adaptive testing involves completing groups of questions, with each group's difficulty tailored based on your performance in the preceding group.

Assessments related to the SAT and PSAT employ a multistage adaptive approach. These tests are structured into sections (Reading and Writing and Math), each split into two modules of equal length and timing. After finishing a set of questions in the initial module, you progress to the subsequent module, where the questions are selected based on your initial module's performance.

Here are three key advantages of the multistage adaptive format that enhance your testing experience:

1. It allows for a more efficient assessment of the same skills and knowledge, reducing the SAT's duration to just over two hours from three.

2. Unlike many question-level adaptive tests, this format permits you to navigate between questions within a module, enabling you to review or return to questions as needed without any penalties for incorrect guesses, thus encouraging you to attempt every question.

3. This testing method does not require a constant internet connection, allowing you to proceed with the test even if you experience connectivity issues.

The initial module in each section (Reading and Writing, Math) contains half of the section's total questions, presenting a diverse array of question difficulties and topics. Your performance in this module determines whether the subsequent module will predominantly feature questions of higher or lower difficulty. After completing the second module, your score for the section is computed based on your responses to all questions in both modules.

PART 2

Mastering Reading and Writing

Strategies for Reading Comprehension

Developing strong reading comprehension skills is essential for success in the Evidence-Based Reading and Writing (EBRW) section of the Digital SAT. Here are some effective strategies to help you better understand and analyze the passages you'll encounter:

PREVIEW THE PASSAGE

Before diving into the details, take a moment to preview the passage by reading the introduction and conclusion. This will give you a general idea of the main topic and the author's purpose, helping you to understand the context better as you read through the entire text.

ACTIVELY ENGAGE WITH THE TEXT

Reading actively means being fully present and engaged with the material. As you read, ask yourself questions about the content, make predictions about what might come next, and try to connect the ideas presented to your knowledge and experiences. This process of active reading will help you to retain and comprehend the information better.

IDENTIFY KEY INFORMATION

Keep an eye out for important details such as names, dates, figures, and other specific information that might be referenced in the questions. Underlining or taking brief notes can help you quickly locate these key points when needed.

USE CONTEXT CLUES

When you come across unfamiliar words or phrases, try to decipher their meaning by examining the context in which they appear. Look for clues in the surrounding sentences or paragraphs that can help you infer the meaning of the unknown term.

BREAK DOWN COMPLEX SENTENCES

If you encounter a particularly lengthy or convoluted sentence, try breaking it down into smaller, more manageable parts. Identify the main subject and verb, and then separate any subordinate clauses or modifying phrases. This will help you to grasp the core meaning of the sentence better.

SUMMARIZE AND PARAPHRASE

After reading each paragraph or section, take a moment to summarize the main points in your own words. This process of paraphrasing helps to reinforce your understanding of the material and can make it easier to recall the information later.

MANAGE YOUR TIME EFFECTIVELY

The EBRW section is timed, so it's crucial to pace yourself appropriately. Don't get bogged down on any one question or passage. If you're stuck, make an educated guess and move on. You can always come back to challenging questions if time allows.

PRACTICE ACTIVE READING REGULARLY

The more you practice active reading techniques, the more natural and effective they will become. Make a habit of applying these strategies whenever you read, whether it's for school, work, or personal enjoyment. Regular practice will help you to build your comprehension skills over time.

Mastering Vocabulary in Context

A strong vocabulary is a key component of success in the Evidence-Based Reading and Writing (EBRW) section of the Digital SAT. However, memorizing long lists of words and definitions is not the most effective approach. Instead, focus on mastering vocabulary in context by learning to decipher the meaning of unfamiliar words based on the information provided in the passage. Here are some strategies to help you build your contextual vocabulary skills:

PAY ATTENTION TO CONTEXT CLUES

When you encounter an unfamiliar word, look for clues in the surrounding sentences or paragraphs that can help you infer its meaning. These clues might include synonyms (words with similar meanings), antonyms (words with opposite meanings), or examples that illustrate the word's definition.

Example: "The politician's platitudes, filled with overused and insincere statements, failed to impress the audience." In this sentence, the word "platitudes" is unfamiliar, but the context clues "overused" and "insincere statements" help to reveal its meaning.

EXAMINE WORD ROOTS, PREFIXES, AND SUFFIXES

Many English words are formed by combining smaller parts, such as roots, prefixes, and suffixes. Familiarizing yourself with these components can help you to decipher the meaning of unfamiliar words more easily.

Example: The word "malevolent" consists of the prefix "mal-" (bad or evil) and the root "volent" (wishing or desiring). By understanding these parts, you can infer that "malevolent" means having or showing a desire to cause harm.

USE THE PROCESS OF ELIMINATION

When answering vocabulary questions on the Digital SAT, you can often use the process of elimination to narrow down the answer choices. Start by eliminating any options that are clearly incorrect based on the context of the passage. Then, carefully consider the remaining choices to determine the best fit.

READ WIDELY AND REGULARLY

One of the most effective ways to build your vocabulary is to read extensively across a variety of genres and subjects. As you read, make a habit of looking up unfamiliar words and recording them in a vocabulary journal along with their definitions and example sentences. Regular exposure to a wide range of texts will help you to encounter new words in context and reinforce your understanding of their meanings.

PRACTICE USING NEW WORDS

Once you've learned a new word, try to incorporate it into your own speaking and writing. Using a word in context helps to solidify your understanding of its meaning and makes it more likely that you'll remember it in the future. Look for opportunities to use your newly acquired vocabulary in conversations, essays, or even social media posts.

CREATE VISUAL ASSOCIATIONS

Some people find it helpful to create visual associations or mnemonic devices to remember new words. For example, you might associate the word "incandescent" (glowing with intense heat) with the image of a brightly burning light bulb. These visual cues can make it easier to recall the word and its meaning when you encounter it in the future.

REVIEW AND REINFORCE REGULARLY

Building a strong vocabulary is an ongoing process that requires regular review and reinforcement. Set aside time each day or week to review the words you've learned using flashcards, quizzes, or other study tools. Consistently revisiting and applying your vocabulary knowledge will help to ensure that it sticks with you over time.

Effective Writing and Language Techniques

The Writing and Language section of the Digital SAT assesses your ability to recognize and correct errors in grammar, punctuation, and style, as well as to improve the overall clarity and effectiveness of a given passage. To excel in this section, it's essential to master a range of writing and language techniques. Here are some key strategies to keep in mind:

ENSURE SUBJECT-VERB AGREEMENT

One of the most common errors tested in the Writing and Language section is subject-verb agreement. Make sure that the verb in each sentence agrees with its subject in number (singular or plural) and person (first, second, or third).

Example: "The committee is meeting today to discuss the proposal." (The singular subject "committee" agrees with singular verb "is.")

MAINTAIN CONSISTENT VERB TENSES

Verb tenses should remain consistent throughout a passage unless there is a clear reason for a shift. Pay attention to the overall context and timeline of the passage to determine which tense is most appropriate.

Example: "The researcher conducted the experiment last month and is currently analyzing the results." (The past tense "conducted" is used for the completed action, while the present tense "is analyzing" is used for the ongoing action.)

USE PRECISE AND CONCISE LANGUAGE

The Writing and Language section often tests your ability to recognize and eliminate redundant, vague, or irrelevant language. Look for opportunities to replace weak or repetitive phrasing with more precise and concise alternatives.

Example: "The very tall skyscraper towered over the city." (The phrase "very tall" is redundant and can be eliminated: "The skyscraper towered over the city.")

VARY SENTENCE STRUCTURE

To improve the flow and readability of a passage, look for opportunities to vary the structure and length of sentences. Combine short, choppy sentences or break up long, complex ones to create a more balanced and engaging text.

Example: "The team worked diligently. They completed the project ahead of schedule." (These two short sentences can be combined into one: "The team worked diligently and completed the project ahead of schedule.")

MAINTAIN A FORMAL AND OBJECTIVE TONE

The Writing and Language section often includes passages from academic or professional contexts, which require a formal and objective tone. Avoid using slang, colloquialisms, or personal opinions unless they are specifically appropriate for the given context.

Example: "The research findings suggest that the hypothesis is supported." (This sentence maintains a formal, objective tone appropriate for a scientific context.)

ENSURE LOGICAL AND COHESIVE ORGANIZATION

Pay attention to the overall structure and organization of the passage. Each paragraph should have a clear topic sentence and support its main idea with relevant details and examples. Transitions between paragraphs should be smooth and logical, guiding the reader through the text.

PRACTICE ACTIVE READING AND EDITING

As you read through the passages in the Writing and Language section, actively look for potential errors and opportunities for improvement. Read each sentence carefully, considering its grammar, clarity, and effectiveness in the context of the overall passage. Practice making quick, decisive edits to strengthen the text.

REVIEW AND APPLY GRAMMAR RULES CONSISTENTLY

Familiarize yourself with the key grammar rules tested on the SAT, such as those related to pronoun usage, parallel structure, and misplaced modifiers. Consistently review and apply these rules in your own writing practice to reinforce your understanding.

By mastering these writing and language techniques, you'll be better prepared to identify and correct errors, improve the clarity and coherence of passages, and demonstrate your command of standard English conventions on the Digital SAT. Remember, the key to success in this section is not just knowing the rules but being able to apply them effectively in context. Regular practice with a variety of passages and question types will help you to build your skills and confidence over time.

Tackling Craft and Structure Questions

The Craft and Structure questions in the Evidence-Based Reading and Writing (EBRW) section of the Digital SAT assess your understanding of how an author constructs a passage and conveys meaning through various literary devices, word choices, and structural elements. To effectively tackle these questions, you'll need to develop a keen eye for analyzing the writer's craft and the overall structure of the text. Here are some strategies to help you approach Craft and Structure questions with confidence:

IDENTIFY THE AUTHOR'S PURPOSE AND MAIN IDEA

Before diving into the specific details of a passage, take a moment to consider the author's overall purpose and the main idea they are trying to convey. Is the passage meant to inform, persuade, entertain, or some combination of these? Understanding the author's intent will help you to analyze the choices they make throughout the text better.

Pay attention to how the author organizes the information in the passage. Is it a straightforward, chronological narrative, or does it follow a more complex structure with flashbacks, parallel storylines, or shifting perspectives? Look for key structural elements such as the introduction, body paragraphs, and conclusion, and consider how they work together to support the main idea.

Analyze the author's tone and perspective: Tone refers to the author's attitude or stance towards the subject matter, while perspective encompasses their unique point of view. Consider how the author's word choices, sentence structures, and rhetorical devices contribute to the overall tone and perspective of the passage. Is the tone serious, humorous, sarcastic, or objective? Does the author present a biased or neutral perspective?

IDENTIFY AND INTERPRET FIGURATIVE LANGUAGE

Authors often use figurative language, such as metaphors, similes, and personification, to add depth and meaning to their writing. When you encounter these devices, take a moment to consider how they enhance the passage's themes or ideas. What comparisons are being made, and what insights do they offer into the subject matter?

Example: "The sun was a fiery orb, casting its scorching rays upon the parched earth." In this sentence, the sun is personified as a "fiery orb," emphasizing its intense heat and the dry, lifeless state of the earth.

CONSIDER THE CONNOTATIONS OF WORD CHOICES

Authors often choose words with specific connotations or emotional associations to convey a particular mood or meaning. Pay attention to the subtle implications of the words used in the passage, and consider how they contribute to the overall tone and theme.

Example: "The politician's speech was filled with grandiose promises and lofty ideals." The words "grandiose" and "lofty" suggest that the politician's promises are exaggerated and unrealistic, casting doubt on their sincerity.

ANALYZE THE FUNCTION OF SPECIFIC DETAILS

Craft and Structure questions may ask you to determine the purpose or function of a particular detail, example, or piece of evidence in the passage. Consider how each element contributes to the author's overall argument or message. Does it provide supporting evidence, illustrate a key concept, or offer a counterargument?

PRACTICE CLOSE READING AND ANNOTATION

To effectively analyze a passage's craft and structure, you'll need to engage in close reading and active annotation. As you read, underline or highlight keywords, phrases, and structural elements that stand out to you. Make notes in the margins about the author's choices and their effects on the overall meaning of the passage. This process of active reading will help you to internalize the text's key features and make connections between ideas.

Familiarize yourself with common literary terms and concepts, such as theme, tone, irony, and point of view. Practice identifying and analyzing these elements in a variety of texts, from short stories and poems to non-fiction articles and essays. The more comfortable you become with these concepts, the easier it will be to recognize and interpret them on the Digital SAT.

The key is not just recognizing literary devices and structural elements but understanding how they work together to create meaning and convey the author's purpose. With regular practice and close reading, you'll be able to approach Craft and Structure questions with greater insight and confidence.

Deciphering Information and Ideas in Texts

As you read through a passage, try to identify the author's central claim or main argument. This is the overarching point they are trying to make, which various pieces of evidence and reasoning should support throughout the text. Understanding the central claim will help you better grasp the passage's key ideas and how they are developed.

In addition to the central claim, passages will typically include several main ideas that contribute to the overall argument. Specific details, examples, or pieces of evidence usually support these main ideas. As you read, try to differentiate between the broader main ideas and the more specific supporting details. This will help you to understand the hierarchy of information in the passage and how the various parts work together. Authors may use various types of evidence to support their claims, such as facts, statistics, expert opinions, anecdotes, or logical reasoning. As you encounter these different forms of evidence, consider their relevance, credibility, and persuasive power. How effectively does each piece of evidence support the author's main points?

Every author brings their own assumptions, biases, and perspectives to their writing. As you read, try to identify any underlying assumptions or biases that may be shaping the author's arguments or influencing their interpretation of evidence. Recognizing these biases can help you to evaluate the strengths and limitations of the author's reasoning.

Some questions may ask you to consider the implications or consequences of the ideas presented in the passage. To answer these questions effectively, think about how the author's arguments or conclusions might play out in real-world situations. What would be the likely results or effects of implementing the ideas discussed?

Deciphering information and ideas often requires you to synthesize information from different parts of the passage. As you read, look for connections and relationships between ideas that may be presented in separate paragraphs or sections. Consider how these various pieces of information work together to support the author's overall message. To effectively decipher information and ideas, engage in active reading and take notes as you go. Underline or highlight key claims, main ideas, and supporting details. Jot down brief summaries or questions in the margins to help you process and retain the information. This active engagement with the text will make it easier to locate and analyze key points when answering questions.

When faced with a challenging question, use the process of elimination to narrow down the answer choices. Start by identifying any options that are clearly inconsistent with the information provided in the passage. Then, carefully evaluate the remaining choices, looking for the one that best aligns with the key ideas and evidence presented.

Advanced Reading Skills and Practice Drills

One advanced reading skill to focus on is the ability to identify and analyze the author's purpose and perspective. As you read, ask yourself questions such as: Why did the author write this passage? What message are they trying to convey? How does their perspective shape the way they present information? For example, consider a passage about the benefits of renewable energy written by an environmental activist. The author's purpose may be to persuade readers to support clean energy initiatives, and their perspective as activists may lead them to emphasize the positive aspects of renewable energy while downplaying any potential drawbacks.

Another important skill is the ability to recognize and interpret figurative language and rhetorical devices. Authors often use techniques such as metaphors, similes, irony, and repetition to add depth and meaning to their writing. For instance, a passage might describe a person's emotions as "a rollercoaster ride, with soaring highs and plummeting lows." This metaphor helps to convey the intensity and unpredictability of the person's feelings in a vivid, relatable way. By identifying and analyzing these devices, you can better understand the author's intended meaning and appreciate the artistry of their language.

To practice these advanced reading skills, engage in targeted reading drills that challenge you to read critically and analytically. One effective drill is to read a short passage and then write a brief summary or analysis of its key points, purpose, and perspective. Another useful exercise is to identify and interpret examples of figurative language or rhetorical devices in a text, explaining how they contribute to the overall meaning. As you practice these drills, aim to read a diverse range of texts, including literary fiction, non-fiction articles, and persuasive essays, to expose yourself to a variety of writing styles and techniques.

Reading and Writing: Comprehensive Review and Practice Tests

For the reading comprehension component, start by reviewing the main question types you'll encounter, such as those related to main ideas, details, inferences, and vocabulary in context. Practice identifying these question types in sample passages and developing strategies for addressing them efficiently. For example, when tackling a main idea question, focus on the passage's introduction and conclusion, as well as any topic sentences in the body paragraphs, to grasp the overarching message quickly.

Next, review the key reading skills and techniques covered in the previous sections, such as active reading, annotating, and using context clues to decipher unfamiliar words. Apply these techniques to a variety of practice passages, focusing on improving your speed and accuracy. For instance, when encountering a challenging vocabulary word, look for clues in the surrounding sentences that might help you infer its meaning, such as synonyms, antonyms, or examples.

For the writing and language component, review the main grammar, usage, and style concepts tested, such as subject-verb agreement, pronoun reference, and parallel structure. Familiarize yourself with the types of questions you'll face, such as those asking you to improve the clarity, concision, or organization of a passage. Practice applying these concepts to sample questions, paying close attention to the specific errors and improvement opportunities presented.

As you review, make use of comprehensive study resources such as grammar guides, vocabulary lists, and practice tests. These resources can help you reinforce your understanding of key concepts and build your familiarity with the format and content of the EBRW section. For example, regularly reviewing a list of commonly tested vocabulary words can help you expand your lexicon and improve your performance on questions related to word choice and meaning.

Finally, prioritize regular, timed practice to build your stamina and time management skills. Set aside dedicated study sessions to complete full-length practice tests under realistic conditions, simulating the timing and format of the actual Digital SAT. After each practice test, carefully review your answers, analyze your errors, and identify areas for improvement. By consistently practicing and reviewing, you'll develop a strong foundation in the reading and writing skills needed to succeed on test day.

PART 3

Excelling in Mathematics

Fundamental Math Concepts for the Digital SAT

To excel in the Mathematics sections of the Digital SAT, it is crucial to have a solid grasp of fundamental math concepts. These foundational skills will help you tackle a wide range of problems and provide a basis for more advanced topics. Let's review some of the key areas you should focus on:

ARITHMETIC

Brush up on your basic arithmetic skills, including operations with integers, fractions, decimals, and percentages. Make sure you are comfortable with the order of operations (PEMDAS) and can perform calculations quickly and accurately.

Example

Simplify

$(2 / 3 \times 1.5) + 0.25$

Solution:

$(2/3 \times 1.5) + 0.25$

$= 1 + 0.25$

$= 1.25$

RATIOS AND PROPORTIONS

Understand how to set up and solve proportions, as well as how to work with ratios and rates. Practice converting between fractions, decimals, and percentages.

Example

If the ratio of boys to girls in a class is 3:2 and there are 30 students in total, how many girls are in the class?

Solution:

Let x be the number of girls.

Then,

$3/2 = (30-x)/x$.

Solve for x to get x = 12 girls.

EXPONENTS AND RADICAL

Know the properties of exponents and how to simplify expressions involving them. Be comfortable working with square roots and other radicals, including rationalizing denominators.

Example

Simplify $(3^4 \times 3^{-2})^{1/2}$

Solution:

When we multiply powers with the same base, we add their exponents according to the laws of exponents. Therefore, we can combine 3^4 and 3^{-2} as follows:

$(3^4 \times 3^{-2}) = 3^{(4+(-2))} = 3^2$

Now we have the expression $(3^2)^{1/2}$. According to the power of a power rule, when we raise a power to another power, we multiply the exponents. Thus,

$(3^2)^{1/2} = 3^{2 \times 1/2} = 3^1$

Since 31 is simply 3, the simplified form of the original expression is: 3.

So, the simplified form of the expression (34×3-2)1/2 is indeed 3.

ABSOLUTE VALUE AND INEQUALITIES

Understand the concept of absolute value and how to solve equations and inequalities involving absolute value expressions. Be able to graph inequalities on a number line.

Example

Solve $|2x - 3| \leq 5$

Solution: $-5 \leq 2x - 3 \leq 5$.

Add 3 to all parts of the inequality:

$-2 \leq 2x \leq 8$.

Divide by 2:

$-1 \leq x \leq 4$.

Algebra: Strategies and Practice

Algebra is a significant component of the Digital SAT's Math sections, and having a solid understanding of algebraic concepts and strategies will greatly benefit your performance. Let's explore some key topics and practice techniques:

LINEAR EQUATIONS AND INEQUALITIES

Learn to solve linear equations and inequalities in one variable, including those involving absolute value. Practice manipulating equations to isolate the variable and interpreting the solutions.

Example

Solve $3(2x - 1) + 4 = 19$

Solution: $3(2x - 1) + 4 = 19$

$6x - 3 + 4 = 19$

$6x + 1 = 19$

$6x = 18$

$x = 3$

SYSTEMS OF LINEAR EQUATIONS

Understand how to solve systems of linear equations using substitution, elimination, or graphing. Be able to interpret the solutions in context.

Example

Solve the system of equations:

$2x + 3y = 11 \quad x - y = 1$

Solution: Using substitution, solve the second equation for x: x = y + 1. Substitute into the first equation:

2(y + 1) + 3y = 11

2y + 2 + 3y = 11

5y + 2 = 11

5y = 9

y = 9/5

Substitute y = 9/5 into x = y + 1 to find x:

x = 9/5 + 1 = 14/5

The solution is (x, y) = (14/5, 9/5).

QUADRATIC EQUATIONS

Learn to solve quadratic equations by factoring, using the quadratic formula, or completing the square. Understand the relationship between the coefficients and the roots of a quadratic equation.

Example

Solve $x^2 - 5x + 6 = 0$

Solution:

By factoring, (x - 2) (x - 3) = 0.

The solutions are x = 2 and x = 3.

FUNCTIONS

Understand the concept of functions, including domain, range, and function notation. Be able to evaluate functions and interpret their graphs.

Example

Given the function f(x) = 2x - 1, find f(3).

Solution:

f (3) = 2(3) - 1

= 6 - 1

= 5

EXPONENTIAL AND LOGARITHMIC FUNCTIONS

Familiarize yourself with the properties of exponential and logarithmic functions, and learn to solve equations involving them.

Example

Solve $2^{(x+1)} = 16$

Solution: Using the properties of logarithms, $\log_2 (2^{(x+1)}) = \log_2 (16)$.

Simplify: x + 1 = 4.

Solve for x:

x = 3.

To strengthen your algebra skills, practice a wide variety of problems and focus on understanding the underlying concepts. Develop a systematic approach to solving equations and identifying key information in word problems. Regularly review and reinforce your knowledge to maintain your proficiency.

Problem Solving with Geometry and Trigonometry

Geometry and trigonometry are important areas of the Digital SAT Math sections, and mastering these concepts will help you tackle a variety of problems. Let's review some key strategies and practice examples:

TRIANGLES AND CONGRUENCE

Understand the properties of triangles, including angle relationships and congruence theorems (SSS, SAS, ASA, AAS). Use these properties to solve problems involving triangles.

Example

In $\triangle ABC$, if AB = 5, BC = 7, and AC = 8, find the cosine of angle A.

Solution:

Using the law of cosines

$\cos(A) = (5^2 + 8^2 - 7^2) / (2 \times 5 \times 8) \approx 0.5625$

RIGHT TRIANGLES AND TRIGONOMETRY

Know the Pythagorean theorem and its applications in solving right triangle problems. Understand trigonometric ratios (sine, cosine, tangent) and how to use them to find missing side lengths and angles.

Example

In a right triangle with hypotenuse 13 and one leg 5, find the sine and cosine of the smallest angle.

Solution:

Let the smallest angle be θ.

The opposite side to θ is 5, and the hypotenuse is 13.

$\sin(\theta) = 5/13$, and

$\cos(\theta) = \sqrt{13^2 - 5^2}/13$

$= 12/13$.

CIRCLES AND THEIR PROPERTIES

Understand the properties of circles, including central and inscribed angles, chords, and tangents. Know how to find the area and circumference of a circle.

Example

If a circle has an area of 64π square units, find its circumference.

Solution:

Area = $\pi r^2 = 64\pi$

So

$r^2 = 64$.

The radius r = 8 units.

Circumference = $2\pi r = 16\pi$ units.

COORDINATE GEOMETRY

Be comfortable working with points, lines, and shapes on the coordinate plane. Know how to find the distance between two points, the midpoint of a line segment, and the slope of a line.

Example

Find the distance between points A(1, 4) and B(4, 2).

Solution:

Using the distance formula,

d = sqrt((4 - 1)^2 + (2 - 4)^2)

= sqrt(3^2 + (-2)^2)

= sqrt(13).

SOLID GEOMETRY

Understand the properties of three-dimensional shapes, such as prisms, cylinders, and spheres. Know how to calculate their surface areas and volumes.

Example

Find the volume of a cylinder with a height of 6 units and a base radius of 3 units.

Solution:

Volume = πr^2h

= π(3^2)(6)

= 54π cubic units.

Data Analysis, Statistics, and Probability

Data analysis, statistics, and probability are increasingly important areas of the Digital SAT Math sections, as they assess your ability to interpret and work with real-world data. Let's explore some key concepts and practice strategies:

MEASURES OF CENTER AND SPREAD

Understand how to calculate and interpret measures of central tendency (mean, median, mode) and measures of spread (range, standard deviation).

Example

Find the mean and median of the following dataset: {12, 7, 9, 12, 8, 11, 9}

Solution:

To find the mean, add all the values and divide by the number of values:

(12 + 7 + 9 + 12 + 8 + 11 + 9) / 7 = 68 / 7 ≈ 9.71.

To find the median, arrange the values in ascending order:

{7, 8, 9, 9, 11, 12, 12}.

The median is the middle value, 9.

INTERPRETING GRAPHS AND CHARTS

Be able to read and interpret various types of graphs and charts, such as line graphs, bar graphs, histograms, and box plots. Understand how to draw conclusions and make comparisons based on the data presented.

Example

Given a histogram of test scores, determine the percentage of students who scored between 70 and 90.

Solution: Identify the bins that include the scores between 70 and 90.

Add the frequencies (heights) of those bins and divide by the total number of students.

For example, if there are 50 students total and the bins for scores 70-79 and 80-89 have heights of 12 and 15, respectively, the percentage would be.

(12 + 15) / 50

= 54%.

PROBABILITY CONCEPTS

Understand the fundamental concepts of probability, such as sample spaces, events, and the complement of an event. Know how to calculate probabilities using the addition rule and the multiplication rule.

Example

A bag contains 4 red marbles, 6 blue marbles, and 2 green marbles. If two marbles are drawn at random without replacement, what is the probability of drawing a red marble and then a blue marble?

Solution:

P(red then blue) = P(red on first draw) × P(blue on second draw given red on first draw)

= (4/12) × (6/11)

= 2/11.

CONDITIONAL PROBABILITY AND INDEPENDENCE

Understand the concept of conditional probability and how to calculate it using the formula P(A|B) = P(A and B) / P(B). Know how to determine if two events are independent.

Example

In a group of 100 students, 60 play sports, and 45 are in the band. If 20 students play sports and are in the band, find the probability that a randomly chosen student plays sports, given that they are in the band.

Solution:

Let S be the event of playing sports and B be the event of being in the band.

P(S|B) = P(S and B) / P(B)

= 20/100 / 45/100

= 20/45

= 4/9.

SAMPLING AND INFERENCE

Be familiar with the concepts of sampling, random sampling, and sampling bias. Understand how to make inferences about a population based on sample data.

Example

A poll of 500 randomly selected adults found that 60% support a new law. Determine a 95% confidence interval for the true proportion of adults who support the law.

Solution:

The formula for a 95% confidence interval is $\hat{p} \pm 1.96 \times \sqrt{\hat{p}(1-\hat{p})/n}$, where $\hat{p}$ is the sample proportion and n is the sample size.

Here, $\hat{p}$ = 0.6 and n = 500.

The confidence interval is $0.6 \pm 1.96 \times \sqrt{0.6 \times 0.4 / 500} \approx (0.564, 0.636)$.

Calculator Tips and Tricks for the Digital SAT (Desmos)

The Digital SAT allows the use of a specific online calculator, the Desmos graphing calculator, during the Math with Calculator section. Familiarizing yourself with the features and functionalities of Desmos can save you valuable time and help you solve problems more efficiently. Let's explore some tips and tricks for using the Desmos calculator:

GRAPHING FUNCTIONS

Desmos allows you to easily graph functions by entering them in the input bar. You can graph multiple functions simultaneously by separating them with commas.

Example

To graph the functions y = x^2 and y = x + 1,

enter "y = x^2, y = x + 1" in the input bar.

SOLVING EQUATIONS

You can use Desmos to solve algebraic equations. Enter the equation, set it equal to zero, and press Enter. Desmos will display the solution(s).

Example

To solve the equation 2x^2 - 5x - 3 = 0,

enter "2x^2 - 5x - 3 = 0" in the input bar.

FINDING INTERSECTIONS

Desmos can find the intersection points of two or more functions. Graph the functions and then use the "Intersection" tool from the menu to select the curves. Desmos will display the coordinates of the intersection point(s).

Example

To find the intersection of y = x^2 and y = x + 1, graph both functions and use the "Intersection" tool to select the curves.

EVALUATING EXPRESSIONS

You can use Desmos as a basic calculator to evaluate expressions. Simply enter the expression in the input bar and press Enter.

Example

To evaluate 2^3 + sqrt(16),

enter "2^3 + sqrt(16)" in the input bar.

USING SLIDERS

Desmos allows you to create sliders to change the values of variables in functions or expressions dynamically. This can be helpful for exploring how changes in parameters affect graphs or solutions.

Example

To create a slider for the variable "a" in the function y = ax^2,

enter "y = ax^2" in the input bar,

then click on the "a" and select "Add Slider."

CALCULATING DERIVATIVES AND INTEGRALS

Desmos can calculate derivatives and definite integrals of functions. Use the "Derivative" or "Integral" tools from the menu, or enter the appropriate notation in the input bar.

Example

To find the derivative of y = x^3, enter "d/dx(x^3)" in the input bar.

To find the definite integral of y = x^2 from 0 to 1, enter "integral_0^1(x^2)dx" in the input bar.

CREATING TABLES

Desmos can generate tables of values for functions. After graphing a function, click on the function and select "Add Table." You can customize the table by specifying the starting value, ending value, and step size.

Example

To create a table for the function y = x^2 from x = 0 to x = 5 with a step size of 1, graph the function, click on it, select "Add Table," and set the appropriate values.

Remember, while the Desmos calculator is a powerful tool, it's essential to have a strong understanding of the mathematical concepts being tested. Use the calculator to supplement your problem-solving skills, not to replace them. Practice using the calculator alongside traditional problem-solving methods to develop a balanced approach.

Mathematics: In-Depth Review and Practice Tests

As you prepare for the Digital SAT Math sections, it's crucial to conduct an in-depth review of the key concepts and skills tested. This review should cover all the major topics, helping you identify your strengths and weaknesses and focus your study efforts where they are most needed. Let's discuss some strategies for an effective in-depth math review:

1. Identify Key Concepts: Begin by reviewing the main math concepts covered on the Digital SAT, such as algebra, geometry, trigonometry, and data analysis. Make a list of the specific topics within each area, ensuring that you have a comprehensive understanding of what will be tested.

2. Assess Your Strengths and Weaknesses: Take a diagnostic practice test to evaluate your current performance level in each math topic. Analyze your results to identify areas where you excel and areas that require more attention and practice. This self-assessment will help you prioritize your study plan and allocate your time effectively.

3. Review Formulas and Theorems: Compile a list of essential formulas and theorems for each math topic, such as the quadratic formula, the Pythagorean theorem, and the laws of sines and cosines. Review these formulas regularly and practice applying them to a variety of problems. Ensure that you understand the conditions under which each formula or theorem is applicable.

Example The quadratic formula, $x = (-b \pm sqrt(b^2 - 4ac)) / (2a)$, is used to solve quadratic equations of the form $ax^2 + bx + c = 0$, where $a \neq 0$.

4. Study with Quality Resources: Utilize high-quality study materials, such as official SAT practice tests, reputable study guides, and online resources. These materials should provide clear explanations of concepts, problem-solving strategies, and practice problems with detailed solutions. Focus on resources that closely align with the format and content of the Digital SAT.

5. Practice Problem-Solving Strategies: In addition to reviewing concepts, focus on developing and refining your problem-solving strategies. Learn to identify key information, break down complex problems into manageable steps, and apply appropriate formulas or techniques. Practice solving problems systematically and efficiently, and always double-check your work.

Example: When solving a word problem, first identify the given information and the unknown variable. Then, an equation or system of equations can be set up based on the relationships described in the problem. Solve the equation(s) and interpret the solution in the context of the problem.

6. Tackle a Variety of Problems: Expose yourself to a wide range of problem types and difficulty levels within each math topic. Practice with multiple-choice questions, student-produced response questions (grid-ins), and extended thinking problems. By encountering diverse problems, you'll develop the flexibility and adaptability needed to succeed on the Digital SAT.

7. Analyze Mistakes and Learn from Them: When reviewing your practice test results or homework assignments, carefully analyze your mistakes. Identify the concepts or skills that caused difficulty and focus on strengthening those areas. Learn from your errors by understanding why you made them and how to avoid similar mistakes in the future.

8. Review Regularly and Consistently: Effective math review is an ongoing process that requires regular practice and reinforcement. Set aside dedicated study time each week to review concepts, practice problems, and assess your progress. Consistent review will help you retain information, maintain your skills, and build your confidence leading up to test day.

PART 4

Test-Taking Strategies and Practice

Time Management and Test-Taking Strategies

Effective time management and test-taking strategies are crucial for success on the Digital SAT. With a well-planned approach, you can maximize your performance and minimize stress on test day. Here are some essential strategies to help you manage your time and tackle the test with confidence.

1. Familiarize yourself with the test structure and timing: Understand the format of the Digital SAT, including the number of sections, question types, and time allotted for each section. Knowing the test structure will help you create a pacing strategy and allocate your time effectively.

2. Practice with timed sections: During your preparation, simulate the test conditions by completing practice sections within the allotted time. This will help you develop a sense of pacing and identify areas where you may need to adjust your strategy.

3. Prioritize easier questions: When you encounter a challenging question, don't get bogged down. Move on to the next question and come back to the difficult ones later. This approach ensures that you have time to answer as many questions as possible and don't miss out on easier points.

4. Read questions carefully: Take the time to read each question thoroughly and understand what is being asked. Rushing through questions can lead to careless errors and misinterpretations. Pay attention to key phrases and details that can help you identify the correct answer.

5. Eliminate incorrect answers: When you're unsure about a question, use the process of elimination to narrow down your choices. Cross out options that are clearly incorrect or irrelevant to the question. This strategy increases your chances of selecting the correct answer, even if you're not entirely certain.

6. Manage your time strategically: Keep track of your progress throughout the test and adjust your pacing as needed. If you find yourself running behind, focus on answering the easier questions first and come back to the more time-consuming ones later.

7. Use educated guessing: If you're unable to eliminate any answer choices and time is running short, make an educated guess. There's no penalty for incorrect answers on the Digital SAT, so it's better to attempt a question than to leave it blank.

8. Take brief breaks: During the test, take short mental breaks between sections or when you need to recharge. Close your eyes, take a few deep breaths, and relax your mind for a moment. These brief breaks can help you maintain focus and reduce fatigue.

9. Review your answers: If you have time remaining at the end of a section, go back and review your answers. Double-check your calculations, ensure you've answered every question, and make any necessary changes.

10. Trust your instincts: If you've prepared well and have a strong understanding of the material, trust your instincts when answering questions. Second-guessing yourself can lead to unnecessary changes and may result in selecting the incorrect answer.

Adaptive Testing: How to Approach Each Module

The Digital SAT introduces adaptive testing in the Reading and Math sections, presenting a unique challenge for test-takers. Understanding how to approach each module effectively is key to maximizing your performance and achieving your best possible score.

In the adaptive testing format, each Reading and Math section is divided into two modules. The first module consists of a set of questions that cover a range of difficulties, serving as a baseline assessment of your proficiency. Your performance in the first module determines the difficulty level of the questions presented in the second module.

Here are some strategies to help you approach each module effectively:

MODULE 1

1. **Start strong:** The first module sets the tone for your performance in the section. Approach each question with focus and give your best effort, as your performance in Module 1 directly impacts the difficulty of questions you'll face in Module 2.

2. **Pace yourself:** While it's important to start strong, don't rush through the questions in Module 1. Take the time to read each question carefully, understand what is being asked, and select the best answer.

3. **Don't dwell on difficult questions:** If you encounter a challenging question in Module 1, don't spend too much time on it. Make an educated guess and move on to the next question. You can always come back to it later if time permits.

4. **Focus on accuracy:** In the adaptive testing format, accuracy is more important than speed. It's better to take your time and answer questions correctly than to rush through and make careless errors.

MODULE 2

1. **Adapt to the difficulty:** Based on your performance in Module 1, the questions in Module 2 will be tailored to your skill level. If you performed well in Module 1, expect more challenging questions in Module 2. Conversely, if you struggled in Module 1, the questions in Module 2 will be more aligned with your current proficiency level.

2. **Maintain your focus:** Regardless of the difficulty of the questions in Module 2, maintain your focus and approach each question with the same level of effort and attention. Don't let the adaptive format distract you from giving your best performance.

3. **Use test-taking strategies:** Apply the same test-taking strategies you used in Module 1, such as reading questions carefully, eliminating incorrect answers, and managing your time effectively.

4. **Stay positive:** If you encounter challenging questions in Module 2, don't get discouraged. The adaptive format ensures that you're being presented with questions that are appropriate for your skill level. Trust in your abilities and continue to give your best effort.

HOW TO TYPE YOUR MATH ANSWERS

In the SAT Math section, out of the 44 questions, many are the traditional multiple-choice type, but there are also places where you need to enter your own answers, known as fill-in questions. These fill-in questions function similarly to multiple-choice questions, except you input your answer directly.

Here are some guidelines for handling fill-in math questions:

* Avoid entering mixed numbers. For example, if you calculate an answer as 5_2^1, don't enter it as 51/2.

The system misinterprets this format as "51 over 2." Instead, convert it to an improper fraction like 11/2, or simply use the decimal equivalent, 5.5.

- If multiple answers are possible, choose any one correct option. For instance, if both 4 and 5 are acceptable, you can enter either. Similarly, if the answer falls within a range (say, between 3 and 7), any number within this range is acceptable.

- Be attentive to rounding instructions. If the answer needs to be rounded to a specific decimal place, ensure your response adheres to this. For example, if you get 1.75 but need to round it to one decimal place, then 1.8 is the correct entry, not 1.75.

- For repeating decimals, include several decimal places and round only the final digit as necessary. For example, instead of entering .3 for one-third, you should type .3333, .6666 for two-thirds, or even.6667 if rounding up the last digit.

Remember, in fill-in questions where multiple correct answers are acknowledged (typically phrased as "what is one possible value of..."), just submit one valid answer to meet the question's requirement.

Stress Management and Mental Preparation

It's completely normal to feel anxious when you arrive at the test center. Keep in mind once the exam begins, you'll recognize the material from your preparation, which should help ease your nerves. To alleviate tension, perform some simple stretches and gentle head shakes. During the test, shift your position slightly by wiggling your toes and moving your shoulders to relax any stiffness. If you need to roll your neck, close your eyes and face away from other students to avoid any misunderstandings about cheating. Taking deep, slow breaths can also help calm your mind.

The mental rigors of SAT preparation extend beyond the mere accumulation of knowledge and the honing of test-taking skills. At the heart of a successful SAT strategy lies a well-thought-out plan for stress management and mental preparation. The weeks and days leading up to the test can be fraught with anxiety and tension, which, if not properly managed, can undermine even the most thorough academic preparation. It's essential, therefore, to incorporate stress-relief techniques into your study regimen.

How to mentally prepare for the SAT:

- **Practice mindfulness meditation:**

  - Set aside 10-15 minutes each day for meditation.

  - Find a quiet space where you won't be disturbed.

  - Sit comfortably with your eyes closed and focus on your breath.

  - Notice any thoughts or sensations that arise without judgment, and gently redirect your attention back to your breath.

  - Consistency is key; make meditation a regular part of your routine.

- **Develop a positive attitude:**

  - Identify your strengths and the areas in which you've improved during your SAT preparation.

  - Celebrate your progress and acknowledge the effort you've put in.

- Replace negative self-talk with constructive thoughts, such as "I am capable of handling challenges" or "I will learn from this experience."

- Surround yourself with motivational quotes or images that inspire confidence.

- **Visualize success:**

  - Set aside time each day to practice visualization.

  - Close your eyes and imagine yourself walking into the test center feeling calm, confident, and well-prepared.

  - Picture yourself reading questions carefully, eliminating incorrect answers, and selecting the best option.

  - Visualize yourself maintaining focus and energy throughout the test, and completing each section with a sense of accomplishment.

  - Imagine receiving your desired score and feeling proud of your achievement.

- **Take care of your physical well-being:**

  - Establish a consistent sleep schedule in the weeks leading up to the test, aiming for 7-9 hours per night.

  - Avoid caffeine and electronic devices close to bedtime, as they can interfere with sleep quality.

  - Eat a balanced diet rich in fruits, vegetables, whole grains, and lean proteins to nourish your brain and body.

  - Stay hydrated by drinking plenty of water throughout the day.

  - Engage in regular physical activity, such as jogging, swimming, or yoga, to reduce stress and improve overall well-being.

- **Establish a support system:**

  - Identify trusted friends, family members, or mentors who can offer encouragement and support throughout your SAT journey.

  - Share your goals, progress, and concerns with them regularly.

  - Consider joining a study group or connecting with other students preparing for the SAT to share experiences and strategies.

  - Don't hesitate to reach out for help or guidance when needed, whether from a teacher, tutor, or counselor.

- **Manage your time effectively:**

  - Break your study schedule into manageable chunks, with clear goals for each session.

  - Use a planner or calendar to keep track of important deadlines and milestones.

  - Prioritize tasks based on their importance and urgency, focusing on your weakest areas first.

  - Take regular breaks to avoid burnout and maintain mental freshness.

  - Reward yourself for achieving goals and staying on track with your study plan.

ADVICE ON WHAT TO WEAR

The temperature in test centers can be unpredictable, so it's wise to dress in layers. Testing rooms can sometimes be overly air-conditioned or unexpectedly warm. Layering your clothing allows you to adjust comfortably to whatever conditions you encounter. Start with a light, short-sleeved shirt; add a heavier top like a long-sleeved shirt, and bring a sweater or sweatshirt. You can remove layers if you get too warm. Typically, jackets and caps might not be allowed, but sweaters and sweatshirts generally are.

SETTING YOUR ALARM AND ENSURING YOU WAKE UP

It's crucial to set your alarm to wake up early on the test day, even though you might already be aware of this. Additionally, it's a good idea to have a backup plan to ensure you wake up on time. You could ask a parent, guardian, or a reliable friend to check that you're awake. If you're on your own, consider setting multiple alarms as a precaution.

PREPARING YOUR JOURNEY TO THE TEST CENTER

To avoid any last-minute rush, thoroughly plan your travel to the test center:

- Confirm your transportation method: Whether you're driving, catching a ride, or using public transport or ride-sharing, make sure everything is set. If you're driving, ensure your car is functional and fueled. If someone else is driving you, double-check your plans with them the night before.

- Know your route: Review the route to the test center beforehand and check it again on the morning of the test to avoid unexpected delays caused by traffic, accidents, or road construction.

- Plan your departure and arrival times: Aim to leave with enough cushion to handle unforeseen delays, and plan to arrive at the test center about 30 minutes early. This gives you ample time to check in and settle in without feeling rushed.

Practice Test 1 with Detailed Answers and Explanations

SECTION 1

MODULE 1: 27 QUESTIONS

DIRECTIONS

This section's questions cover a variety of crucial writing and reading abilities. There are one or more texts in each question, some of which may contain a table or graph. After carefully reading each excerpt and question, select the appropriate response to the question based on the relevant passage or passages. This section's questions are all multiple-choice, with four possible answers. Every question has a one optimal response.

1. Hedgehog tenrecs in Madagascar, while not closely related to true hedgehogs, have evolved to share certain fundamental characteristics, such as defensive spines, sharply pointed snouts, and diminutive size, demonstrating that the two mammalian groups independently acquired these traits as adaptations to comparable ecological niches. Fill in the blank with the most coherent and accurate word or phrase choice:

A. examples of

B. concerns about

C. indications of

D. similarities with

2. In the introduction to her anthology titled The Future Is Female! More Classic Science Fiction Stories by Women, editor Lisa Yaszek notes a growing inclination towards a _____ feminist writing style in the 1970s, differing from many science fiction stories authored by women from the 1920s to the 1960s, which exhibited politics that were conveyed less intentionally. Choose the most logical and exact term or phrase to complete the passage:

A. a prudently

B. an overtly

C. a cordially

D. an inadvertently

3. _____ the enduring pattern of disproportionately focusing on adolescents and young adults in studies examining social media usage, researchers have recently started broadening their scope to encompass the most rapidly expanding demographic of social media users: older adults. Select the word or phrase that finishes the excerpt with the highest degree of coherence and precision:

A. Exacerbating

B. Redressing

C. Epitomizing

D. Precluding

4. Although contemporary research has called into question assertions that 12th-century Islamic philosopher Ibn Rushd's writings were _____ other Muslim thinkers of his era, it remains incontrovertible that his presence in the Muslim-controlled region of what is now Spain meant his works were chiefly accessible thousands of miles west of the period's hub of Islamic thought. Identify the most sensible and accurate word or phrase to fill in the blank:

A. controversial among

B. antagonistic toward

C. imitated by

D. inconsequential to

5. The following excerpt is adapted from James Baldwin's 1956 novel Giovanni's Room. The narrator is traveling by taxi along a Parisian street lined with food sellers and customers.

The multitude of Paris seems to be dressed in blue every day but Sunday, when, for the most part, they put on an unbelievably festive black. Here they were now, in blue, disputing, every inch, our passage, with their wagons, handtrucks, their bursting baskets carried at an angle steeply self-confident on the back. ©1956 by James Baldwin

In the context of the excerpt, the term "disputing" is closest in meaning to:

A. Arguing about

B. Disapproving of

C. Asserting possession of

D. Providing resistance to

6. When painter William H. Johnson returned to the United States in 1938 following a ten-year period in Europe, his artistic approach underwent a dramatic shift. Moving away from landscapes rendered in an expressionist manner—a style frequently characterized by the use of fluid, distorted forms and thick, textured brushstrokes to convey the artist's personal perception of reality—Johnson started creating portraits of African Americans in a striking new fashion. Reminiscent of African sculpture as well as American and Scandinavian folk art traditions, these portraits depict flat, purposefully simplified figures using a bold but restricted color scheme.

Which option most accurately describes how the underlined sentence functions within the overall text?

A. It elaborates on the previous sentence's statement about a transitional moment in Johnson's artistic career.

B. It provides information about Johnson's travels in support of a claim about his artistic influences, which is advanced in the following sentence.

C. It recounts a moment in Johnson's personal life that enabled the success of his subsequent career, which is summarized in the following sentence.

D. It presents evidence that calls into question the previous sentence's characterization of Johnson's artistic development.

7. When classical pianist Martha Argerich gives a performance, the music appears to flow from her spontaneously. Despite her exceptional technical abilities, her uninhibited playing style and openness to taking chances make her seem at ease and authentic. This apparent effortlessness, however, stems from an immense amount of preparation. Regardless of Argerich's expertise and virtuosity, she never assumes her mastery of a piece of music. Rather, she engages with the composition as if discovering it anew and strives to grasp it with fresh perspective.

Which statement best captures the primary purpose of the passage?

A. To provide details about how Argerich identifies which pieces of music she will perform

B. To assert that Argerich's performances look effortless because of how she prepares for them

C. To discuss the kinds of music Argerich feels most comfortable encountering for the first time

D. To describe the unique way that Argerich approaches music she hasn't performed before

8. The following text is adapted from Herman Melville's 1855 novel Israel Potter. Israel is a young man wandering through New England during the late eighteenth century.

He hired himself out for three months; at the end of that time to receive for his wages two hundred acres of land lying in New Hampshire. [...] His employer proving false to the contract in the matter of the land, and there being no law in the country to force him to fulfil it, Israel—who, however brave-hearted, and even much of a dare-devil upon a pinch, seems nevertheless to have evinced, throughout many parts of his career, a singular patience and mildness—was obliged to look round for other means of livelihood than clearing out a farm for himself in the wilderness.

Which choice best describes the function of the underlined portion in the text as a whole?

A. It implies that Israel treasures a particular characteristic of his personality when that characteristic should usually be regarded as a flaw.

B. It suggests that if not for a certain aspect of his character, Israel might not have been as easily thwarted in his ambition to establish a farm.

C. It shows why Israel would not have been able to undertake the enormous amount of labor necessary to run a farm even if he had owned the necessary property.

D. It explains why, when the situation requires it, Israel is able to undertake courageous acts that others would generally avoid.

9.

Text 1

In 1954, choreographer George Balanchine staged a production of Pyotr Ilyich Tchaikovsky's ballet The Nutcracker. Since then, it has become customary for hundreds of dance companies across North America to mount their own versions of The Nutcracker annually. However, the ballet is mired in the past, with an antiquated narrative and allusions, and should no longer be produced. If ballet wishes to remain relevant to modern audiences, it must forge new traditions.

Text 2

While The Nutcracker may be outdated, it should be preserved as a beloved holiday tradition that generates substantial revenue for some dance companies. Despite its potential to seem behind the times, there are imaginative ways to modernize the production. Debbie Allen, for instance, successfully updated the story in her show Hot Chocolate Nutcracker, which blends ballet, tap, hip-hop, and other dance styles. This innovative version has been growing in popularity since its 2009 premiere.

Based on the texts, how would the author of Text 2 most likely respond to the underlined claim in Text 1?

A. By questioning the idea that the story of The Nutcracker is stuck in the past and by rejecting the suggestion that contemporary audiences would enjoy an updated version

B. By agreeing that contemporary audiences have largely stopped going to see performances of The Nutcracker because it's so old-fashioned

C. By pointing out that most dance companies could increase their incomes by offering modernized versions of The Nutcracker

D. By suggesting that dance companies should consider offering revised versions of The Nutcracker instead of completely rejecting the show

10.
To gain insight into how Paleolithic artists navigated dark caves, archaeologist Ma Ángeles Medina-Alcaide and her team conducted experiments in a cave in Spain using replicas of artifacts discovered in European caves containing artwork. They tested three different Paleolithic light sources—torches, animal-fat lamps, and fireplaces—and concluded that each likely served a distinct purpose. For example, the team found that animal-fat lamps were less effective than torches for illuminating the cave floor while walking.

Which statement best encapsulates the main idea of the passage?

A. Medina-Alcaide and her team's study demonstrated that fireplaces were essential to the creators of Paleolithic cave art.

B. Medina-Alcaide and her team discovered that Paleolithic cave artists in Spain used animal-fat lamps more often than they used torches.

C. Medina-Alcaide and her team were reluctant to draw many conclusions from their study because of the difficulty they had replicating light sources based on known artifacts.

D. Medina-Alcaide and her team tested Paleolithic light sources and learned some details about how Paleolithic artists traveled within dark caves.

11.
Annual Car Production in the United States, 1910–1925

Year	Number of cars produced	Number of companies producing cars
1910	123,990	320
1915	548,139	224
1920	1,651,625	197
1925	3,185,881	80

A student is using the table as part of a social studies class presentation on the US auto industry in the early twentieth century. The student notes that, according to the table, from 1910 to 1925 _____

Which choice most effectively uses data from the table to complete the statement?

A. the number of cars produced increased but the number of companies producing cars decreased.

B. both the number of cars produced and the number of companies producing cars remained unchanged.

C. the number of cars produced decreased but the number of companies producing cars remained unchanged.

D. both the number of cars produced and the number of companies producing cars increased.

12. 12. External shopping cues are a form of marketing that employs conspicuous messaging—such as a display featuring a new product or a "buy one, get one free" promotion—to entice consumers to make impulsive purchases. In a study conducted by data scientist Sam K. Hui and colleagues, it was discovered that this effect can also be achieved through a less apparent cue: altering a store's layout. The researchers explain that attempting to locate items in unfamiliar places prompts shoppers to traverse more of the store, exposing them to a greater number of products and increasing the probability that they will purchase an item they had not initially intended to buy.

Which response from a survey given to shoppers who made a purchase at a retail store best supports the researchers' explanation?

A. I needed to buy some cleaning supplies, but they weren't in their regular place. While I was looking for them, I saw this interesting notebook and decided to buy it, too."

B. "I didn't buy everything on my shopping list today. I couldn't find a couple of the items in the store, even though I looked all over for them."

C. "The store sent me a coupon for a new brand of soup, so I came here to find out what kinds of soup that brand offers. I decided to buy a few cans because I had the coupon."

D. "This store is larger than one that's closer to where I live, and it carries more products. I came here to buy some things that the other store doesn't always have."

13. Arkansas's Crystal Bridges Museum of American Art hosted the 2021 exhibition This Is the Day, which showcased works exploring expressions of faith and spirituality within the Black community. In 2022, the museum presented The Dirty South, an exhibition centered on Black culture in the American South from 1920 to 2020, with a specific emphasis on the intersections between visual arts and music.

Together, these exhibitions not only underscore the diversity of the Black experience in the United States but also highlight the wide range of media through which artists have portrayed and engaged with that experience.

Which statement about the exhibitions, if true, would most directly support the underlined claim?

A. Between them, This Is the Day and The Dirty South included drawings, paintings, photographs, sculptures, textiles, videos, costumes, and music.

B. This Is the Day included works by fewer than two dozen artists, whereas The Dirty South included works by more than 80 artists.

C. This Is the Day exclusively included works in the permanent collection of the museum, whereas The Dirty South included works from multiple sources outside the museum.

D. Between them, This Is the Day and The Dirty South included works depicting more than 300 years of Black experience in the United States.

14. 14. Researchers Jan Packer and colleagues examined the potential cognitive advantages of taking time off work in a six-month study involving Australian university employees. Participants were divided into three groups: those who took no leave, those who took 2-4 days off, and those who took 1-5 weeks off. Attentiveness tests were conducted three times: randomly for the no-leave group, and for the others, a week before their leave, a week after returning to work, and a week following the second test. The researchers concluded that more extended leave durations might not provide superior cognitive benefits compared to shorter leave periods.

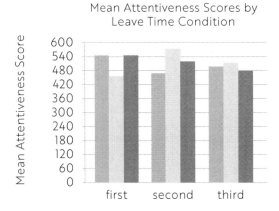

Mean Attentiveness Scores by Leave Time Condition

Test administration
- no leave
- 2-4 days leave
- 1-5 weeks leave

Which data points from the graph best support the researchers' conclusion?

A. In the second test, participants with 2-4 days of leave scored higher on average attentiveness than those with no leave. However, in the third test, the no-leave group outperformed the 1-5 week leave group.

B. During the first test, participants who took 2-4 days off had lower average attentiveness scores than both the 1-5 week leave and no-leave groups.

C. Participants who took 2-4 days of leave consistently demonstrated higher average attentiveness scores than those who took 1-5 weeks off in the second and third test administrations.

D. In both the second and third tests, participants with 2-4 days of leave exhibited higher average attentiveness scores compared to those who took no leave.

15. 15. Pursuing prey or fleeing from predators at top speed may appear to be the best approach for animals. However, the energy cost of utilizing maximum speed capacity can discourage this strategy, even in escape situations, as demonstrated by the fact that_____.

Which option most effectively utilizes the graph's data to finish the passage?

A. The majority of lizard species employ a similar percentage of their top speed when escaping predation and when chasing prey.

B. Several lizard species move at an average speed less than 90% of their maximum while evading predation.

C. More lizard species use, on average, 90%-100% of their top speed while fleeing predation compared to any other percentage of their maximum speed.

D. At least 4 lizard species utilize, on average, less than 100% of their top speed while pursuing prey.

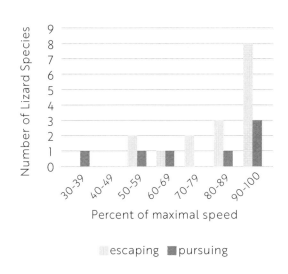

Number of Lizard Species by Average Percent of Maximal Speed Used

escaping   pursuing

16. The Boston Saloon was one of the most popular African American–owned establishments in nineteen-th-century Nevada. _____ by businessman William A.G. Brown, the saloon was known to offer elegant accommodations and an inclusive environment.

Which choice completes the text so that it conforms to the conventions of Standard English?

A. Created

B. Creates

C. Creating

D. Create

17. "He was just the man for such a place, and it was just the place for such a man." This line is from Frederick Douglass's autobiography Narrative of the Life of Frederick Douglass (1845). It's an example of antimetabole, a writing technique that _____ emphasis by repeating a statement in a reversed order.

Which choice completes the text so that it conforms to the conventions of Standard English?

A. create

B. are creating

C. have created

D. creates

18. Louise Bennett (1919–2006), also known as "Miss Lou," was an influential Jamaican poet and folklorist. Her innovative poems _____ the use of Jamaican Creole (a spoken language) in literature.

Which choice completes the text so that it conforms to the conventions of Standard English?

A. popularized;

B. popularized,

C. popularized

D. popularized:

19. Researchers Amit Kumar and Nicholas Epley investigated how _____ In a series of experiments conducted in 2022, they found that people performing small acts of kindness underestimated the positive effect their actions had on others.

Which choice completes the text so that it conforms to the conventions of Standard English?

A. do people perceive acts of kindness.

B. do people perceive acts of kindness?

C. people perceive acts of kindness?

D. people perceive acts of kindness.

20. In a painting titled "The Milkmaid" by Johannes Vermeer, the artist prominently features a bread basket, milk pitcher, and bowl. Such quotidian objects, depicted in exquisite detail by Vermeer, a painter celebrated for his naturalism, _____ the daily minutiae of a seventeenth-century Dutch household.

Which choice completes the text so that it conforms to the conventions of Standard English?

A. was revealing

B. has revealed

C. reveals

D. reveal

21. Consider the mechanics of the pinhole camera: light passes through a small hole, resulting in a focused projected image. A ray diagram reveals how this _____ the hole's small size restricts light to a single ray, all light passing through the hole can only arrive at a single destination, eliminating diffraction and ensuring a clear image.

Which choice completes the text so that it conforms to the conventions of Standard English?

A. works because

B. works. Because

C. works, it's because

D. works: it's because

22. Jamaican British artist Willard Wigan is known for his remarkable _____ so small that they are best viewed through a microscope, Wigan's sculptures are made from tiny natural materials, such as spiderweb strands.

Which choice completes the text so that it conforms to the conventions of Standard English?

A. microsculptures creations

B. microsculptures, creations

C. microsculptures. Creations

D. microsculptures and creations

23. In the search for extraterrestrial life, astrobiologists Stuart Bartlett and Michael L. Wong propose that scientists avoid using the term "life." _____ researchers should use another word: "lyfe." This new term, they argue, could be used to draw distinctions between the known characteristics of life on Earth and the potentially differing characteristics of lyfe on other planets.

Which choice completes the text with the most logical transition?

A. Previously,

B. Regardless,

C. There,

D. Instead,

24. Before it unveiled a massive new gallery in 2009, the Art Institute of Chicago was only able to display about 5% of its art collection. _____ the museum is able to display close to 30% of its collection.

Which choice completes the text with the most logical transition?

A. Additionally,

B. For example,

C. Nevertheless,

D. Today,

25.   The Inca of South America used intricately knotted string devices called quipus to record countable information, like population data and payments. _____ they may have used quipus to record more complex information, like stories and myths, according to researchers.

Which choice completes the text with the most logical transition?

A. As a result,

B. In other words,

C. In addition,

D. For example,

26.   Working together with the Navajo Nation Department of Water Resources, Dr. Lani Tsinnajinnie analyzed data about snowpack levels in the Chuska Mountains. She found that the snowpack (the amount of snow on the ground) was deepest in early March at lower elevations. At higher elevations, _____ the snowpack was deepest in mid-March.

Which choice completes the text with the most logical transition?

A. in other words,

B. for instance,

C. on the other hand,

D. in summary,

27.   In hindsight, given the ideas about the natural world circulating among British scientists in the 1800s, the theory of natural selection was an obvious next step. It may not have been a coincidence, _____ that Charles Darwin and Alfred Wallace arrived at the concept independently. Indeed, contrary to the popular myth of the lone genius, theirs is not the first paradigm-shifting theory to have emerged from multiple scholars working in parallel.

Which choice completes the text with the most logical transition?

A. however,

B. then,

C. moreover,

D. for example,

MODULE 2: 27 QUESTIONS

DIRECTIONS

This section consists of questions that test key reading and writing skills. Each question is accompanied by one or more texts, which may also feature tables or graphs. Please read each text and accompanying question thoroughly before selecting the most appropriate answer from the four multiple-choice options provided. Note that there is only one correct answer for each question.

1. The artworks of Chicana artist Ester Hernandez can now be found _____ in museums across the United States and internationally, but early in her career, the murals she contributed to as part of Las Mujeres Muralistas were exhibited in public outdoor locations throughout San Francisco. Select the most coherent and accurate word or phrase to fill in the blank:

A. invented

B. adjusted

C. featured

D. recommended

2. Whether creating small-scale paintings and illustrations or large-scale public works like Baile, a copper cutout depicting traditional Mexican dance at the San Francisco International Airport, Carmen Lomas Garza draws _____ personal experience, deriving inspiration from childhood memories in Texas or aspects of her present life in California. Choose the most logical and precise term or phrase to complete the passage:

A. complimented by

B. uncertain about

C. unbothered by

D. inspired by

3. In a 2021 study led by animal researcher Amalia P.M. Bastos, a wild kea parrot was observed using small stones as tools for preening its feathers. Initially, skeptical colleagues suggested to Bastos that the kea's stone interactions might merely be _____, but Bastos and her team demonstrated the kea's intentional use of the stones. Identify the most sensible and exact word or phrase to complete the text:

A. intriguing

B. obvious

C. accidental

D. observable

4. While Mary Engle Pennington, a chemist who contributed to the advancement of home refrigeration, undeniably had a significant societal impact, her position in our collective historical memory is perhaps more _____ compared to that of Stephanie Kwolek, who will long be remembered for inventing the exceptionally strong material known as Kevlar. Select the word or phrase that finishes the excerpt with the highest degree of coherence and precision:

A. permanent

B. tentative

C. warranted

D. prominent

5. Design artist William Morris cofounded the Kelmscott Press in 1891, which printed book editions using pre-industrial techniques. Historians contend that Morris's rejection of industrialization is _____ the Kelmscott editions' use of handcrafted materials and elaborate ornamentation reminiscent of medieval manuscripts, as these painstakingly handmade elements exemplify the artistry involved. Choose the most logical and precise term or phrase to fill in the blank:

A. insensible to

B. manifest in

C. scrutinized by

D. complicated by

6. Researchers have long hypothesized that woolly mammoths in North America were hunted to extinction by humans using spears with grooved tips known as Clovis points. To test this hypothesis, one anthropologist used a mechanical spear-thrower to launch spears with Clovis points into mounds of clay, which served as substitutes for the animals' large bodies. The projectiles generally penetrated only a few inches into the clay, an insufficient depth to have harmed most woolly mammoths. Based on these results, the anthropologist concluded that hunters using spears with Clovis points were likely not the primary cause of the extinction.

Which option most accurately describes the main purpose of the text?

A. To argue for the significance of new findings amid an ongoing debate among researchers

B. To discuss the advantages and disadvantages of the method used in an experiment

C. To summarize two competing hypotheses and a major finding associated with each one

D. To describe an experiment whose results cast doubt on an established hypothesis

7. Medieval Europeans have traditionally been portrayed as uninterested in cleanliness and hygiene, but recent research has largely debunked this misconception. Historian Eleanor Janega notes that most medieval European towns had at least one public bathhouse, which typically offered both full-immersion baths and, more affordably, steam baths. Although these amenities were primarily accessible to urban residents, regular bathing in rivers and streams or daily sponge baths at home were common practices throughout medieval Europe.

Which statement best describes the role of the underlined sentence?

A. It asserts that in medieval Europe steam baths were more popular in rural areas than in urban ones.

B. It describes a limitation of earlier historians' studies of medieval European bathing habits.

C. It concedes that not all people in medieval Europe had access to public bathhouses.

D. It explains why Janega decided to study the popularity of public bathhouses in medieval Europe.

8. Academic studies of the Chicano movement—a movement that advocated for the social, political, and cultural empowerment of Mexican Americans and reached its peak in the 1960s and 1970s—often emphasize the most militant, outspoken figures in the movement, portraying it as uniformly radical. However, geographer Juan Herrera has demonstrated that by shifting our focus to the way the movement manifested in comparatively low-profile neighborhood institutions and projects, we observe participants advocating a range of political orientations and approaches to community activism.

Which choice best describes the function of the underlined portion in the text as a whole?

A. It presents a trend in scholarship on the Chicano movement that the text claims has been reevaluated by researchers in light of Herrera's work on the movement's participants.

B. It identifies an aspect of the Chicano movement that the text implies was overemphasized by scholars due to their own political orientations.

C. It describes a common approach to studying the Chicano movement that, according to the text, obscures the ideological diversity of the movement's participants.

D. It summarizes the conventional method for analyzing the Chicano movement, which the text suggests creates a misleading impression of the effectiveness of neighborhood institutions and projects.

9. Elizabeth Asiedu has observed a negative correlation between the proportion of developing countries' economies derived from natural-resource extraction and those countries' receipts of foreign investment. While this may seem counterintuitive—resource extraction necessitates initial investments (e.g., in extractive technology) at scales best provided by multinational corporations—Asiedu points out that the boom-bust cycle of natural-resource industries can destabilize local currencies and increase developing countries' susceptibility to external shocks, creating levels of uncertainty that foreign investors typically find unappealing.

Which statement best encapsulates the main idea of the passage?

A. Although it may seem surprising that foreign investment declines in developing countries as natural-resource extraction makes up a larger share of those countries' economies, that decline happens because resource extraction requires initial investments too large for foreign investors to supply.

B. Although developing countries tend to become less dependent on foreign investment as natural-resource industries make up a larger share of their economies, this change may not occur if the boom-bust cycle of those industries destabilizes local currencies or increases countries' vulnerability to external shocks.

C. Although one might expect that foreign investment would increase as natural-resource extraction makes up a larger share of developing countries' economies, the opposite happens because heavy reliance on natural resources can lead to unattractive conditions for investors.

D. Although foreign investors tend to avoid initial investments in natural-resource industries in developing countries, foreign investment may increase significantly as those industries stabilize and the risks associated with them decline.

10. To investigate how temperature change impacts microorganism-mediated cycling of soil nutrients in alpine ecosystems, Eva Kaštovská et al. collected plant-soil cores in the Tatra Mountains at elevations around 2,100 meters and transplanted them to elevations of 1,700–1,800 meters, where the mean air temperature was 2°C warmer. In the transplanted cores, microorganism-mediated nutrient cycling was accelerated; importantly, microorganism community composition remained unchanged, allowing Kaštovská et al. to attribute the acceleration to temperature-induced increases in microorganism activity.

Based on the text, it can most reasonably be inferred that the finding about the microorganism community composition was significant for which reason?

A. It provided preliminary evidence that microorganism-mediated nutrient cycling was accelerated in the transplanted cores.

B. It suggested that temperature-induced changes in microorganism activity may be occurring at increasingly high elevations.

C. It ruled out a potential alternative explanation for the acceleration in microorganism-mediated nutrient cycling.

D. It clarified that microorganism activity levels in the plant-soil cores varied depending on which microorganisms comprised the community.

11. Some astronomers searching for extraterrestrial life have suggested that atmospheric NH_3 (ammonia) can serve as a biosignature gas—an indication that a planet harbors life. Jingcheng Huang, Sara Seager, and colleagues evaluated this possibility and found that on rocky planets, atmospheric NH_3 likely couldn't reach detectably high levels in the absence of biological activity. However, the team also discovered that on so-called mini-Neptunes—gas planets smaller than Neptune but with atmospheres similar to Neptune's—atmospheric pressure and temperature can be high enough to produce atmospheric NH_3. Based on the text, Huang, Seager, and colleagues would most likely agree with which statement about atmospheric NH_3?

A. Its presence is more likely to indicate that a planet is a mini-Neptune than that the planet is a rocky planet that could support life.

B. Its absence from a planet that's not a mini-Neptune indicates that the planet probably doesn't have life.

C. It should be treated as a biosignature gas if detected in the atmosphere of a rocky planet but not if detected in the atmosphere of a mini-Neptune.

D. It doesn't reliably reach high enough concentrations in the atmospheres of rocky planets or mini-Neptunes to be treated as a biosignature gas.

12. 12. To evaluate a medication's effectiveness, scientists compare outcomes for patients taking the medication and those taking a placebo (a medically inactive substance). Patients are typically unaware that they are receiving a placebo, but a research team conducted a study to explore the potential medical benefit of informing them. The team used various measures to assess participants, with higher ratings indicating greater well-being in each measure. Compared to the mean ratings after 21 days for participants in the control group, the mean ratings for participants who were aware of taking a placebo _____

MEASURE	Mean rating for participants aware of taking a placebo	mean rating for participants in the control group
Global improvement	5.0	3.9
Symptom severity reduction	92.00	46.00
Quality of life improvement	11.4	5.4

Which choice most effectively uses data from the table to complete the statement?

A. ranged from 5.0 to 92.00, indicating that well-being varied widely from participant to participant.

B. were lower for two measures, with the rating for only one measure indicating greater well-being for these participants.

C. ranged from 3.9 to 46.00, with no rating indicating greater well-being in any measure for these participants.

D. were higher for all three measures, indicating greater overall well-being for these participants.

13. Some biologists have argued that reptiles in the Triassic period were not a particularly _____ group. However, Dr. Elena Ramirez's research suggests that these ancient reptiles displayed a remarkable variety of forms and behaviors. Fossils found in Argentina reveal species with unique adaptations, such as Gliding Lizardus, which Dr. Ramirez believes could glide between trees. Which choice completes the text with the most logical and precise word or phrase?

A) diverse

B) singular

C) typical

D) mundane

14. As media consumption has become increasingly multiplatform and socially mediated, active news acquisition has diminished in favor of an attitude known as "news finds me" (NFM), in which people passively rely on their social networks and ambient media environments for information about current events. Homero Gil de Zúñiga and Trevor Diehl examined data on a representative group of adults in the United States to determine participants' strength of NFM attitude, political knowledge, and political interest. Although no major election took place sufficiently near the study for Gil de Zúñiga and Diehl to identify causality between NFM and voting behavior, they did posit that NFM may reduce voting probability through an indirect effect.

Which finding, if true, would most directly support the idea advanced by Gil de Zúñiga and Diehl?

A. NF-M attitude tends to increase in strength as major elections approach, and people are significantly more likely to vote in major elections than in minor elections.

B. NFM attitude has a strong negative effect on political knowledge and interest, and there is known to be a strong positive correlation between political knowledge and interest and the likelihood of voting.

C. Political interest is known to have a strong positive effect on likelihood of voting but shows only a weak positive effect on political knowledge, and NFM attitude shows little correlation with either political knowledge or political interest.

D. The likelihood of voting increases as political knowledge increases, and the relationship between NFM attitude and political knowledge tends to strengthen as the size of people's social networks increases.

15. The practice of logging (cutting down trees for commercial and other uses) is often thought to be at odds with forest conservation (the work of preserving forests). However, a massive study in forest management and preservation spanning 700,000 hectares in Oregon's Malheur National Forest challenges that view. Thus far, results of the study suggest that forest plots that have undergone limited logging (the careful removal of a controlled number of trees) may be more robust than plots that haven't been logged at all. These results, in turn, imply that _____

Which statement most logically completes the passage?

A. logging may be useful for maintaining healthy forests, provided it is limited.

B. other forest management strategies are more effective than limited logging.

C. as time passes, it will be difficult to know whether limited logging has any benefits.

D. the best way to support forest health may be to leave large forests entirely untouched.

16. Even with the widespread adoption of personal computers, many authors still choose to write and revise their novels by hand and only then transcribe the final version on a computer. It may be tempting to speculate about how a novel written this way would be affected if it had been exclusively typed instead, but each novel is a unique entity resulting from a specific set of circumstances. Therefore, _____

Which statement most logically concludes the text?

A. in order to increase their efficiency, authors who currently write their novels largely by hand should instead work only on a computer.

B. authors who do most of their drafting and revising by hand likely have more success than those who work entirely on a computer.

C. novels written by hand take less time to produce, on average, than novels written on a computer do.

D. there is no way to reasonably evaluate how a work would be different if it had been written by other means.

17. In forecasting weather events, meteorologists sometimes discuss the role of atmospheric rivers. What are atmospheric rivers, and how _____ Part of the water cycle, atmospheric rivers are narrow channels of moisture moving through the atmosphere. In certain conditions, these "rivers" can release some of their moisture as precipitation.

Which choice completes the text so that it conforms to the conventions of Standard English?

A. do they affect our weather.

B. they do affect our weather.

C. do they affect our weather?

D. they do affect our weather?

18. One of the few African American global explorers during the turn of the 20th century, _____

Which choice completes the text so that it conforms to the conventions of Standard English?

A. Matthew Henson made several treks across Greenland between 1891 and 1909.

B. 1891 and 1909 were the years between which Matthew Henson made several treks across Greenland.

C. Greenland was where Matthew Henson made several treks between 1891 and 1909.

D. several treks across Greenland were made by Matthew Henson between 1891 and 1909.

19. Woven from recycled yarn and hand tufted using a carpet weaving technique passed down by the artist's Turkish grandmother, _____ so lush and tactilely inviting that you are tempted to reach out and touch them.

Which choice completes the text so that it conforms to the conventions of Standard English?

A. the topological tapestries of Argentine textile artist Alexandra Kehayoglou are

B. the Argentine textile artist Alexandra Kehayoglou creates topological tapestries that are

C. when she creates her topological tapestries, Argentine textile artist Alexandra Kehayoglou makes them

D. Alexandra Kehayoglou is an Argentine textile artist whose topological tapestries are

20. Physical materials can be classified by how much light passes through them. Clear glass, which is classified as transparent, allows all (or almost all) light to pass _____ wax paper, which is classified as translucent, allows only some light to pass through.

Which choice completes the text so that it conforms to the conventions of Standard English?

A. through,

B. through

C. through;

D. through and

21. Latin America is known to have dozens, if not hundreds, of popular dance forms. Only five of these dances are included in international ballroom dance competitions _____ rumba, samba, cha-cha-cha, paso doble, and jive—the last of which is grouped with the other Latin dances despite not having Latin roots.

Which choice completes the text so that it conforms to the conventions of Standard English?

A. competitions, however:

B. competitions, however,

C. competitions, however;

D. competitions; however,

22. Using natural debris, such as dried _____ such as plastic bags; and more traditional art supplies, such as tree glue, Ghanaian artist Ed Franklin Gavua creates his striking Yiiiiikakaii African masks, which he hopes can help viewers rethink how waste is used in their communities.

Which choice completes the text so that it conforms to the conventions of Standard English?

A. leaves, man-made trash:

B. leaves; man-made trash,

C. leaves, man-made trash,

D. leaves; man-made trash;

23. For thousands of years, humans have used domesticated goats (Capra hircus) to clear land of unwanted vegetation. When it comes to their diets, goats are notoriously _____ they will devour all kinds of shrubs and weeds, leaving virtually no part of any plant unconsumed.

Which choice completes the text so that it conforms to the conventions of Standard English?

A. indiscriminate and

B. indiscriminate,

C. indiscriminate

D. indiscriminate:

24. A species of Byropsis algae produces toxins to avoid being eaten by predators. However, in some cases, the toxins the organism uses to protect itself from predation actually _____ its attractiveness to predators. The Hawaiian sea slug, for example, not only tolerates Byropsis toxins but actually uses them for protection in the same way the algae does.

Which choice completes the text so that it conforms to the conventions of Standard English?

A. is increasing

B. increase

C. increases

D. has increased

25. The liquid metals in Earth's core circulate constantly, and this circulation generates electrical currents that flow between Earth's North and South magnetic poles. These electrical currents, _____ create a barrier around Earth that protects us from radiation and charged particles coming from space.

Which choice completes the text with the most logical transition?

A. in turn,

B. likewise,

C. nevertheless,

D. in reality,

26. After appropriate permissions are granted, a typical archaeological dig begins with a surveyor making a detailed grid of the excavation site. Then, the site is carefully dug, and any artifacts found are recorded and mapped onto the site grid. _____ the artifacts are removed, cataloged, and analyzed in a laboratory.

Which choice completes the text with the most logical transition?

A. For instance,

B. On the contrary,

C. Earlier,

D. Finally,

27. Some biologists have argued that reptiles in the Triassic period were not a particularly _____ group. However, Dr. Elena Ramirez's research suggests that these ancient reptiles displayed a remarkable variety of forms and behaviors. Fossils found in Argentina reveal species with unique adaptations, such as Gliding Lizardus, which Dr. Ramirez believes could glide between trees. Which choice completes the text with the most logical and precise word or phrase?

A. diverse

B. singular

C. typical

D. mundane

STOP IF YOU COMPLETE BEFORE THE TIME LIMIT, YOU MAY JUST REVIEW YOUR WORK ON THIS MODULE. AVOID SWITCHING TO ANY OTHER TEST MODULE.

SECTION 2: MATH TEST

MODULE 1: 22 QUESTIONS

DIRECTIONS

The problems in this area cover a variety of key math concepts. Calculators are authorized for all questions.

Notes

Unless otherwise stated:

· All variables and expressions contain real numbers.

· The figures presented are drawn to scale.

· All of the figures are on the same plane.

· The domain of a given function f is the set of all real integers x that have a real value.

For multiple-choice questions, solve each issue, select the correct answer from the options supplied, and circle it in this book. Circle just one answer to each question. If you change your mind, delete the entire circle. You will not receive credit for questions with multiple circled answers or questions with no circled answers.

For student-generated response questions, solve each issue and record your solution next to or underneath the question in the exam book as stated below.

· After you've typed your response, circle it clearly. You will not be given credit for anything written outside the circle, or for questions having more than one marked answer.

· If you discover many right answers, write and circle only one.

· You can respond with up to 5 characters for a positive response and 6 characters (with the negative sign) for a negative answer, but no more.

· If your answer is a lengthy fraction (more than 5 characters for positive and 6 characters for negative), enter the decimal equivalent.

· If your answer is a large decimal (more than 5 characters for positive and 6 characters for negative), truncate it or round to the fourth number.

· If your answer is a mixed number (e.g. 3½), express it as an improper fraction (7/2) or decimal equivalent (3.5).

· Avoid using symbols like a percent sign, comma, or dollar sign in your highlighted response.

1. **If (2x + 3) / 4 = l and l = 4, what is the value of x?**

    2.5

    6.5

    7.5

    10

2. **For i = $\sqrt{(-1)}$, what is the sum (9 - 4i) + (-7 + 6i)?**

    2 + 2i

    2 - 10i

    16 + 2i

    16 - 10i

3. **$(2x^2z - 4z^3 + 6xz^2) - (-2x^2z + 4xz^2 - 5z^2)$ Which of the following is equal to the given expression?**

$6x^2z^2$
$10xz^2 - 9z^2$
$4x^2z + 2xz^2$
$4x^2z - 4z^3 + 2xz^2 + 5z^2$

4. $k = 4b + 35.2$ The formula above is used by a pediatrician to predict the height k of a girl in inches, based on the girl's age b in years, for ages between 3 and 6 years. According to this model, what is the yearly estimated growth in height, measured in inches, for a girl?

4
8.8
11.7
17.6

5. $m = ((s/1500)/((1+s/1500)^M-1)) P$

The given formula calculates the monthly payment m required to repay a loan amount P in dollars, with an annual interest rate of s percent, over a period of M months. Which of the options expresses the principal amount P as a function of m, s, and M?

$P = ((s/1500)/((1+s/1500)^M-1)) m$
$P = m((1+s/1500)^M-1)(1500/s)$
$P = (s / 1500) m$
$P = (1500 / s) m$

6. If $c/d = 3$, what is the value of $5d/c$?

0
1.67
3
5

7. Solve the given set of equations for x and y:

$4x - 5y = -28$

$3y - 2x = -23$

(−7, −3)
(4, −9)
(−99.5, −74)
((34, -74)]

8. $f(x)=bx2+36$ Given the function f as described, where b is a constant and f (3) =9, what is the value of f (-3)?

| 9 |
| 0 |
| -3 |
| -9 |

9.   In a certain town, the cost per pound of beef (b) and chicken (c) in dollars is given by the equations b = 3.2 + 0.05x and c = 2.5 + 0.1x, where x represents the number of weeks after January 1, 2024. At what price per pound will beef and chicken cost the same?

A) 3.9

B) 4.6

C) 2.9

D) 3.5

10.   A line on the xy-plane passes through the point (2, -1) with a slope of 3/5. Which of the listed points is located on this line?

A) (-3, 4)

B) (0, -1)

C) (7, 2)

D) (8, -1)

11.   If x > 5, which of the following expressions is equal to $(x^2 - 25)/(x - 5)$?

A) x + 5

B) x^2 - 25

C) x - 5

D) x + 5

12.   Given the table:

x	2	4	6	8
y	8	16	24	32

If y = ax + b, what is the value of a + b?

A) 10

B) 12

C) 4

D) The value cannot be determined from the information given.

13.   The product of (ax + 2) and (bx+7) equals $15x^2 + cx + 14$ for any value of x. If the sum of a and b is 8, find the two possible values of c.

A) 3, 5

B) 31, 41

C) 41, 35

D) -21, -10

14. The graph y = kx. If y = 18 when x = 6, find the value of y when x = 9.

A) 12

B) 18

C) 24

D) 27

15. If 20 + 3x is 8 more than 2x, find the value of 6x.

A) 2

B) 6

C) -80

D) -72

16. For what value of n is |n + 2| + 2 equal to 4?

A) 0

B) -4

C) option a & b

D) There is no such value of n.

17. Which of the following values of x does not satisfy the inequality 2x - 3 ≥ 5x - 7?

A) -1

B) 0

C) 1

D) 2

18. At what air temperature would the velocity of a sound wave be most comparable to 1,100 feet per second?

A) −44°F

B) −45°F

C) −47°F

D) −51°F

19. A right triangle has a hypotenuse of length 10 and one leg of length 6. What is the length of the other leg?

A) 4

B) 6

C) 8

D) 9

20. The cost C of renting a bike is related to the number of hours h the bike is rented. Which of the following equations best illustrates the relationship between C and h?

A) C = 4h

B) C = 20 + 4h

C) C = 20h + 4

D) h = 4C

21. A food truck vends sandwiches at $7.50 apiece and drinks at $2.50 each. In a single day, the food truck generated $925.00 in revenue from selling a combined total of 225 sandwiches and drinks. How many sandwiches were sold on that particular day?

A) 85

B) 72

C) 95

D) 100

22. The following table shows the yearly budget for public safety in Kansas (in millions of dollars) from 2015 to 2018:

Year	Budget (in millions of dollars)
2015	320
2016	360
2017	410
2018	480

Which of the following options most closely estimates the average rate of change in the yearly budget for public safety in Kansas between 2015 and 2018?

A) $50,000,000 per year

B) $53,000,000 per year

C) $55,000,000 per year

D) $60,000,000 per year

MODULE 2: 22 QUESTIONS

DIRECTIONS

The problems in this area cover a variety of key math concepts. Calculators are authorized for all questions.

Notes

Unless otherwise stated:

· All variables and expressions contain real numbers.

· The figures presented are drawn to scale.

· All of the figures are on the same plane.

· The domain of a given function f is the set of all real integers x that have a real value.

For multiple-choice questions, solve each issue, select the correct answer from the options supplied, and circle it in this book. Circle just one answer to each question. If you change your mind, delete the entire circle. You will not receive credit for questions with multiple circled answers or questions with no circled answers.

For student-generated response questions, solve each issue and record your solution next to or underneath the question in the exam book as stated below.

· After you've typed your response, circle it clearly. You will not be given credit for anything written outside the circle, or for questions having more than one marked answer.

· If you discover many right answers, write and circle only one.

· You can respond with up to 5 characters for a positive response and 6 characters (with the negative sign) for a negative answer, but no more.

· If your answer is a lengthy fraction (more than 5 characters for positive and 6 characters for negative), enter the decimal equivalent.

· If your answer is a large decimal (more than 5 characters for positive and 6 characters for negative), truncate it or round to the fourth number.

· If your answer is a mixed number (e.g. 3½), express it as an improper fraction (7/2) or decimal equivalent (3.5).

· Avoid using symbols like a percent sign, comma, or dollar sign in your highlighted response.

1. David is a botanist studying the production of apples by two types of apple trees. He noticed that Type A trees produced 25 percent more apples than Type B trees did. Based on David's observation, if the Type A trees produced 150 apples, how many apples did the Type B trees produce?

A) 112

B) 120

C) 125

D) 188

2. A rectangular field measures 12 meters by 8 meters. Twelve students each mark off a randomly selected region of the field; each region is rectangular and has side lengths of 1 meter and 0.5 meters, and no two regions overlap. The students count the earthworms contained in the soil to a depth of 10 centimeters beneath the ground's surface in each region. The results are shown in the table below.

Which of the following is a reasonable approximation of the number of earthworms to a depth of 10 centimeters beneath the ground's surface in the entire field?

A) 130

B) 1,300

C) 13,000

D) 130,000

Region	Number of earthworms
A	120
B	135
C	128
D	142
E	118
F	130
G	125
H	133
I	140
J	137
K	145
L	129

3. A right triangle has a hypotenuse of length 10 and one leg of length 6. What is the length of the other leg?

A) 4

B) 6

C) 8

D) 9

4. The Eco-Friendly Skyscraper Corporation is designing a new building with a novel energy-efficient cooling system. The system's efficiency (E) is modeled by the function $E(x,y) = 0.8x^2 - 0.05xy + 1.2y - 10$, where x represents the number of cooling units installed (in hundreds) and y represents the average daily temperature (in °C). The corporation wants to maximize efficiency while keeping costs reasonable. They've determined that the number of cooling units must be between 300 and 700, the system should be optimized for temperatures between 20°C and 35°C, and to be cost-effective, the efficiency must be at least 15 units.

What is the maximum number of cooling units that can be installed while meeting all the given constraints when the average daily temperature is 30°C?

A) 500 units

B) 600 units

C) 700 units

D) 650 units

5. A food truck vends sandwiches at $7.50 apiece and drinks at $2.50 each. In a single day, the food truck generated $925.00 in revenue from selling a combined total of 225 sandwiches and drinks. How many sandwiches were sold on that particular day?

A) 85

B) 90

C) 95

D) 72.5

6. y < -2x + a   y > 2x + b

If (0, 0) is a solution to the system of inequalities provided, which of the subsequent relationships between a and b must hold true in the xy-plane?

A) a > b

B) b > a

C) |a| > |b|

D) a = -b

7. A local charity organization is planning a fundraising event. They have found that the total amount of money raised, R(x), in thousands of dollars, can be modeled by the function R(x) = 2x² + 5x, where x is the number of hours the event lasts.

If the event lasts for 4 hours, how much money will be raised in total?

A) $42,000

B) $52,000

C) $62,000

D) $72,000

8. What is the value of x in the equation 3(2x - 5) + 4(x + 3) = 22?

A) 1.5

B) 2.5

C) 3

D) 4.5

9. If the area of a triangle is 48 cm² and its height is 8 cm, what is the length of its base?

A) 6 cm

B) 10 cm

C) 12 cm

D) 16 cm

10. Simplify the expression: (2√3 + 5√2) - (3√3 - 2√2)

A) -√3 + 3√2

B) -√3 + 7√2

C) 5√3 + 3√2

D) 5√3 + 7√2

11. The volume of a cylinder with a radius of 5 cm is 942 cm³. What is the height of the cylinder? (Use π ≈ 3.14)

A) 6 cm

B) 8 cm

C) 10 cm

D) 12 cm

12. Solve the system of equations: 3x + 2y = 8 5x - 3y = 5

A) x = 1, y = 4

B) x = 2, y = 1

C) x = 3, y = 2

D) x = 4, y = 1

13. Simplify the expression: $(3x^2 - 5x + 2) - (2x^2 + 3x - 4)$

A) $x^2 - 2x + 6$

B) $x^2 - 8x + 6$

C) $5x^2 - 2x + 6$

D) $5x^2 - 8x + 6$

14. If 25% of x is equal to 40% of 75, what is the value of x?

A) 90

B) 100

C) 110

D) 120

15. What is the perimeter of a rectangle with a length of 15 cm and a width of 8 cm?

A) 23 cm

B) 30 cm

C) 38 cm

D) 46 cm

16. Simplify the expression: (2/3) ÷ (1/4)

A) 1/6

B) 2/3

C) 1 1/3

D) 2 2/3

17. If the ratio of boys to girls in a class is 3:2 and there are 30 students in the class, how many girls are there?

A) 6

B) 10

C) 12

D) 18

18. The function f(x) = ax + b passes through the points (1, 5) and (2, 8). What is the value of a + b?

A) 4

B) 5

C) 6

D) 8

19. If 3x - 5 = 16, what is the value of x?

A) 5

B) 6

C) 7

D) 8

20. In the given system of equations, r is a constant. If the system has no solution, what is the value of r?

48x - 64y = 48y + 24

ry = 1/8 - 12x

21. The scatterplot shows the relationship between two variables, x and y, for data set E. A line of best fit is shown. Data set F is created by multiplying the y-coordinate of each data point from data set E by 3.9.

Which of the following could be an equation of a line of best fit for data set F?

A. y = 46.8 + 5.9x

B. y = 46.8 + 1.5x

C. y = 12 + 5.9x

D. y = 12 + 1.5x

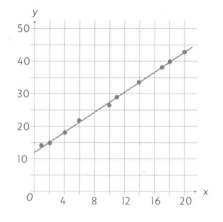

22. A rectangle has an area of 155 square inches. If the length of the rectangle is 4 inches less than 7 times its width, what is the width of the rectangle in inches?

STOP

Practice Test 1 Answers

SECTION 1 READING AND WRITING

MODULE 1:

1. **D** is correct. The phrase "similarities with" accurately completes the sentence because it describes the traits that hedgehog tenrecs in Madagascar and true hedgehogs share, despite not being closely related, indicating that they independently acquired these traits as adaptations to comparable ecological niches.

2. **B** is correct. The phrase "an overtly" completes the sentence logically by describing a shift toward a more explicitly feminist writing style in the 1970s, contrasting with earlier science fiction stories by women that conveyed political themes less directly.

3. **B** is correct. The word "Redressing" completes the sentence accurately, indicating that researchers have started to address the previous focus on adolescents and young adults in social media studies by broadening their scope to include older adults.

4. **C** is correct. The phrase "imitated by" completes the sentence sensibly, suggesting that contemporary research questions whether Ibn Rushd's writings were copied by other Muslim thinkers of his era.

5. **D** is correct. In the context of the excerpt, "disputing" means "providing resistance to," as the multitude in Paris is making it difficult for the taxi to pass through the street.

6. **A** is correct. The underlined sentence elaborates on the previous sentence by explaining how William H. Johnson's artistic approach shifted after returning to the United States, detailing the new style he adopted for his portraits.

7. **B** is correct. The passage explains that Argerich's performances appear effortless due to her immense preparation, highlighting that her technical abilities and spontaneous style are the result of diligent practice and a fresh engagement with each piece.

8. **B** is correct. The underlined portion implies that if not for Israel's characteristic patience and mildness, he might not have been as easily thwarted in his ambition to establish a farm, suggesting that his personality played a role in his response to the contract breach.

9. **D** is correct. The author of Text 2 would likely respond to the claim in Text 1 by suggesting that instead of completely rejecting The Nutcracker, dance companies should consider offering revised versions to keep the tradition alive while modernizing it.

10. **D** is correct. The main idea of the passage is that Medina-Alcaide and her team tested Paleolithic light sources and learned some details about how Paleolithic artists navigated dark caves, using different light sources for distinct purposes.

11. **A** is correct. From 1910 to 1925, the number of cars produced increased significantly, while the number of companies producing cars decreased, as shown by the data in the table.

12. **A** is correct. The response "I needed to buy some cleaning supplies, but they weren't in their regular place. While I was looking for them, I saw this interesting notebook and decided to buy it, too." supports the researchers' explanation that altering a store's layout can prompt shoppers to traverse more of the store and make impulsive purchases.

13. A is correct. The statement "Between them, This Is the Day and The Dirty South included drawings, paintings, photographs, sculptures, textiles, videos, costumes, and music." directly supports the claim that these exhibitions underscore the diversity of the Black experience and highlight the wide range of media used by artists.

14. C is correct. The data points showing that participants who took 2-4 days of leave consistently demonstrated higher average attentiveness scores than those who took 1-5 weeks off in the second and third test administrations support the researchers' conclusion that shorter leave periods may provide similar cognitive benefits as longer ones.

15. B is correct. The statement "Several lizard species move at an average speed less than 90% of their maximum while evading predation." effectively utilizes the graph's data to demonstrate that animals may avoid using maximum speed capacity due to the high energy cost, even in escape situations.

16. A is correct. The word "Created" completes the text so that it conforms to the conventions of Standard English, indicating that William A.G. Brown founded the Boston Saloon.

17. D is correct. The word "creates" completes the text so that it conforms to the conventions of Standard English, describing how antimetabole emphasizes by repeating a statement in a reversed order.

18. C is correct. The word "popularized" completes the text so that it conforms to the conventions of Standard English, describing how Louise Bennett promoted the use of Jamaican Creole in literature.

19. D is correct. The phrase "people perceive acts of kindness." completes the text so that it conforms to the conventions of Standard English, indicating what Kumar and Epley investigated.

20. D is correct. The word "reveal" completes the text so that it conforms to the conventions of Standard English, describing how Vermeer's detailed depiction of quotidian objects highlights the daily minutiae of a seventeenth-century Dutch household.

21. A is correct. The phrase "works because" completes the text so that it conforms to the conventions of Standard English, explaining the mechanism of the pinhole camera.

22. B is correct. The phrase "microsculptures, creations" completes the text so that it conforms to the conventions of Standard English, describing Willard Wigan's work.

23. D is correct. The word "Instead," completes the text with the most logical transition, suggesting that researchers should use the term "lyfe" instead of "life."

24. D is correct. The word "Today," completes the text with the most logical transition, indicating the current ability of the Art Institute of Chicago to display more of its collection.

25. C is correct. The phrase "In addition," completes the text with the most logical transition, indicating that quipus may have been used to record more complex information beyond countable data.

26. C is correct. The phrase "on the other hand," completes the text with the most logical transition, contrasting the snowpack levels at different elevations.

27. B is correct. The word "then," completes the text with the most logical transition, suggesting that it may not have been a coincidence that Darwin and Wallace arrived at the theory of natural selection independently.

SECTION 1 READING AND WRITING TEST

MODULE 2:

1. **C** is correct. "featured" accurately completes the sentence, describing the current status of Ester Hernandez's artworks in museums.

2. **D** is correct. "inspired by" correctly completes the sentence, indicating that Carmen Lomas Garza draws inspiration from personal experience.

3. **C** is correct. "accidental" correctly completes the sentence, suggesting that the kea's stone interactions might have been unintentional.

4. **B** is correct. "tentative" correctly completes the sentence, indicating that Mary Engle Pennington's position in historical memory is less certain compared to Stephanie Kwolek's.

5. **B** is correct. "manifest in" accurately completes the sentence, suggesting that William Morris's rejection of industrialization is evident in the handcrafted elements of the Kelmscott editions.

6. **D** is correct. The text describes an experiment whose results cast doubt on the established hypothesis that hunters using spears with Clovis points were the primary cause of the woolly mammoths' extinction.

7. **C** is correct. The sentence concedes that not all people in medieval Europe had access to public bathhouses, acknowledging the limitation in accessibility.

8. **C** is correct. The underlined portion describes a common approach to studying the Chicano movement that, according to the text, obscures the ideological diversity of the movement's participants.

9. **C** is correct. Although one might expect that foreign investment would increase as natural-resource extraction makes up a larger share of developing countries' economies, the opposite happens because heavy reliance on natural resources can lead to unattractive conditions for investors.

10. **C** is correct. The finding about the microorganism community composition ruled out a potential alternative explanation for the acceleration in microorganism-mediated nutrient cycling, attributing the acceleration to temperature-induced increases in microorganism activity.

11. **C** is correct. "It should be treated as a biosignature gas if detected in the atmosphere of a rocky planet but not if detected in the atmosphere of a mini-Neptune" aligns with Huang, Seager, and colleagues' findings on atmospheric NH_3.

12. **D** is correct. "were higher for all three measures, indicating greater overall well-being for these participants" most effectively uses data from the table to complete the statement.

13. **A** is correct. "diverse" logically and precisely completes the text, indicating the variety of forms and behaviors displayed by Triassic period reptiles.

14. **B** is correct. "NFM attitude has a strong negative effect on political knowledge and interest, and there is known to be a strong positive correlation between political knowledge and interest and the likelihood of voting" supports the idea advanced by Gil de Zúñiga and Diehl.

15. **A** is correct. "logging may be useful for maintaining healthy forests provided it is limited" logically completes the passage, implying the potential benefits of limited logging for forest health.

16. **D** is correct. "there is no way to reasonably evaluate how a work would be different if it had been written by other means" logically concludes the text, emphasizing the uniqueness of each novel.

17. **C** is correct. "do they affect our weather?" completes the text so that it conforms to the conventions of Standard English.

18. **A** is correct. "Matthew Henson made several treks across Greenland between 1891 and 1909" completes the text so that it conforms to the conventions of Standard English.

19. A is correct. "the topological tapestries of Argentine textile artist Alexandra Kehayoglou are" completes the text so that it conforms to the conventions of Standard English.

20. C is correct. "through;" completes the text so that it conforms to the conventions of Standard English.

21. A is correct. "competitions; however," completes the text so that it conforms to the conventions of Standard English.

22. B is correct. "leaves; man-made trash" completes the text so that it conforms to the conventions of Standard English.

23. B is correct. "indiscriminate" completes the text so that it conforms to the conventions of Standard English.

24. B is correct. increase" completes the text so that it conforms to the conventions of Standard English.

25. A is correct. "in turn" completes the text with the most logical transition.

26. D is correct. "Finally" completes the text with the most logical transition.

27. A is correct. "diverse" logically and precisely completes the text, indicating the variety of forms and behaviors displayed by Triassic period reptiles.

SECTION 2

MODULE 1: MATH TEST

QUESTION 1

Option B is correct. Given $(2x + 3)/4 = l$ and $l = 4$:

$(2x + 3)/4 = 4$

$2x + 3 = 16$

$2x = 13$

$x = 6.5$

QUESTION 2

Option A is correct. For $i = \sqrt{(-1)}$, the sum of $(9 - 4i) + (-7 + 6i)$:

Combine the real parts:

$9+(-7)=2$

Combine the imaginary parts:

$-4i+6i=2i$

So, the sum is:

$= 2 + 2i$

QUESTION 3

Option D is correct. Simplify the expression:

Distribute the negative sign through the second set of parentheses:

$(2x^2 z-4z^3+6xz^2)-(-2x^2 z+4xz^2-5z^2)$

$=2x^2 z - 4z^3 + 6xz^2 + 2x^2 z - 4xz^2 + 5z^2$

Combine the $x2\ z$ terms:

$2x^2 z + 2x^2 z = 4x^2 z$

Combine the $z3$ terms:

$-4z^3$

Combine the $xz2$ terms:

$6xz^2 - 4xz^2 = 2xz^2$

Combine the $z2$ terms:

$5z^2$

So, the simplified expression is:

$4x^2 z - 4z^3 + 2xz^2 + 5z^2$

QUESTION 4

Option A is correct. In the equation $k = 4b + 35.2$, This formula predicts the height k of a girl in inches based on her age b in years. The coefficient of b in the formula represents the yearly growth in height. In this formula, the coefficient of b is 4, which means that for each additional year of age b, the height k increases by 4 inches.

QUESTION 5

Option B is correct.

To express P as a function of m, s, and M, we need to solve this equation for P:

$$m = \left(\frac{\frac{s}{1500}}{\left(1 + \frac{s}{1500}\right)^M - 1} \right) P$$

We want to isolate P. Let's go through the steps:

1)   Start with the given formula:

$$m = \left(\frac{\frac{s}{1500}}{\left(1 + \frac{s}{1500}\right)^M - 1} \right) P$$

2)   Isolate P:

First, multiply both sides by the denominator (1+s/1500)^M-1 to get rid of the fraction:

$$m \left(\left(1 + \frac{s}{1500}\right)^M - 1 \right) = \frac{s}{1500} P$$

3)   Solve for P:

Now, divide both sides by s/1500 :

$$P = \frac{m \left(\left(1 + \frac{s}{1500}\right)^M - 1 \right)}{\frac{s}{1500}}$$

Since dividing by a fraction is the same as multiplying by its reciprocal, we have:

$$P = m \left(\left(1 + \frac{s}{1500}\right)^M - 1 \right) \left(\frac{1500}{s} \right)$$

QUESTION 6

Option B is correct. Given c / d = 3, the value of 5d / c is:

First rewrite the given question *c/d=3*

c= 3d

Now substitute c into *5d/c*

5d/c =5d/3d

Cancel d with each other we left with *5/3*

5/3=1.67

QUESTION 7

Option C is correct. Solve the given set of equations for x and y:

4x - 5y = -28

3y - 2x = -23

Multiply the 2nd equation by 2:

$6y-4x=-46$

Add the equations:

$(4x-5y)+(-4x+6y)= -28+(-46)$

$4x-4x-5y+6y=-28-46$

$y=-74$

Substitute y value into first equation

$5x-5(-74)=-28$

$4x+370=-28$

$4x=-398$

$x=-398/4$

$x=-99.5$

So the answer for (x,y) is (-99.5,-74)

QUESTION 8

Option A is correct.

Given $f(x) = bx^2 + 36$ and $f(3) = 9$, solve for b:

$9 = b(3)^2 + 36$

$9=9b + 36$

$9b= 9 - 36$

$b = -3$

The value of f(-3) is:

$f(-3) = -3(-3)^2 + 36$

$f(-3)= -27 + 36$

$= 9$

QUESTION 9

Option A is correct. In the given cost equations for beef (b) and chicken (c):

$b = 3.2 + 0.05x$

$c = 2.5 + 0.1x$

Set b equal to c to find the price per pound where they cost the same:

$3.2 + 0.05x = 2.5 + 0.1x$

Subtract 0.05x from both sides:

$3.2 = 2.5 + 0.05x$

Now subtract 2.5 from both sides:

$0.7 = 0.05x$

Divide both sides with 0.05x:

$x=0.7/0.05$

$x=14$

Substitute x = 14 back into either equation to find the price per pound:

b = 3.2 + 0.05(14)

= 3.2 + 0.7

= 3.9

So the answer will be the same for both equations.

QUESTION 10

Option C is correct. A line passes through (2, -1) with a slope of 3/5. Using the point-slope form:

$y - y_1 = m(x - x_1)$ Where (x_1, y_1) is a point on the line and m is the slope.

Substituting our known values (2,-1) and 3/5:

y + 1 = 3/5 (x - 2)

y = 3/5 x - 6/5 -1

y = 3/5 x - 11/5

Check which point c satisfies the equation:

Point (7,2):

For x=2

y = 3/5 (2) – 11/5 = 6/5 – 11/5 = -1

For x=7

y = 3/5 (7) – 11/5 = 21/5 – 11/5 = 2

So point (7,2) satisfies (2,-1) so its passing the line as well.

QUESTION 11

Option A is correct.

For x > 5, the expression $\frac{x^2 - 25}{x - 5}$ can be simplified:

The numerator x^2-25 is a difference of squares and can be factored as:

(x² - 25) = (x - 5)(x + 5)

Using factorization the original expression will become:

$$\frac{(x - 5)(x + 5)}{x - 5}$$

Cancel x-5 with each other left with:

(x + 5)

QUESTION 12

Option C is correct.

Find the Slope a

The slope a of the line is given by:

$$a = \frac{\Delta y}{\Delta x}$$

Using two points from the table, such as (2,8) and (4,16):

$$a = \frac{16-8}{4-2} = \frac{8}{2} = 4$$

Find the Y-Intercept b:

Using the slope-intercept form y=ax+b, substitute one of the points into the equation to solve for b.

Using the point (2,8):

8=4·2+b

8=8+b

b=8-8

b=0

Calculate a+b:

With a=4 and b=0:

a+b=4+0=4

Result will be the same with any points from the table.

QUESTION 13

Option B is correct. The product of (ax + 2)and (bx+7)= 15x2   + cx + 14.
Find the two possible values of c:
(ax + 2)(bx+ 7)= abx² +(7a+2b)x+14
Math the coefficients with right side of equations:
abx² +(7a+2b)x+14= 15x² + cx + 14
From this, we can compare the coefficients of x², x, and the constant term on both sides of the equation.
·   The coefficient of x² gives us: ab=15
·   The coefficient of x gives us: 7a+2b=c
Solve for a and b Given a+b=8 and ab=15:
To find a and b, solve the quadratic equation:
t² - (a+b)t + ab = 0
Substitute a+b=8 and ab=15:
t² - 8t + 15 = 0

Solve this quadratic equation using the quadratic formula:

$$t = \frac{8 \pm \sqrt{8^2 - 4.15}}{2} = \frac{8 \pm \sqrt{64 - 60}}{2} = \frac{8 \pm \sqrt{4}}{2} = \frac{8 \pm 2}{2}$$

So $t = \frac{10}{2} = 5$ and $t = \frac{6}{2} = 3$

Calculate c for Each Pair (a,b):

·   For a=5 and b=3: c=7a+2b=7(5)+2(3)=35+6=41

·   For a=3 and b=5: c=7a+2b=7(3)+2(5)=21+10=31

QUESTION 14

Option D is correct. Given the equation y = kx, find the value of y when x = 9:
y = 18 when x = 6
k =y/x =18/6 = 3
When x = 9:
y = 3 * 9 = 27

QUESTION 15

Option D is correct. Given 20 + 3x is 8 more than 2x:

20 + 3x = 2x + 8
3x - 2x = 8 - 20
x = -12

Find the value of 6x:

6x = 6(-12) = -72

QUESTION 16

Option C is correct. Solve the equation for the value of n:

Subtract 2 from both sides

|n + 2| + 2-2 = 4 -2
|n + 2|= 2

Now lets solve for 2 possible cases:

· Case 1: n+2=2

n=2-2
n=0

· Case 2: n+2=-2

n + 2 = -2
n = -2-2
n = -4

QUESTION 17

Option D is correct.

1) Solve the inequality for xxx:

$2x-3 \geq 5x-7$

Subtract 2x2x2x from both sides:

$-3 \geq 3x-7$

Add 7 to both sides:

$4 \geq 3x$

Divide by 3:

$4/3 \geq x$

Or equivalently:

$x \leq 4/3$

2) Check each value of xxx to see if it satisfies $x \leq 4/3$:

· For x=−1:

$-1 \leq 4/3$ *(True)*

· For x=0:

$0 \leq 4/3$ *(True)*

· For x=1:

$1 \leq 4/3$ *(True)*

· For x=2:

$2 \leq 4/3$ *(False)*

Therefore, the value of xxx that does not satisfy the inequality is 222, which corresponds to option D.

QUESTION 18

Option B is correct. The velocity of sound waves at different air temperatures: v = 331.3 + 0.606 * T For velocity of sound waves to be comparable to 1100 feet per second: 331.3 + 0.606 * T = 1100 T = (1100 - 331.3) / 0.606 = -45

QUESTION 19

Option C is correct. Using the Pythagorean theorem:

$a^2 + b^2 = c^2$

Given hypotenuse c = 10 and one leg a = 6:

$6^2 + b^2 = 10^2$
$36 + b^2 = 100$
$b^2 = 64$
$b = 8$

QUESTION 20

Option B is correct. The correlation between h and C can be expressed as: C = 20 + 4h

QUESTION 21

Option B is correct.
Let:
- s be the number of sandwiches sold.
- d be the number of drinks sold.

From the problem, we have two pieces of information:
1. The total number of items sold is 225.
2. The total revenue generated is $925.00.

We can write the following equations:
1. s+d=225 (total number of sandwiches and drinks)
2. 7.50s+2.50d=925 (total revenue)

Solve the system of equations:

Step 1: Solve the first equation for d:
   d=225-s
Step 2: Substitute d into the second equation:
   7.50s+2.50(225−s)=925
Step 3: Distribute and simplify:
   7.50 s+562.50-2.50 s=925

   5.00 s+562.50=925
Step 4: Isolate s: ·

   5.00 s=925-562.50

   5.00 s=362.5

   s=362.50/5.00

   s=72.5

QUESTION 22

Option B is correct. To determine the average rate of change in the yearly budget for public safety in Kansas between 2015 and 2018, we first calculate the difference in the budget over the years and divide it by the number of years.

The table provides the following information:
- 2015: $320 million
- 2018: $480 million

First, find the difference in the budget between 2018 and 2015: 480−320=160 million dollars

Next, determine the number of years between 2015 and 2018: 2018−2015=3 years

Now, divide the difference by the number of years to find the average rate of change: 160 million dollars / 3 years ≈ 53.33 million dollars per year

The closest estimate to this calculation is $53,000,000 per year (Option B), making it the most accurate choice.

SECTION 2
MODULE 2: MATH TEST

QUESTION 1

Option B is correct. Let B be the number of apples produced by Type B trees. Given A = 150 and Type A produced 25% more apples than Type B: 150 = 1.25B B = 150 / 1.25 = 120

QUESTION 2

Option D is correct. The total area of the field is 12 meters × 8 meters, which is 96 square meters. Each student marks off an area of 1 meter × 0.5 meters, so the total sampled area is 12 × 0.5 = 6 square meters. The average number of earthworms per region is: Average = (120 + 135 + 128 + 142 + 118 + 130 + 125 + 133 + 140 + 137 + 145 + 129) / 12 = 131.83 Approximate total number of earthworms in the entire field: Total = Average × 96 / 6 = 131.83 × 16 ≈ 130,000

QUESTION 3

Option C is correct. In a right triangle, using the Pythagorean theorem: $a^2 + b^2 = c^2$ Given hypotenuse c = 10 and one leg a = 6:

$6^2 + b^2 = 10^2$

$36 + b^2 = 100$

$b^2 = 64$

$b = \sqrt{64} = 8$

QUESTION 4

Option C is correct. To solve this problem, we need to use the given efficiency function E(x,y) = 0.8x² - 0.05xy + 1.2y - 10 and substitute y = 30 for the average daily temperature. We then need to find the largest value of x between 3 and 7 (remember, x is in hundreds of units) that satisfies the efficiency constraint of E ≥ 15.
Let's set up the inequality:

0.8x² - 0.05(30x) + 1.2(30) - 10 ≥ 15

0.8x² - 1.5x + 26 ≥ 15

0.8x² - 1.5x - 11 ≥ 0

Solving this quadratic inequality, we find that x ≥ 6.96. Since x must be between 3 and 7, and we're looking for the maximum value, we choose 7. This corresponds to 700 cooling units.

QUESTION 5

Option D is correct. Let S be the number of sandwiches sold and D be the number of drinks sold. Given that each sandwich costs $7.50 and each drink costs $2.50, and the total revenue is $925 from a total of 225 items: 7.50S + 2.50D = 925 S + D = 225 Solving the system of equations: 7.50S + 2.50(225 - S) = 925 7.50S + 562.50 - 2.50S = 925 5S = 362.50 S = 362.50 / 5 = 72.5

QUESTION 6

Option A is correct. If (0, 0) is a solution to the system of inequalities: y < -2x + a y > 2x + b Substituting (0, 0) into both inequalities: 0 < a 0 > b Thus, a > b

QUESTION 7

Option B is correct. Here's how we arrive at this answer: We are given the function R(x) = 2x² + 5x, where R(x) is in thousands of dollars and x is the number of hours. We need to find R(4), as the question asks how much money will be raised if the event lasts 4 hours.

Let's substitute x = 4 into the function: R(4) = 2(4²) + 5(4)

Let's calculate step by step: R(4) = 2(16) + 5(4) R(4) = 32 + 20 R(4) = 52

Remember, R(x) is in thousands of dollars. So R(4) = 52 means 52 thousand dollars or $52,000.

Therefore, if the fundraising event lasts for 4 hours, the organization will raise $52,000 in total.

QUESTION 8
Option B is correct. Solving the equation: 3(2x - 5) + 4(x + 3) = 22 6x - 15 + 4x + 12 = 22 10x - 3 = 22 10x = 25 x = 25 / 10 = 2.5

QUESTION 9
Option C is correct. Given the area of a triangle and its height: Area = 48 cm², height = 8 cm Using the formula for the area of a triangle: Area = (base × height) / 2 48 = (base × 8) / 2 48 × 2 = base × 8 96 = base × 8 base = 96 / 8 = 12 cm

QUESTION 10
Option B is correct. Simplify the expression: (2√3 + 5√2) - (3√3 - 2√2) = 2√3 + 5√2 - 3√3 + 2√2 = -√3 + 7√2

QUESTION 11
Option D is correct. Given the volume of a cylinder and its radius: Volume = 942 cm³, radius = 5 cm Using the formula for the volume of a cylinder: Volume = πr²h

942 = 3.14 × (5)² × h

942 = 3.14 × 25 × h

942 = 78.5h h =

942 / 78.5 = 12 cm

QUESTION 12
Option B is correct. Solving the system of equations: 3x + 2y = 8 4x - 3y = 5 Multiply the first equation by 3 and the second by 2 to eliminate y: 9x + 6y = 24   8x - 6y = 10 Add the two equations: 17x = 34 x = 34 / 17 = 2 3x+2y=8   3(2) + 2y = 8   2y = 8-6   2y = 2 y= 1

So x = 2, y = 1

QUESTION 13
Option B is correct. Simplifying the expression: (3x² - 5x + 2) - (2x² + 3x - 4) = 3x² - 5x + 2 - 2x² - 3x + 4 = x² - 8x + 6

QUESTION 14
Option D is correct. Solving the equation: 25% of x = 40% of 75 0.25x = 0.40 × 75 0.25x = 30 x = 30 / 0.25 = 120

QUESTION 15
Option D is correct. Finding the perimeter of a rectangle with given length and width: Length = 15 cm, Width = 8 cm Using the formula for perimeter: Perimeter = 2(length + width) = 2(15 + 8) = 2(23) = 46 cm

QUESTION 16
Option D is correct. Simplifying the expression: (2/3) ÷ (1/4) = (2/3) × (4/1) = 8/3 = 2 2/3

QUESTION 17
Option C is correct. Finding the number of girls in the class with given ratio: Ratio of boys to girls = 3:2, Total students = 30 Let number of boys = 3x and number of girls = 2x 3x + 2x = 30 5x = 30 x = 30 / 5 = 6 Number of girls = 2 × 6 = 12

QUESTION 18

Option B is correct. Given points (1, 5) and (2, 8): Using the formula for the slope (a): a = (8 - 5) / (2 - 1) = 3 / 1 = 3 Using point (1, 5) to find b: 5 = 3(1) + b 5 = 3 + b b = 2 a + b = 3 + 2 = 5

QUESTION 19

Option C is correct. Solving the equation: 3x - 5 = 16 3x = 16 + 5 3x = 21 x = 21 / 3 = 7

QUESTION 20

To solve the system of equations:

48x - 64y = 48y + 24

ry = 1/8 - 12x

First, simplify the first equation: 48x - 64y = 48y + 24

48x - 64y - 48y = 24

48x - 112y = 24

Divide by 8: 6x - 14y = 3

Next, consider the second equation: ry = 1/8 - 12x

For the system to have no solution, the lines must be parallel, meaning they must have the same slope but different intercepts. Therefore, we need to compare the coefficients of x and y in both equations.

Rearrange the 2nd equation for match the form: Ax + By = C

ry + 12x = 1/8

For the lines to be parallel, the ratio of the coefficients of x and y in both equations must be equal. Therefore:

Comparing slopes: **6/12 = -14/r   r = -28**

QUESTION 21

Option A is correct. Given that data set F is created by multiplying the y-coordinate of each data point from data set E by 3.9, the equation of the line of best fit for data set F would also have its y-intercept and slope multiplied by 3.9: If the line of best fit for data set E is y = 12 + 1.5x, For data set F: y = 12 × 3.9 + 1.5 × 3.9x   y = 46.8 + 5.85x

QUESTION 22

Given the area of a rectangle and its relationship between length and width: Area = 155 square inches Let w be the width.

Then the length is 7w - 4:

Area = w(7w - 4)

155 = 7w^2 - 4w

Solving the quadratic equation:

7w^2 - 4w - 155 = 0

Using the quadratic formula $\quad w = \frac{-b \pm \sqrt{(b^2 - 4ac)}}{2a}$

where a = 7, b = -4, and c = -155:

$$w = \frac{4 \pm \sqrt{((-4)^2 - 4(7)(-155))}}{2.7}$$

$$w = \frac{4 \pm \sqrt{(16 + 4340)}}{14}$$

$$w = \frac{4 \pm \sqrt{(4356)}}{14}$$

w = [4 ± 66] / 14 Taking the positive solution: w = (4 + 66) / 14 w = 70 / 14 w = 5 inches

Practice Test 2 with Detailed Answers and Explanations

SECTION 1 > READING AND WRITING

MODULE 1: 27 QUESTIONS

DIRECTIONS

This section focuses on various essential reading and writing abilities. Each question contains one or more passages, which might feature a table or graph. Thoroughly read each passage and question, then select the most suitable answer based on the passage(s). All questions in this section are multiple-choice with four options. There's one correct answer for each question.

1. Which word or phrase most accurately characterizes Benito Juarez, who, as Mexico's first Indigenous president, became one of the most _____ figures in his country's history, consolidating national authority and advancing the rights of Indigenous peoples during his lengthy tenure in office from 1858 to 1872?

The options are:

A) unpredictable

B) important

C) secretive

D) ordinary

2.   Many of John Ashbery's poems can be quite challenging to _____ due to their unusual imagery, highly experimental syntax, and opaque subject matter, making them the focus of heated debate among scholars.

The options are:

A) delegate

B) compose

C) interpret

D) renounce

3.   The term "Cambrian explosion" refers to the sudden emergence and rapid diversification of animal fossil remains approximately 541 million years ago during the Cambrian period. Certain scientists contend that this _____ transformation in the fossil record could be attributed to a transition in numerous organisms to physical forms that were more prone to fossilization.

Which option most logically and accurately fills in the blank?

A) catastrophic

B) elusive

C) abrupt

D) imminent

4.   In 2014, during an archaeological excavation in Spain, Vicente Lull and his team discovered the skeletal remains of a woman from El Algar, an Early Bronze Age civilization, interred with valuable artifacts indicating a position of significant authority. This discovery may convince researchers who have contended that Bronze Age societies were governed by men to _____ that women may have also occupied leadership roles.

Which option most logically and accurately fills in the blank?

A) waive

B) concede

C) refute

D) require

5.   Among baleen whale species, certain individuals develop an auxiliary spleen—a seemingly non-functional accumulation of splenic tissue separate from the regular spleen. Considering the formation's higher prevalence among whales known for undertaking deeper dives, some researchers hypothesize that its purpose is not _____; instead, the auxiliary spleen may actively facilitate diving mechanisms.

Which choice most logically and precisely fills in the blank?

A) replicable

B) predetermined

C) operative

D) latent

6. As per a US tax policy expert, state taxes are _____ compared to other factors when contemplating an interstate relocation. Even substantial variations in state taxation have almost no impact on most individuals' decisions, while disparities in employment prospects, housing availability, and climate play a significant and influential role.

Which choice logically and precisely completes the text?

A) consistent with

B) representative of

C) overshadowed by

D) irrelevant to

7. The author's assertion about the relationship between Neanderthals and Homo sapiens is _____, as it fails to take into account several recent archaeological discoveries. For the argument to be persuasive, it would need to address recent findings of additional hominid fossils, such as the latest Denisovan specimens and Homo longi.

A) disorienting

B) tenuous

C) nuanced

D) unoriginal

8. The following excerpt is from Georgia Douglas Johnson's 1922 poem "Benediction." "Venture forth, my child, Propelled by my heartfelt aspirations! Vast unexplored territories Await your claiming. I cannot, even if I wished, Retrace the path alongside you, My journey has concluded, But life beckons you!"

Which choice best encapsulates the primary intent of the text?

A) To convey a hope that a child will achieve identical accomplishments as the parent

B) To imply that nurturing a child entails numerous hardships

C) To caution a child that they will confront myriad challenges throughout their life

D) To inspire a child to wholeheartedly embrace the experiences life presents

9. The following passage is adapted from the 1902 memoir "Indian Boyhood" by Ohiyesa (Charles A. Eastman), a Santee Dakota author. In the text, Ohiyesa recounts how the women in his tribe harvested maple sap during his childhood years.

The women commenced testing the trees - moving at a leisurely pace among them, axe in hand, and striking a single swift blow to observe if sap would emerge. The trees, akin to humans, possessed distinctive characteristics; some were prepared to yield their life essence, while others exhibited greater reluctance. One of the birchen vessels was then positioned beneath each tree, and a hardwood chip driven deeply into the cut made by the axe. From the corners of this chip - initially drop by drop, then more freely - the sap trickled into the small receptacles.

Which choice best describes the function of the underlined sentence within the overall text?

A) It depicts the range of personality traits displayed by the women as they worked.

B) It highlights the beneficial relationship between humans and maple trees.

C) It demonstrates how human behavior can be influenced by the natural environment.

D) It elaborates on an aspect of the maple trees that the women evaluated.

10. Text 1: Ecologists have long pondered how thousands of microscopic phytoplankton species can coexist near ocean surfaces, vying for the same resources. Conventional understanding suggests that a single species should emerge triumphant after outcompeting the rest. So why do so many species persist? Despite numerous attempts, ecologists have yet to uncover a satisfactory explanation for this phenomenon.

Text 2: Ecologist Michael Behrenfeld and colleagues have linked phytoplankton's diversity to their minuscule size. Since these organisms are so tiny, they are relatively distant from one another in ocean water and, moreover, experience that water as a comparatively dense medium. This, in turn, makes it challenging for them to move around and interact with each other. Therefore, according to Behrenfeld's team, direct competition among phytoplankton likely occurs much less than previously thought.

Based on the texts, how would Behrenfeld and colleagues (Text 2) most likely respond to the "conventional wisdom" discussed in Text 1?

A) By arguing that it is based on a misconception about phytoplankton species competing with one another

B) By asserting that it fails to recognize that routine replenishment of ocean nutrients prevents competition between phytoplankton species

C) By suggesting that their own findings help clarify how phytoplankton species are able to compete with larger organisms

D) By recommending that more ecologists focus their research on how competition among phytoplankton species is increased with water density

11. In 2014, Amelia Quon and her team at NASA embarked on building a helicopter capable of flying on Mars. Since Mars's atmosphere is only one percent as dense as Earth's, the Martian air would not provide sufficient resistance to the rotating blades of a conventional helicopter for the aircraft to remain airborne. For five years, Quon's team tested designs in a laboratory that simulated Mars's atmospheric conditions. The craft the team ultimately engineered can fly on Mars because its blades are longer and rotate at a higher speed than those of a similarly sized helicopter designed for Earth.

According to the text, what is the reason a helicopter built for Earth would be unable to operate on Mars?

A) Because Mars and Earth have differing atmospheric conditions

B) Because the blades of Earth-built helicopters are too large to function on Mars

C) Because the gravity of Mars is significantly weaker than Earth's gravity

D) Because Earth-built helicopters are too small to handle the conditions on Mars

12. In West Africa, jalis have traditionally been the custodians of information regarding family histories and records of significant events. They have often served as educators and advisers as well. While new technologies may have altered certain facets of their role today, jalis continue to be esteemed for their knowledge and preservation of their peoples' narratives.

Which choice best captures the main idea of the text?

A) Despite some changes in their role, jalis continue to safeguard their communities' histories.

B) Although jalis have multiple roles, many prefer teaching above all.

C) Jalis have been entertaining members within their communities for centuries.

D) Technology can now fulfill some of the responsibilities previously held by jalis.

13. In 1934, physicist Eugene Wigner hypothesized the existence of a crystal composed entirely of electrons arranged in a honeycomb-like structure. However, the so-called Wigner crystal remained largely theoretical until Feng Wang and colleagues announced in 2021 that they had captured an image of one. The researchers trapped electrons between two semiconductors and then cooled the apparatus, causing the electrons to settle into a crystalline arrangement. By inserting an ultrathin sheet of graphene above the crystal, the researchers obtained an impression—the first visual confirmation of the Wigner crystal.

Which choice best encapsulates the main idea of the text?

A) Researchers have obtained the most conclusive evidence to date of the Wigner crystal's existence.

B) Researchers have identified an innovative new method for working with unusual crystalline structures.

C) Graphene is the most crucial of the components required to capture an image of a Wigner crystal.

D) It's challenging to acquire an image of a Wigner crystal due to the crystal's honeycomb structure.

14. Examining a large sample of companies, economic experts Maria Guadalupe, Julie Wulf, and Raghuram Rajan evaluated the number of managers and leaders from various departments who reported directly to a chief executive officer (CEO). According to the researchers, the findings indicate that across the years studied, there was an increasing inclination among CEOs to connect with more departments within their companies.

Which choice best describes the data from the graph corroborates the researchers' conclusion?

A) The average numbers of managers and department leaders reporting directly to their CEO did not vary from the 1991-1995 period to the 2001-2008 period.

B) The average number of managers reporting directly to their CEO was highest during the 1996-2001 period.

C) The average number of department leaders reporting directly to their CEO exceeded the average number of managers reporting directly in each of the three periods analyzed.

D) The average number of department leaders reporting directly to their CEO increased over the three periods studied.

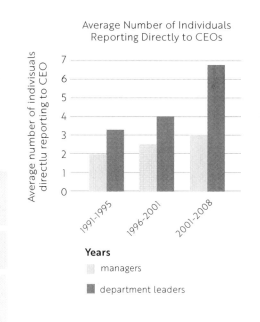

Average Number of Individuals Reporting Directly to CEOs

Years

managers

department leaders

15. When searching for clams, which are their main source of sustenance, sea otters inflict damage upon the roots of eelgrass plants flourishing on the seafloor. In the vicinity of Vancouver Island in Canada, the otter populace is substantial and well-entrenched, yet the eelgrass meadows exhibit superior vitality in comparison to those situated elsewhere along Canada's coastal regions. To elucidate this phenomenon, conservation scientist Erin Foster and her colleagues drew comparisons between the Vancouver Island meadows and meadows where otters are either entirely absent or have been recently reintroduced. Upon discerning that the Vancouver Island meadows boast a more diverse genetic pool than the others, Foster hypothesized that the damage inflicted upon eelgrass roots amplifies the plant's rate of sexual reproduction; this, in turn, augments genetic diversity, thereby benefiting the overall well-being of the meadow.

Which finding, if proven to be factual, would most directly undermine Foster's hypothesis?

A) At certain locales encompassed within the study, eelgrass meadows are proximate to otter populations that are diminutive in size and have only recently been reintroduced.

B) At several sites not incorporated into the study, there exist sizable, well-established sea otter populations, yet eelgrass meadows are conspicuously absent.

C) At several sites not incorporated into the study, the health of eelgrass meadows exhibits a negative correlation with the duration of residence and magnitude of otter populations.

D) At certain locales encompassed within the study, the health of plant species unrelated to eelgrass exhibits a negative correlation with the duration of residence and magnitude of otter populations.

16. Researchers have noted that the literary works of F. Scott Fitzgerald were likely shaped, to some degree, by his marital relationship with Zelda Fitzgerald, yet many neglect to recognize Zelda as an author in her own right. The truth is, Zelda herself penned several compositions, such as the novel Save Me the Waltz and numerous short stories. Thus, those who primarily perceive Zelda's role as a source of inspiration for F. Scott's writings _____

Which choice completes the passage most logically?

A) overlook the multitude of other factors that inspired F. Scott's writing

B) risk understating the full breadth of Zelda's literary contributions

C) may arrive at mistaken judgments about how F. Scott and Zelda viewed one another's works

D) tend to interpret the writings of F. Scott and Zelda through an excessively autobiographical lens

17. Among socially-inclined creatures that nurture their offspring, such as chickens, macaque primates, and humans, newborns appear to exhibit an innate attraction towards faces and face-resembling stimuli. Elisabetta Versace and her colleagues utilized an image depicting three black dots arranged in a pattern resembling eyes and a nose or mouth to test whether this trait is also present in Testudo tortoises, solitary creatures that do not engage in parental care behaviors. They discovered that tortoise hatchlings demonstrated a significant preference for the image, suggesting _____

Which choice logically concludes the passage?

A) Face-like stimuli are likely perceived as non-threatening by newborns of social species that practice parental care but as menacing by newborns of solitary species lacking parental care.

B) Researchers should not assume that an innate attraction to face-like stimuli is necessarily an adaptation related to social interaction or parental care behaviors.

C) Researchers can assume that the attraction to face-like stimuli observed in social species that practice parental care is a learned behavior rather than innate.

D) Newly hatched Testudo tortoises exhibit a stronger preference for face-like stimuli compared to adult Testudo tortoises.

18. Assembled in the late 1500s, primarily through the efforts of Indigenous scribes, Cantares Mexicanos stands as the most significant compilation of poetry composed in Classical Nahuatl, the principal tongue of the Aztec Empire. The poems depict Aztec society prior to the occupation of the empire by the Spanish military forces, and marginalia within Cantares Mexicanos indicates that a substantial portion of the collection's content predates the initial invasion. Nonetheless, certain poems undeniably contain references to beliefs and customs prevalent in Spain during this era. Consequently, some scholars have concluded that _____

Which choice most logically concludes the passage?

A) While its content is largely pre-invasion, Cantares Mexicanos also incorporates additions made following the invasion.

B) Although those who compiled Cantares Mexicanos were fluent in Nahuatl, their knowledge of the Spanish language was limited.

C) Prior to the Spanish invasion, the poets of the Aztec Empire borrowed from the literary traditions of other societies.

D) The references to beliefs and customs in Spain should be attributed to a coincidental resemblance between the societies of Spain and the Aztec Empire.

19. In a study examining the cognitive capabilities of white-faced capuchin monkeys (Cebus imitator), researchers failed to account for the physical difficulty of the tasks utilized to assess the monkeys. The cognitive abilities of monkeys presented with problems requiring minimal dexterity, such as sliding a panel to obtain food, were evaluated using the same criteria as those of monkeys faced with physically demanding problems, such as unscrewing a bottle and inserting a straw. Consequently, the results of the study _____
Which choice logically completes the text?

A) could suggest the existence of differences in cognitive ability among the monkeys, even though such differences may not actually be present.

B) are useful for identifying tasks that exceed the cognitive capacities of the monkeys, but not for identifying tasks within their cognitive abilities.

C) should not be considered indicative of the cognitive abilities of any monkey species other than C. imitator.

D) reveal more about the monkeys' cognitive abilities when solving artificial problems than when solving problems encountered in their natural habitats.

20.   In order to endure periods of water scarcity, embryos encased within the eggs of African turquoise killifish _____ a dormant condition termed diapause. During this state, embryonic development is suspended for a duration spanning up to two years—exceeding the lifespan of an adult killifish. Which choice completes the text in conformity with the conventions of Standard English?

A) enter

B) to enter

C) having entered

D) entering

21. Established in 1967 with the aim of promoting political and economic stability within the Asia-Pacific region, the Association of Southeast Asian Nations initially comprised five member nations: Thailand, the Philippines, Singapore, Malaysia, and Indonesia. By the conclusion of the 1990s, the organization _____ its original membership.

Which choice completes the text in accordance with the conventions of Standard English?

A) has doubled

B) had doubled

C) doubles

D) will double

22. The immense pressure present in the deep ocean can impact the structure of proteins within the cells of fish, distorting the proteins' shape. The chemical compound trimethylamine N-oxide (TMAO) counteracts this effect, ensuring that proteins retain their original _____ and is found in high concentrations in the cells of the deepest-dwelling fish species.

Which choice completes the text in accordance with the conventions of Standard English?

A) configurations. TMAO

B) configurations TMAO

C) configurations, TMAO

D) configurations and TMAO

23. Food and the sense of taste hold a central place in Monique Truong's novels. In The Book of Salt, for instance, the exiled character Bình maintains a connection to his native Saigon through the cuisine he prepares, while in Bitter in the Mouth, the character Linda _____ a form of synesthesia in which the words she hears evoke specific tastes.

Which choice completes the text in accordance with the conventions of Standard English?

A) experienced

B) had experienced

C) experiences

D) will be experiencing

24. Inventor John Friedman devised the initial version of the inaugural flexible straw by placing a screw into a paper straw and tightly wrapping the straw around it using dental floss. Once the floss and screw were taken out, the resulting ridges in the paper enabled the straw to bend effortlessly over the rim of a glass.

Which option completes the sentence in accordance with Standard English conventions?

A) screw's thread's.

B) screws' threads.

C) screw's threads.

D) screws threads'.

25. In her examination of Edith Wharton's The House of Mirth (1905), academic Candace Waid notes that the book portrays the elite circles of New York society as "engulfed by the hunger of a heartless _____," a fitting evaluation considering The House of Mirth is situated within the Gilded Age, characterized by swift industrialization, financial avarice, and increasing wealth discrepancies.

Which option properly completes the sentence according to the norms of Standard English?

A) materialism"; and

B) materialism" and

C) materialism,"

D) materialism"

26. To humans, it seems that the golden orb-weaver spider doesn't employ camouflage to catch its _____ instead, the brightly colored arachnid appears to conspicuously wait in the center of its expansive circular web for insects to approach. Researcher Po Peng of the University of Melbourne has suggested that the spider's unique coloration might actually contribute to its allure.

Which option correctly completes the sentence following the standards of Standard English?

A) prey, rather,

B) prey rather,

C) prey, rather;

D) prey; rather,

27. In Death Valley National Park's Racetrack Playa, a flat, dry lakebed, there are 162 rocks—some weighing less than a pound but others almost 700 pounds—that move periodically from place to place, seemingly of their own volition. Racetrack-like trails in the _____ mysterious migration.

Which option properly completes the sentence according to the norms of Standard English?

A) playas sediment mark the rock's

B) playa's sediment mark the rocks

C) playa's sediment mark the rocks'

D) playas' sediment mark the rocks

STOP IF YOU COMPLETE BEFORE THE TIME LIMIT, YOU MAY JUST REVIEW YOUR WORK ON THIS MODULE. AVOID SWITCHING TO ANY OTHER TEST MODULE

MODULE 2: 27 QUESTIONS

1. The play "The Mule Bone," penned jointly by Zora Neale Hurston and Langston Hughes in 1930, stands out as perhaps the most prominent illustration of _____ among literary works. The majority of authors prefer toiling solo, and considering the fact that their collaborative effort cost Hurston and Hughes their friendship, it's understandable why this approach is often eschewed.

Which choice fills the blank with the most logical and precise word or phrase?

A) characterization

B) interpretation

C) collaboration

D) commercialization

2. The mechanical recycling of plastics is frequently regarded as _____ due to the environmental toll it exacts and the degradation in material quality that frequently ensues. However, chemist Takunda Chazovachii has been instrumental in developing a more eco-friendly chemical recycling process that transforms the superabsorbent polymers found in diapers into a coveted reusable adhesive.

Which choice fills the blank with the most logical and precise word or phrase?

A) resilient

B) inadequate

C) dynamic

D) satisfactory

3. Disruptions in the supply chain for the microchips utilized in personal electronic devices have posed a challenge to an economist's assertion that retailers can anticipate robust growth in sales of those products in the forthcoming months. The delays are improbable to _____ her projection altogether, but they will almost certainly extend its timeframe.

Which choice completes the text most logically and precisely?

A) dispute

B) withdraw

C) underscore

D) invalidate

4. For her 2021 art installation titled "Anthem," Wu Tsang collaborated with singer and composer Beverly Glenn-Copeland to craft a piece that critics found genuinely _____: they commended Tsang for her inventive transformation of a museum rotunda into a dynamic exhibit by projecting filmed visuals of Glenn-Copeland onto a massive 84-foot curtain and filling the space with the sounds of his and other vocalists' singing.

Which choice completes the text most logically and precisely?

A) restrained

B) inventive

C) inexplicable

D) mystifying

5. Some scientists have posited that mammals in the Mesozoic era did not constitute a particularly
_____ group, but paleontologist Zhe-Xi Luo's research indicates that early mammals living in the
shadow of dinosaurs were not all ground-dwelling insectivores. Fossils of various plant-eating mammalian
species have been uncovered in China, including creatures like Vilevolodon diplomylos, which Luo asserts
could glide akin to a flying squirrel.

Which choice completes the text most logically and precisely?

A) predatory

B) obscure

C) diverse

D) localized

6. The poem "Street Lamps in Early Spring," written by Gwendolyn Bennett in 1926, is the source of the
language that follows. Night puts on an article of clothing. Soft as velvet, as blue as violet... She then pulls a
veil, as shimmering and delicate as drifting dew, over her face. And occasionally, the delicate hands of Night
move softly with their gem-starred light in the darkness of her hair.

Which option best sums up the text's general organization?

A) It alternates between describing nighttime scenes in a city and a rural location.

B) It draws a picture of dusk and, subsequently, a picture of dawn.

C) It compares the night to a human being in detail.

D) It illustrates the way that darkness varies with the seasons.

7. Historian Vicki L. Ruiz claims that during World War II, Mexican American women played a significant
role in the labor movement. Food processing businesses at the time signed contracts to provide canned products to the US military. Increased output targets gave the company's workers, many of whom were Mexican
American women, additional negotiating leverage. Workers demanded better benefits, and bosses, eager to
meet their obligations under the contracts, obliged. Mexican American women therefore used labor action
as a forum to claim their agency.

Which option best sums up the underlined section's purpose throughout the entire text?

A) It provides further details on an earlier allegation made in the text regarding labor
relations in a certain sector.

B) It provides an illustration of a pattern in the post-World War II economy that was
previously covered in the book.

C) It draws attention to a potential deviation from the historical account of labor activism that
was previously outlined in the text.

D) It offers more information on the identity of the employees that was previously covered in
the text.

8. The short tale "John Redding Goes to Sea" by Zora Neale Hurston, published in 1921, is the source of the prose that follows. A little boy named John lives in a village in the woods. Given that John was a creative youngster who enjoyed daydreaming, it's possible that the people in the Florida woods were perplexed by the ten-year-old. Only around three hundred feet separated his back door from the St. John River. At this point, a profusion of palm trees, lush magnolias, and bay trees flourish along its banks. Millions of exquisitely colored hyacinths float on the stream's bosom. When [John Redding] would stroll to the edge of the water, he would love to watch them float away down stream to Jacksonville, the sea, and the big world while tossing in some dry twigs. He wanted to follow them. Which option best sums up how the underlined sentence fits within the overall structure of the text?

A) It gives a detailed account of a place that John enjoys going to.

B) It demonstrates that John's actions have confused some of the town's citizens.

C) It demonstrates how distinct John's imagination is from other kids' imaginations.

D) It implies that John aspires to live a more fulfilling life outside of the Florida forests.

9. The Picture of Dorian Gray by Oscar Wilde, published in 1891, is the source of the content that follows. Dorian Gray is looking at a painting that Hallward created of him for the first time. Dorian glanced toward his photo after walking by it listlessly. He recoiled in surprise as soon as he saw it, and his cheeks briefly reddened. His eyes took on a happy expression, as though he was finally able to identify himself. He was stunned and astonished as he stood there, vaguely aware that Hallward was addressing him but unable to understand what he was saying. It was as though he had come to the realization that he was beautiful. He'd never experienced it before. And what is true about Dorian as described in the text?

A) He's curious about Hallward's thoughts on the portrait.

B) He finds the portrait's contents to be delightful.

C) Compared to other painting styles, he favors portraiture.

D) He has doubts about Hallward's artistic ability.

10. Melvin Stephens Jr. and Kerwin Kofi Charles, two economists, looked at a range of factors that affect American voting turnout. Charles and Stephens assert that the likelihood of voting is influenced by potential voters' confidence in their assessments of candidates, using survey data that revealed whether respondents voted in national elections and their level of political knowledge. In other words, the more informed voters are about politics, the more confident they are in determining whether candidates share their views, and consequently, the more likely they are to vote.

Which option most accurately sums up the graph's statistics that back up Charles and Stephens' assertion?

A) Voters with more knowledge were more likely to cast a ballot than voters with less information at every position on the political orientation scale.

B) The only voters with a voting probability below 50% were those who identified as independents and had limited knowledge.

C) Voters with poor information were more likely to cast a ballot if they were between the extremes of the political orientation spectrum.

D) Compared to low-information voters, high-information respondents were more likely to identify as strong Republicans or Democrats.

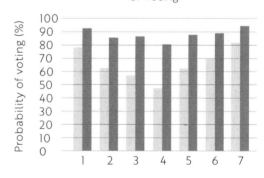

Voters' Political Orientation, Level of Political Information, and Probability of Voting

Voters' Political Orientation
(1 = strong Democrat/liberal;
4 = independent;
7 = strong Republican/conservative)

low information
high information

11. 11. A biology student put spiders in two enclosures—one with lizards and the other without—and counted the number of spiders in each enclosure for thirty days to look into the impact of lizard predation on spider populations. The student came to the conclusion that the lizards' presence was solely responsible for the decrease in the number of spiders in the cage by day thirty.

Which option best sums up the graph's statistics that contradict the student's conclusion?

A) On the first day, the number of spiders in both cages was the same.

B) In the enclosure lacking lizards, the number of spiders had likewise significantly decreased by day thirty.

C) From day 1 to day 10, there was the biggest drop in the number of spiders in the lizard cage.

D) Compared to the enclosure without lizards, the spider population count on day 30 was lower in the enclosure with lizards.

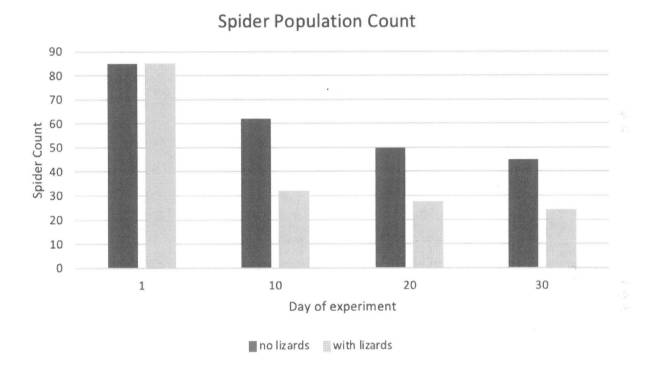

12. Xinyi Liu, an anthropologist, and archaeologist Petra Vaiglova conducted research on the domestication of farm animals in China during the Bronze Age (c. 2000–1000 BCE). Through a detailed examination of the chemical makeup of the bones belonging to sheep, goats, and cattle from this historical period, the researchers concluded that the majority of the diets of the sheep and goats were composed of wild plants, whereas the cattle ate mostly human-cultivated millet. The researchers came to the conclusion that whereas sheep and goats were free to roam farther, cattle were probably reared closer to human settlements.

Which discovery, if accurate, would lend the greatest weight to the team's conclusion?

A) An examination of the animal bones revealed that wheat, which was extensively farmed by people in China throughout the Bronze Age, was also a part of the cattle's diet.

B) Additional analysis of the bones of sheep and goats showed that they also consumed tiny amounts of millet in their diets.

C) Compared to the diets of sheep and goats, the diets of cattle often call for higher food intake and a wider range of nutrients.

D) It was discovered that the diets of cattle, sheep, and goats differed according on what the farmers in each Bronze Age community could cultivate.

13. Approximately 100 million to 66 million years ago, during the Late Cretaceous period, enormous sea reptiles called mosasaurs existed. In order to estimate the likely body temperatures of mosasaurs, Celina Suarez, Alberto Pérez-Huerta, and T. Lynn Harrell Jr. studied oxygen-18 isotopes in mosasaur tooth enamel. They found that mosasaurs were endothermic, meaning they relied on internal metabolic processes to maintain a stable body temperature in a range of ambient temperatures. Endothermy, according to Suarez, Pérez-Huerta, and Harrell, would have allowed mosasaurs to wander over rather frigid arctic seas.

Which conclusion, if accurate, would most strongly bolster the assertion made by Suarez, Pérez-Huerta, and Harrell?

A) It is simpler to estimate the probable body temperatures of molasisaurs using tooth enamel oxygen-18 isotope data than it is to estimate the body temperatures of nonendothermic sea reptiles from the Late Cretaceous.

B) Although in lesser quantities than elsewhere, fossils of both nonendothermic sea reptiles and mosasaurs have been discovered in areas that are thought to have been close to the poles during the Late Cretaceous.

C) While very few fossils of nonendothermic sea reptiles have been discovered in areas known to have been close to the poles during the Late Cretaceous, some mosasaur fossils have been discovered there.

D) Seawater temperatures were probably greater during the Late Cretaceous than they are now across the range of mosasaurs, especially close to the poles.

14. Researchers postulated that a decrease in the number of eastern oysters in the area was caused by a fall in the dusky shark population close to North America's mid-Atlantic coast. Although cownose rays are the primary predators of eastern oysters, dusky sharks do not often eat them.

Which result, if accurate, would most strongly lend credence to the researchers' theory?

A) Regional decreases in the number of dusky sharks are linked to reductions in the quantity of other prey species, such as cownose rays.

B) Compared to places with only dusky sharks, locations containing cownose rays appear to have a higher abundance of eastern oysters.

C) Before the local fall in dusky shark numbers started, cownose rays in the area significantly boosted their consumption of eastern oysters.

D) The regional abundance of cownose rays has grown in tandem with the decline of dusky sharks.

15. Voting in an election does not alter a voter's opinion of the politicians running for office, according to political scientists who support the conventional explanation of voter behavior. Ebonya Washington and Sendhil Mullainathan tested this claim by focusing on every US presidential election from 1976 to 1996 and differentiating between subjects who had just turned 18 (approximately half of whom actually cast ballots) and otherwise similar subjects who were just too young to cast a ballot (none of whom did). Two years after each election, Washington and Mullainathan contrasted the opinions of the various topic groups toward the victor.

Which study conclusion by Washington and Mullainathan, if accurate, would most immediately refute the assertion made by supporters of the conventional view of voter behavior?

A) Regardless of whether the individuals were old enough to vote at the time of the election, their overall political inclination was a robust predictor of their opinions about the victor two years later.

B) Two years after the election, subjects who were too young to cast ballots showed noticeably higher favorable sentiments toward the victor than they did at the time of the election.

C) Two years later, individuals who cast ballots in a particular election were far more divided in their opinions about the victorious candidate than were subjects who were too young to vote in that particular election.

D) Individuals who cast ballots and individuals who were too young to vote had considerably higher odds of expressing unfavorable than positive sentiments on the victorious candidate two years following that election.

16. Compared to older types of solar cells, perovskite solar cells convert light into energy more effectively, and recent advancements in manufacturing have made them more appealing to the commercial world. However, the cells' electron transport layer (ETL), which absorbed electrons must transit through, is one of its limitations. Although spin coating is a common method of applying the ETL, such ETLs are not very effective in converting input power to output power. André Taylor and associates experimented with a new spray coating technique to apply the ETL. The researchers created ETLs of various thicknesses and found that spray coating offers potential for enhancing the power conversion efficiency of ETLs in perovskite solar cells.

Which option most accurately sums up the graph's facts that support Taylor and colleagues' findings?

A) At their lowest performance thickness, the ETL applied by spin coating and the ETL applied by spray coating both demonstrated a power conversion efficiency of more than 10%.

B) Compared to the best-performing ETL applied using spin coating, the lowest-performing ETL applied through spray coating showed a greater power conversion efficiency.

C) roughly 13% of the power conversion efficiency was demonstrated by the best-performing ETL applied by spray coating, and roughly 11% by the best-performing ETL applied using spin coating.

D) The power conversion efficiency of the best and lowest performing ETLs placed using spray coating differed significantly.

17. Although New York City is regarded as one of the greatest sites to view contemporary art from throughout the world, Okwui Enwezor saw few works by African artists in exhibitions during her time as a student there in the 1980s. An arts writer claims that Enwezor attempted to address this shortcoming later in his career as a well-known curator and art historian, not by concentrating just on contemporary African artists but also by demonstrating how their work fits into the greater framework of international modern art and art history.

Which result, if accurate, would lend the most weight to the journalist's assertion?

A) One of the biggest art exhibits honoring a Black artist in European history, El Anatsui: Triumphant Scale, was curated by Enwezor while he was curator of the Haus der Kunst in Munich, Germany. El Anatsui is a Ghanaian sculptor.

B) Enwezor and cocurator Katy Siegel curated the show Postwar: Art Between the Pacific and the Atlantic, 1945–1965, which featured pieces by prominent international artists including Mexico's David Siqueiros and American artist Andy Warhol alongside African artists like Malangatana Ngwenya.

C) Enwezor's work as curator of the 2001 exhibition The Short Century: Independence and

Liberation Movements in Africa, 1945–1994 demonstrated how African artists of the era, including Kamala Ibrahim Ishaq and Thomas Mukarobgwa, were greatly influenced by the continent's movements for independence from European colonial powers after World War II.

D) In order to highlight the variety of ways that African artists have treated the medium of photography, rather than to highlight a certain aesthetic trend, Enwezor curated the exhibition In/sight: African Photographers, 1940 to the Present.

18. The bottle gourd is a huge bitter fruit with a thick skin that has been used for thousands of years by people in the Americas to construct musical instruments, bottles, and other kinds of containers. Strangely, no species of bottle gourd is native to the Western Hemisphere; the fruit and/or seeds must have been brought over from Asia or Africa.

Which option brings the text up to date and into compliance with Standard English conventions?

A) to employ

B) made use of

C) after utilizing

D) using

19. While many video game developers want to provide graphics that are ever more stunning, others take a different approach and create games with graphics that are reminiscent of the "8-bit" games from the 1980s and 1990s. (The phrase "8-bit" describes a console whose CPU could only manage eight data bits simultaneously.)

Which option brings the text up to date and into compliance with Standard English conventions?

A) realistic but

B) realistic

C) realistic,

D) realistic, although

20. Joseph McVicker was having trouble keeping his firm solvent in the 1950s when his sister-in-law Kay Zufall suggested that he use the nontoxic, clay-like material the company produced to remove soot from wallpaper as a kid's modeling putty. Furthermore, Zufall _____ is marketing the product as Play-Doh, which is kid-friendly.

Which option brings the text up to date and into compliance with Standard English conventions?

A) proposed

B) recommends

C) had proposed

D) made a suggestion

21. Beatrix Potter is primarily recognized for her work on children's books, including The Tale of Peter Rabbit (1902). However, she also devoted her life to the study of fungi, studying over 350 different species of fungi that she saw in the wild and presenting her findings on spore germination to the Linnean Society of London.

Which option brings the text up to date and into compliance with Standard English conventions?

A) Fungi; generating

B) Fungi. Generating

C) fungus that produce

D) fungi that produce

22. _____ have overlooked Akira Kurosawa's equally profound involvement with Japanese creative traditions, like Noh theater, while evaluating his films.

Which option brings the text up to date and into compliance with Standard English conventions?

A) Kurosawa's use of Western literary materials has drawn a lot of criticism, yet

B) A lot of reviewers have focused on Kurosawa's usage of Western literature sources, who

C) A lot of commentators have emphasized how Kurosawa used Western literary elements, although they

D) A lot of commentators have emphasized Kurosawa's utilisation of Western literary materials; they

23. The world's first Indigenous language training app, Chickasaw _____ Chickasaw TV, was created in 2010 with assistance from Joshua Hinson, director of the Chickasaw Nation's language revitalization initiative in Oklahoma. In 2015, a Chickasaw language course was developed by Rosetta Stone.

Which option brings the text up to date and into compliance with Standard English conventions?

A) Basic; an internet television network in 2009;

B) Basic: an internet television network launched in 2009,

C) Basic, an internet television network launched in 2009,

D) Basic, an internet television network launched in 2009,

24. Natural groundwater recharge is the mechanism by which precipitation percolates through the soil to feed the 47 geothermal springs in Arkansas's Hot Springs National Park. In this instance, the permeable hills near Hot _____ gather rainwater in a subterranean basin.

Which option brings the text up to date and into compliance with Standard English conventions?

A) Awakens to

B) Springs: to

C) Springs: to

D) Springs, in order to

25. In a seminal study on the psychology of choice more than two decades ago, professor Sheena Iyengar set up a jam-tasting booth at a grocery store. There were _____ jams available for tasting; some customers got twenty-four possibilities, while others only had six. It's interesting to see that customers with fewer options for jam bought more of it.

Which option brings the text up to date and into compliance with Standard English conventions?

A) Changed:

B) changed,

C) changed, although

D) changed as

26. The 2013 book Americanah by Chimamanda Ngozi Adichie recounts the differing lives of Ifemelu and Obinze, a young Nigerian couple, following high school. Ifemelu relocates to the US to study at a famous institution. _____ Obinze goes to London with the intention of launching a career there. But he soon leaves for Nigeria, disillusioned with the lack of chances.

Which option provides the most logical conclusion to the text?

A) In the interim,

B) However,

C) Secondly,

D) Actually,

27. To secure their survival under harsh environments, organisms have evolved a variety of unexpected adaptations. During protracted droughts, tadpole shrimp (Triops longicaudatus) embryos, _____, can halt developing for more than 10 years.

Which option provides the most logical conclusion to the text?

A) Conversely,

B) as an illustration,

C) In the interim,

D) Consequently,

STOP IF YOU COMPLETE BEFORE THE TIME LIMIT, YOU MAY JUST REVIEW YOUR WORK ON THIS MODULE. AVOID SWITCHING TO ANY OTHER TEST MODULE.

SECTION 2: MATH TEST

MODULE 1: 22 QUESTIONS

DIRECTIONS

The problems in this area cover a variety of key math concepts. Calculators are authorized for all questions. .

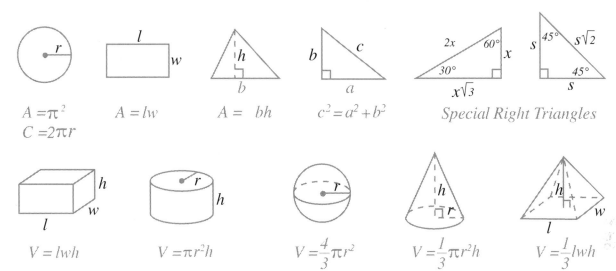

$$A = \pi r^2$$
$$C = 2\pi r$$

$$A = lw$$

$$A = \tfrac{1}{2}bh$$

$$c^2 = a^2 + b^2$$

Special Right Triangles

$$V = lwh$$

$$V = \pi r^2 h$$

$$V = \tfrac{4}{3}\pi r^2$$

$$V = \tfrac{1}{3}\pi r^2 h$$

$$V = \tfrac{1}{3}lwh$$

The number of degrees of arc in a circle is 360.
The number of radians of arc in a circle is 2π.
The sum of the measures in degrees of the angles of a triangle is 180.

Notes

Unless otherwise stated:

· All variables and expressions contain real numbers.

· The figures presented are drawn to scale.

· All of the figures are on the same plane.

· The domain of a given function f is the set of all real integers x that have a real value.

For multiple-choice questions, solve each issue, select the correct answer from the options supplied, and circle it in this book. Circle just one answer to each question. If you change your mind, delete the entire circle. You will not receive credit for questions with multiple circled answers or questions with no circled answers.

For student-generated response questions, solve each issue and record your solution next to or underneath the question in the exam book as stated below.

· After you've typed your response, circle it clearly. You will not be given credit for anything written outside the circle, or for questions having more than one marked answer.

· If you discover many right answers, write and circle only one.

· You can respond with up to 5 characters for a positive response and 6 characters (with the negative sign) for a negative answer, but no more.

· If your answer is a lengthy fraction (more than 5 characters for positive and 6 characters for negative), enter the decimal equivalent.

· If your answer is a large decimal (more than 5 characters for positive and 6 characters for negative), truncate it or round to the fourth number.

· If your answer is a mixed number (e.g. 3½), express it as an improper fraction (7/2) or decimal equivalent (3.5).

· Avoid using symbols like a percent sign, comma, or dollar sign in your highlighted response.

1. A painter will apply a certain brand of paint on n walls of the same size and form of a structure. The painter's charge may be estimated using the formula nKAh, where n is the number of walls, K is a constant in dollars per square foot, A is the length of each wall in feet, and h is the height of each wall. What variables in the phrase would alter if the buyer asked the painter to use a more costly brand of paint?

A) h

B) A

C) K

D) n

2. If 3r equals 18, what is the value of 6r plus 3?

A) 6

B) 27

C) 36

D) 39

3. Which of the following equals $a^{\frac{2}{3}}$ for all values of a?

A) $\sqrt{a^{\frac{1}{3}}}$

B) $\sqrt{a^3}$

C) $\sqrt[3]{a^{\frac{1}{2}}}$

D) $\sqrt[3]{a^2}$

4. There were twice as many states that became members of the Union between 1850 and 1900 as there were between 1776 and 1849. Which of the following equations applies if 30 states entered the union between 1776 and 1849 and x states joined between 1850 and 1900?

A) 30x = 2

B) 2x = 30

C) x/2 = 30

D) x + 30 = 2

5. Given that 5/x = 15/(x+20), what is x/5?

A) 10

B) 5

C) 2

D) 1/2

6. $2x - 3y = -14$

$3x - 2y = -6$

Given that the system of equations above has a solution represented by (x, y), what is the value of $x - y$?

A) −20

B) −8

C) −4

D) 8

7. A polynomial defines the function f. In the table above, a few values for x and f (x) are displayed. Of the following, which one needs to be a factor of f (x)?

A) x − 2

B) x − 3

C) x − 4

D) x − 5

x	F(x)
0	3
2	1
4	0
5	-2

8. The xy-plane is used to graph the line $y = kx + 4$, where k is a constant. What is the slope of the line in terms of c and d if it encompasses the point (c, d) where $c \neq 0$ and $d \neq 0$?

A) (d−4)/c

B) (c−4)/d

C) (4−d)/c

D) (4−c)/d

9. $kx - 3y = 4$

$4x - 5y = 7$

In the given system of equations, x and y are variables and k is a constant. What value of k would the equation system be unable to solve?

A) 12/5

B) 16/5

C) (−16)/7

D) (−12)/7

10. The line with equation $y = 25$ is intersected at points A and B by the parabola with equation $y = [(x-11)]^2$ in the xy-plane. What is AB's length?

A) 10

B) 12

C) 14

D) 16

11. $y = a(x - 2)(x + 4)$

The constant an in the above quadratic equation is nonzero. The equation's graph in the xy plane is a parabola with (c, d) as its vertex. Which of the subsequent terms equals d?

A) −9a

B) −8a

C) −5a

D) −2a

12. $C = \frac{5}{9}(F - 32)$

The relationship between a temperature F, expressed in degrees Fahrenheit, and a temperature C, expressed in degrees Celsius, is demonstrated by the equation above. Which of the following has to be true based on the equation?

I   A 1 degree Fahrenheit rise in temperature is equal to a 5/9 degree Celsius increase in temperature.

II   A one-degree Celsius increase in temperature is equal to a 1.8-degree Fahrenheit increase.

III   A 5/9 degree Fahrenheit temperature rise is equal to a 1 degree Celsius temperature increase.

A) I only

B) II only

C) III only

D) I and II only

13. A few values of the linear function f are displayed in the above table. Which definition of f applies to ?

n	1	2	3	4
F(n)	-2	1	4	7

A) $f(n) = n - 3$

B) $f(n) = 2n - 4$

C) $f(n) = 3n - 5$

D) $f(n) = 4n - 6$

14. About 5% of enrolled seniors and 7% of enrolled juniors at Lincoln High School were admitted into the National Honor Society the previous year. Which of the following best describes the total number of juniors and seniors at Lincoln High School who were inducted into the National Honor Society last year, assuming there were 562 juniors and 602 seniors enrolled?

A) 140

B) 69

C) 39

D) 30

15. 3x^2-5x+2

5x^2-2x-6

Which of the following sums up the two polynomials that were just shown?

A) 8x^2-7x+4

B) 8x^2+7x+4

C) 8x^4-7x^2-4

D) 8x^4+7x^2-4

16. If 3/5 w = 4/3 , What does w stand for?

A) 9/20

B) 4/5

C) 5/4

D) 20/9

17. It takes Nate 13.7 seconds to walk 25 meters. Which of the following best describes the distance he will walk in four minutes if he continues to walk at this pace?

A) 150 meters

B) 450 meters

C) 700 meters

D) 1,400 meters

The following material is referenced in the next two questions.

Planet	Acceleration due to gravity (m/$[sec]^2$)
Mercury	3.6
Venus	8.9
Earth	9.8
Mars	3.8
Jupiter	26.0
Saturn	11.1
Uranus	10.7
Neptune	14.1

The accompanying graphic provides an estimate of the acceleration caused by gravity for each of the eight planets in our solar system, expressed in meters per second squared (m/$\| sec]^2$). The formula W= mg may be used to determine an object's weight on a certain planet. Here, W stands for the object's weight in newtons, m for its mass in kilograms, and g for the planet's acceleration due to gravity, expressed in (m/$\| sec]^2$).

18. What is the mass of an item on Mercury that weighs ninety kilograms, expressed in newtons?

A) 25

B) 86

C) 101

D) 324

19. In a hotel conference room, using a phone costs $0.20 per minute. Which of the subsequent formulas sums up the price of using a phone for h hours, in dollars?

A) c = 0.20(60h)

B) c = 0.20h + 60

C) c = 60h/0.20

D) c = 0.20h/60

20. Graphene, a material used to make integrated circuits, is so thin that it may cover up to seven football fields in a single ounce. What is the approximate area of a football field (one and a third acres) that 48 ounces of graphene could cover?

A) 250

B) 350

C) 448

D) 1,350

21. Which of the following four savings account plan types would result in the account's balance growing exponentially?

A) The account's worth is increased by 2% of the starting funds each year.

B) The account value is increased by $100 and 1.5% of the original funds each year.

C) The account's worth is increased by 1% of its existing value every year after that.

D) The account's worth is increased by $100 per year.

22. Eighty-five is the sum of three numbers. The difference between the sum of the other two numbers and one of the numbers, x, is 50%. What is x's value?

A) 70

B) 51

C) 34

D) 15

STOP IF YOU COMPLETE BEFORE THE TIME LIMIT, YOU MAY JUST REVIEW YOUR WORK ON THIS MODULE. AVOID SWITCHING TO ANY OTHER TEST MODULE.

THE ULTIMATE **DIGITAL SAT** MASTERCLASS

MODULE 2: 22 QUESTIONS

DIRECTIONS

The problems in this area cover a variety of key math concepts. Calculators are authorized for all questions.

Notes

Unless otherwise stated:
· All variables and expressions contain real numbers.
· The figures presented are drawn to scale.
· All of the figures are on the same plane.
· The domain of a given function f is the set of all real integers x that have a real value.

For multiple-choice questions, solve each issue, select the correct answer from the options supplied, and circle it in this book. Circle just one answer to each question. If you change your mind, delete the entire circle. You will not receive credit for questions with multiple circled answers or questions with no circled answers.

For student-generated response questions, solve each issue and record your solution next to or underneath the question in the exam book as stated below.

· After you've typed your response, circle it clearly. You will not be given credit for anything written outside the circle, or for questions having more than one marked answer.

· If you discover many right answers, write and circle only one.

· You can respond with up to 5 characters for a positive response and 6 characters (with the negative sign) for a negative answer, but no more.

· If your answer is a lengthy fraction (more than 5 characters for positive and 6 characters for negative), enter the decimal equivalent.

· If your answer is a large decimal (more than 5 characters for positive and 6 characters for negative), truncate it or round to the fourth number.

· If your answer is a mixed number (e.g. 3½), express it as an improper fraction (7/2) or decimal equivalent (3.5).

· Avoid using symbols like a percent sign, comma, or dollar sign in your highlighted response.

1.   Mr. Kohl is going to give his chemistry students a beaker filled with n milliliters of solution. He will have five milliliters left over if he gives each pupil three milliliters of solution. He will want an extra 21 milliliters to provide each pupil with 4 milliliters of solution. The number of pupils in the class?

A) 16

B) 21

C) 23

D) 26

2.   A rectangle was modified by subtracting p percent from its width and adding 10 percent to its length. What is the value of p if these changes resulted in a 12 percent decrease in the rectangle's area?

A) 12

B) 15

C) 20

D) 22

3. Handedness

The number of right-handed and left-handed pupils at Keisel Middle School by gender is shown in the partial table above for the eighth grade. There are five times as many female students who are right-handed as there are left-handed students, and there are nine times as many male students who are right-handed as there are left-handed. Which of the following best describes the likelihood that a right-handed student chosen at random is a female, given that there are 122 right-handed students and 18 left-handed students in the school?

Gender	Left	Right
Female		
Male		
Total	18	122

(Note: Assume that no kid in the eighth grade is both left- and right-handed.)

A) 0.410

B) 0.357

C) 0.333

D) 0.250

4. The Spanish club consists of 55 students. A random sample of students from the Spanish club was selected and surveyed about their intention to enroll in a new study program. Out of the individuals surveyed, 20% indicated their intention to engage in the study program. According to this survey, what is the most accurate approximation of the total number of students in the Spanish club who plan to participate in the study program?

A) 11

B) 20

C) 44

D) 55

5. 5. Jay's walking pace is 3 miles per hour, but his running speed is 5 miles per hour. He spends w hours walking and r hours running, covering a total distance of 14 miles. Which equation accurately captures this scenario?

A) $3w + 5r = 14$

B) $1w + 1r = 35$

C) $1w + 1r = 1/12$

D) $3w + 5r = 12$

6. What is the equivalent equation of $(m^4 q^4 z^{-1})(mq^5 z^3)$, given that m, q, and z are positive?

A) $m^4 q^{20} z^{-3}$

B) $m^5 q^9 z^2$

C) $m^6 q^8 z^{-1}$

D) $m^{20} q^{12} z^{-2}$

7. 73, 74, 75, 77, 79, 82, 84, 85, 91

What is the median of the data shown?

8. x + 40 = 95

What is the value of x that satisfies the given equation?

9. 9. The solution to the provided system of equations is represented by the coordinates (x, y).

5x = 15

−4x + y = −2

What is the sum of x and y?

A) −17

B) −13

C) 13

D) 17

10.   g (m) = −0.05m + 12.1

The function g is used to model how many gallons of gasoline are left in an automobile after m miles of driving. How many gallons of gasoline are consumed to travel a mile, according to the model?

A) 0.05

B) 12.1

C) 20

D) 242.0

11. The provided equation establishes a relationship between the positive variables b, x, and y. Which equation accurately represents the relationship between x, b, and y?

1/ 7b = 11x / y

A) x = 7by / 11

B) x = y − 77b

C) x = y /77b

D) x = 77by

12.

$$y = 76$$

$$y = x^2 - 5$$

The equations intersect at the coordinates (x, y) in the xy-plane. What is a possible value for x?

A) 76 – 5

B) –9

C) 5

D) 76

13. The point (x, 53) satisfies the system of inequalities in the xy-plane. What are the possible values of x?

$y > 14$
$4 + xy < 18$

A) –9

B) –5

C) 5

D) 9

14. Of the 300 seeds that were planted, 80% germinated. What is the germination rate of these seeds?

15. The function f is defined as $f(x) = 4x$. What is the value of x that makes f(x) equal to 8?

16. The phrase $8x(x-7) - 3(x-7)2 - 14x$, when $x > 7$, is similar to which expression?

A) $(x – 7) / 5$

B) $(8x – 3) / 2$

C) $(8x2 – 3x – 14) / (2x – 14)$

D) $(8x2 – 3x – 77) / (2x – 14)$

17. The equation $2 + 18x + y = 9$ defines line p. Line r is orthogonal to line p in the xy-plane. What is the gradient of line r?

A) –9

B) 1 – 9

C) 19

D) 9

18.

$$f(t) = 8,000(0.65)t$$

The function f reflects the quantity of coupons that a corporation distributed to its clients at the conclusion of each year. In this function, t is the number of years that have passed since the conclusion of 1998, with t ranging from 0 to 5. If the function y = (ft) is plotted on the ty-plane, the most accurate interpretation of the y-intercept of the graph in this case is:

A) The minimum estimated number of coupons the company sent to their customers during the 5 years was 1,428.

B) The minimum estimated number of coupons the company sent to their customers during the 5 years was 8,000.

C) The estimated number of coupons the company sent to their customers at the end of 1998 was 1,428.

D) The estimated number of coupons the company sent to their customers at the end of 1998 was 8,000.

19. Triangle XYZ is identical to triangle RST, with X corresponding to R, Y corresponding to S, and Z corresponding to T. The angle Z measures 20 degrees and the length of 2XY is equal to the length of RS. What is the value of angle T?

A) 2°

B) 10°

C) 20°

D) 40°

20. The equation represents a linear relationship between the variables y and x, where y is equal to 6 times x plus 18. One of the equations in a system of two linear equations is provided. The system is unsolvable. Which equation could serve as the second equation in the system?

A) −6x y + = 18

B) −6x y + = 22

C) −12x y + = 36

D) −12x y + = 18

21. What is the area, in square centimeters, of a rectangle having dimensions 34 cm by 29 cm?

22.
$$y = 4x + 1$$
$$4y = 15x - 8$$

The solution to the provided system of equations is represented by the ordered pair (x, y). What is the difference between x and y?

Practice Test 2 Answers

SECTION 1 READING AND WRITING TEST

MODULE 1:

QUESTION 1

Choice B is the best option because it logically concludes the text's discussion of Juarez. In this context, "important" refers to something that has undergone substantial labor or resulted in significant outcomes. According to the book, Juarez—the first Mexican president to come from an Indigenous community—became a particular sort of character in Mexican history. Then, it provides evidence for that assertion by summarizing a few of Juarez's "many significant accomplishments" over his extensive term in government. This setting portrays Juarez as a pivotal and important character in Mexican history.

QUESTION 2

Choice C is the finest response, as it brings the text's study of John Ashbery's poetry to a logical conclusion. In this situation, "interpret" would imply determining the meaning. According to the text, Ashbery's poetry includes a lot of unique elements; it might be challenging to determine the precise subject matter of the poems; and there is a lot of disagreement among academics regarding the poems. It's clear from this context that interpreting Ashbery's poetry is challenging.

QUESTION 3

Choice C is the best response because it brings the text's consideration of the Cambrian period's fossil record to a logical and accurate conclusion. The word "abrupt" here refers to sudden. The book reflects the sudden arrival and quick diversification—or rise in variety—of animal remains during the Cambrian period in the fossil record. This context demonstrates how abruptly these remnants entered the fossil record.

QUESTION 4

Choice B is the best option since it logically concludes the text's explanation of the significance of the 2014 archeological discovery at El Algar. The word "concede" here refers to giving in to an acceptance of truth after initially opposing it. According to the text, some researchers think that "men ruled Bronze Age societies." However, the discovery of "valuable objects signaling a high position of power" in the Bronze Age tomb of a woman at El Algar suggests that "women may have also held leadership roles." Therefore, the text challenges the idea that men were the only leaders in ancient cultures and raises the possibility that those who maintain this belief may change their mind.

QUESTION 5

Choice D is the best option because it logically concludes the text's description of baleen whale auxiliary spleens. "Latent" here refers to inactive or nonfunctional. The paper presents a contrast between the notion that baleen whales' supplementary spleens appear to serve no purpose and the research suggesting that the spleens may in fact support the whales' diving capabilities. As a result, this context suggests that the notion that baleen whales' spleen accessory is latent may not be accurate.

QUESTION 6

Choice C is the best answer because it logically concludes the text's explanation of the elements that impact people's decisions to relocate to another state. "Overshadowed by," in this sense, refers to being eclipsed by or made to appear less significant than other elements influencing an action. According to a

US tax policy expert quoted in the text, state taxes have relatively little bearing on people's decisions to migrate across state lines, but housing availability, career possibilities, and the environment do. Given the circumstances, it appears that individuals value these other considerations over state taxation.

QUESTION 7

Choice B is the best answer since it most logically concludes the text's examination of the author's assertion regarding the link between Neanderthals and Homo sapiens. "Tenuous" in this sense refers to a lack of strength or substance. According to the text, the author's argument lacks credibility since it ignores several significant recent discoveries and other pieces of evidence. It is clear from the context that the author's assertion is unconvincing.

QUESTION 8

Choice D is the best answer since it appropriately summarizes the text's key point. The speaker of the poem starts off by encouraging a young child to "go forth" by saying, "My heart's desire." The speaker continues by saying that the boy has "life calling" him to pursue new experiences that await him—"great reaches yet unknown." Therefore, encouraging a youngster to accept the experiences that are accessible to him in his life is a major goal.

QUESTION 9

Choice D is the best answer because it best reflects how the highlighted passage fits into the text's broader depiction of how the women in Ohiyesa's tribe gathered maple syrup. According to the narrative, the ladies struck the maple trees with an axe to determine which ones would yield sap. The statement that is underlined draws a comparison between individuals and trees, referring to the sap as the plants' "life blood." A few of the trees are eager to release their sap, while others are not. The line uses personification to provide further information about the feature of the maple trees that the women are assessing, namely their capacity to yield sap.

QUESTION 10

Choice A is the best option because, according to Text 2, that is how Behrenfeld and colleagues would most likely reply to the "conventional wisdom" mentioned in Text 1. The referenced common wisdom states that "one species should emerge after outcompeting the rest"—that is, when the other species go extinct from the population due to intense competition for resources. is theory says that when there is species variety within a phytoplankton population, However, Text 2 adds that, contrary to what scientists had previously believed, there is "much less" direct competition for resources among phytoplankton populations since they are so few and widely distributed in the ocean, according to Behrenfeld and colleagues.

QUESTION 11

Choice A is the best answer since it provides an explanation for a helicopter that is explicitly supported by the text. The text suggests that Mars's atmosphere is significantly thinner than Earth's, implying that it lacks the necessary resistance to sustain the blades of an Earth-made helicopter and keep it in the air. Put another way, due to the atmospheric variations between the two worlds, a helicopter designed for Earth cannot fly on Mars.

QUESTION 12

Choice A is the best answer since it accurately expresses the text's key point. According to the book, Jalis' traditional job has been to keep records of family history and major occurrences. The book goes on to state that, while technological advances have changed the function of jalis, they are still appreciated for preserving their communities' histories.

QUESTION 13

Choice A is the best response since it correctly conveys the text's key point. The book suggests that Eugene Wigner proposed the existence of an electron-based honeycomb-shaped crystal. ding to the article, the existence of the Wigner crystal was unknown until Feng Wang and colleagues created an impression of one using two semiconductors and an ultrathin layer of graphene. Thus, the fundamental point is that researchers have found the most conclusive proof to date of the Wigner crystal's existence.

QUESTION 14

Choice D is the best answer because it describes facts from the graph that support the researchers' conclusion that CEOs are more interested in communicating with additional departments inside their organizations. The graph depicts the average number of personnel reporting directly to CEOs over three time periods: managers and department leaders. The average number of department executives reporting directly to their CEO was slightly more than three from 1991 to 1995, four from 1996 to 2001, and over seven from 2001 to 2008. Thus, the average number of department heads reporting directly to their CEO increased during the three time periods investigated, indicating that CEOs were engaging with more departments.

QUESTION 15

Choice C is the best response because it gives a discovery that, if accurate, calls into question Foster's notion that eelgrass root injury promotes eelgrass meadow health by increasing genetic variety. According to the literature, sea otters harm eelgrass roots, whereas eelgrass meadows on Vancouver Island, where there is a significant otter population, are rather healthy. When Foster and her colleagues compared Vancouver Island eelgrass meadows to those without established otter populations, they discovered that the Vancouver Island meadows were more genetically varied. Foster hypothesized that injury to eelgrass roots promotes eelgrass reproduction, therefore boosting genetic variety and meadow health. On the other hand, if other meadows not included in the study become less healthy as the local otter population grows and the otters stay longer, it suggests that the expected increase in damage to eelgrass roots with otter population size and duration of residence doesn't lead to healthier meadows. Such a discovery would undermine Foster's premise.

QUESTION 16

Choice B is the most logical conclusion to the text's consideration of Zelda Fitzgerald's literary accomplishments. The essay opens by stating that many researchers view Zelda primarily through the lens of her marriage to F. Scott Fitzgerald and "don't recognize Zelda as a writer in her own right." The text then references a novel and "numerous short stories" that she produced, which such researchers often disregard. As a result, academics who focus solely on Zelda as a source of inspiration for F. Scott's writings run the risk of distorting Zelda's entire literary contribution.

QUESTION 17

Choice B is the best answer because it provides the most logical conclusion to the text's summary of Versace and colleagues' study. The article asserts that certain species of newborn animals exhibit a preference for faces and facial-like stimuli. According to the book, these animals have two characteristics in common: they are sociable, and they perform parental care, which means they care for their children. The book then delves into Versace and colleagues' experiment, revealing that turtle hatchlings, despite Testudo tortoises' lack of sociability and parental care, responded to a face-like stimulus. Versace and colleagues showed that a species lacking social interaction and parental care possesses an innate attraction to face-like stimuli; therefore, we should not interpret this characteristic as a social interaction or parental care adaptation.

QUESTION 18

Choice A is the best response because it logically concludes the text. According to the text, the Cantares Mexicanos contain poetry about the Aztec Empire that was written before the Spanish conquest. Furthermore, annotations in the collection show that some of these poems predate the Spanish conquest, while some of the rituals represented are most certainly of Spanish provenance. The collection likely includes both pre-invasion and post-invasion content, with some poems likely written before the invasion and later references to Spanish practices.

QUESTION 19

Choice A is the best answer because it gives the most reasonable conclusion based on the text's examination of capuchin monkey cognitive ability. According to the text, the study did not discriminate between outcomes for the capuchin monkeys' activities; therefore, simpler tasks needing less dexterity, or skill, were scored using the same criteria as ones requiring greater dexterity. Because the study did not account for this mismatch, the researchers may have concluded that the observed disparities in performance were attributable to the monkeys' talents rather than the complexity of the tasks. In other words, the data may indicate cognitive differences among the monkeys, even if such differences do not exist.

QUESTION 20

Choice A is the best option. The convention under consideration consists of finite and nonfinite verb forms within a sentence. A major phrase requires a finite verb to conduct the subject's action (in this example, "embryos"), and this option provides the clause with the finite present tense verb "enter" to describe how the embryos enter diapause.

QUESTION 21

Choice B is the best option. The use of verbs to denote tense is the norm under consideration. The past perfect verb "had doubled" accurately conveys that the organization's original membership doubled within a specified era prior to the present, specifically between the organization's establishment in 1967 and the late 1990s.

QUESTION 22

Choice A is the best option. The standard being examined is the use of punctuation between sentences. The period after "configurations" accurately marks the border between one phrase ("The intense... configurations") and another ("TMAO... fish"). The extra phrase ("ensuring configurations") modifies the main clause of the first sentence ("The chemical effect"), whereas "TMAO" is the subject of the second sentence. Choice B is inappropriate since it creates a run-on phrase. The phrases ("The intense configurations" and "TMAO fish") are combined without punctuation or conjunction.

QUESTION 23

Choice C is the best option. The use of verbs to denote tense is the norm under consideration. In this case, the present tense verb "experiences" is compatible with the other present tense verbs (such as "connects" and "prepares") used to describe events in Truong's novels. Furthermore, it is customary to employ the present tense while discussing a literary work.

QUESTION 24

Choice C is the best option. We are evaluating the convention of using plural and possessive nouns. The singular possessive noun "screw's" and plural noun "threads" accurately convey that there is only one screw with many threads.

QUESTION 25

Choice C is the best option. Punctuation between a main sentence and a supplemental noun phrase is the rule under consideration. This choice utilizes a comma to separate the main clause ("scholar... materialism") from the extra noun phrase ("an apt assessment") that expresses Waid's view of how The House of Mirth portrays the upper strata of New York society.

QUESTION 26

Choice D is the best option. The convention being tested is the synchronization of key clauses within a sentence. The semicolon is used appropriately to connect the first main clause ("To humans, prey") with the second main clause ("rather, approach"). The comma after the adverb "rather" separates it from the main clause ("the brightly...") it modifies. This indicates that the information in this clause (how the spider's behavior appears to humans) contradicts the information in the previous clause (how the spider's behavior does not appear to humans).

QUESTION 27

Choice C is the best option. We are evaluating the use of plural and possessive nouns. The singular possessive word "playa's" and the plural possessive noun "rocks'" accurately imply that the silt is from a single playa (the Racetrack Playa) and that many rocks have strangely traveled across it.

SECTION 1

MODULE 2: READING AND WRITING TEST

QUESTION 1

Choice C is the best answer because it logically and exactly concludes the text's examination of The Mule Bone, a play written by Zora Neale Hurston and Langston Hughes. In this usage, "collaboration" refers to working together with someone to create a literary work. According to the text, most writers prefer to work alone, and working together ended Hurston and Hughes' friendship. This demonstrates that The Mule Bone is a rather uncommon case of cooperation in writing.

QUESTION 2

Choice B is the best answer since it logically concludes the text's topic of recycling plastics. In this sense, "inadequate" denotes unsatisfactory. The article claims that the mechanical plastic recycling method harms the environment and results in "the loss of material quality." It compares this with Chazovachii's chemical plastic-recycling technique, which is cleaner and provides a more desired product. The text's emphasis on the negative features of mechanical recycling indicates that it falls short in terms of environmental effects and the quality of the material produced.

QUESTION 3

Choice D is the best answer since it most logically concludes the text's consideration of the economist's thesis regarding personal electronic gadget sales. In this sense, "invalidate" almost always means to negate or render invalid. According to the text, disruptions in the supply of microchips for personal electronics "have challenged" the economist's assumption that personal electronics sales will increase significantly in the coming months. The paragraph goes on to explain the impact of the delays on the economist's prediction, indicating that the delays are quite likely to lengthen the time frame during which the expected sales growth would materialize. This background shows that the delays are unlikely to completely invalidate the economist's estimate—the delays will most certainly change the time period of the projection but will not cancel or render it invalid.

QUESTION 4

Choice B is the best option since it logically concludes the text's description of the art installation, Anthem. In this sense, "inventive" refers to the quality of being creative and inventive. The essay describes how critics praised Tsang's imaginative makeover of a room into a vibrant show with large pictures and lots of music. This context indicates that the critics regarded the essay as highly inventive.

QUESTION 5

Choice C is the best answer since it most logically concludes the text's explanation of the types of animals that existed throughout the Mesozoic era. In this usage, "diverse" refers to a great quantity of variation. The text indicates that some scientists have suggested that Mesozoic mammals cannot be characterized in a certain way, then contrasts that view with Luo's research, which shows that Mesozoic mammals "weren't all ground-dwelling insectivores" and instead were "various." This context implies that some scientists have viewed Mesozoic mammals as being all alike, or not a very diverse group.

QUESTION 6

Choice C is the best answer since it appropriately defines the text's general structure. Throughout the passage, the speaker describes nightfall as if it were a person wearing clothing ("a garment" that is "velvet soft" and "violet blue") and a veil "over her face" and moving her hands "slowly with their gemstarred light" over her black hair. Thus, the material is organized as an extended analogy of night to a human being.

QUESTION 7

Choice A is the best answer because it better reflects how the underlined piece operates in the context of the entire text. According to the text, greater output quotas in food processing industries during World War II allowed employees to negotiate better terms in exchange for their labor. The highlighted section exemplifies this enhanced negotiating power: employees wanted more favorable perks, and employers responded since they were under pressure to meet the stringent requirements of their contracts. Thus, the highlighted portion of the text expands on a previous argument concerning labor relations in a specific industry (food processing).

QUESTION 8

Choice D is the best answer because it clearly reflects how the underlined statement fits within the overall context of the text. The poem builds John's vivid imagination before describing the St. John River near his house in the Florida forests. The highlighted text portrays John sending twigs down the river, imagining them reaching "Jacksonville, the sea, the wide world," where he hopes he could join. This shows that John wishes to broaden his life experiences outside the Florida forests.

QUESTION 9

Choice B is the best answer since it makes a statement about Dorian that is explicitly supported by the text. The text's narrator says that when Dorian sees his portrait, "his cheeks flushed for a moment with pleasure" and "a look of joy came into his eyes." The narrator goes on to say that Dorian looked at the portrait "in wonder" and presents him as being so entranced by the portrait that he doesn't notice what Hallward is saying to him. These characteristics confirm Dorian's claim of being thrilled by what he sees in the painting.

QUESTION 10

Choice A is the best response since it successfully supports Charles and Stephens' argument regarding the impact of information level on voters. The graph depicts the likelihood of voting for both high- and low-information voters in seven types of political orientations. According to Charles and Stephens, voters who are more informed about politics are more likely to vote. The graph shows that high-information voters are more likely to vote than low-information voters across all seven political orientations. As a result, this remark appropriately uses data from the graph to support Charles and Stephens' argument regarding how degree of knowledge impacts voters.

QUESTION 11

Choice B is the best response since it describes graph data that undermines the student's claim regarding the spider population drop in the lizard cage. The graph demonstrates that the enclosure with lizards and the enclosure without lizards each started with around 85 spiders, and that the number of spiders in each enclosure decreased throughout the course of the 30 days. The student claims that the drop in spiders in the enclosure with lizards is "entirely attributable to the presence of the lizards," implying that the spider population would not have declined without the presence of the lizards. This argument, however, is undermined by the fact that the lizard-free enclosure also observed a significant fall in the number of spiders. Because the number of spiders decreased in both the lizard-free and lizard-infested enclosures, there must have been some other reason contributing to the spider population decline besides the presence of the lizards.

QUESTION 12

Choice A is the best response because it offers a discovery that, if confirmed, would most strongly support the team's conclusion that cattle were grown closer to human settlements than sheep and goats. According to the text, Vaiglova, Liu, and their colleagues examined the chemical composition of sheep, goat, and cattle bones from the Bronze Age in China to investigate the animals' domestication, or adaptation, from a wild state to one in which they lived in close proximity to humans. According to the article, the team's investigation revealed that sheep and goats of the era ate primarily wild vegetation, whereas cattle ate millet—an important grain farmed by people. If analysis of the animal bones shows that the cattle's diet also consisted of wheat, another crop cultivated by humans in China during the Bronze Age, the finding would support the team's conclusion by providing additional evidence that cattle during this era fed on human-grown crops—and, by extension, that humans raised cattle relatively close to the settlements where they grew these crops, leaving goats and sheep to roam farther away in areas with wild vegetation,

QUESTION 13

Choice C is the best response because it gives the result that, if accurate, would most strongly support Suarez, Pérez-Huerta, and Harrell's thesis concerning mosasaurs. According to the text, Suarez, Pérez-Huerta, and Harrell's research on mosasaur tooth enamel led them to the conclusion that mosasaurs were endothermic, which implies they could survive in waters of varying temperatures while maintaining a constant body temperature. The researchers believe that endothermy allowed mosasaurs to survive in relatively chilly seas near the poles. If several mosasaur fossils have been discovered in areas near the poles during the time when mosasaurs were alive, and fossils of nonendothermic marine reptiles are uncommon in such locations, this would support the researchers' claim: it would show that mosasaurs inhabited polar waters but nonendothermic marine mammals did not, implying that endothermy may have been the characteristic that allowed mosasaurs to include polar waters in their range.

QUESTION 14

Choice D is the best response since it gives a fact that, if accurate, directly supports the researchers' hypothesis concerning the link between dusky shark population loss and eastern oyster population decline. According to the text, although dusky sharks do not often eat eastern oysters, they do consume cownose rays, which are the primary predators of eastern oysters. An increase in the quantity of cownose rays in the region as a result of a decrease in the abundance of dusky sharks would directly confirm the researchers' hypothesis: a larger number of cownose rays would devour more eastern oysters, reducing the oyster population.

QUESTION 15

Choice C is the best answer because it gives a result that, if correct, undermines the assertion made by those who support the traditional view of voter behavior. According to the text, supporters of the viewpoint feel that voting in an election has no effect on a voter's attitudes about the candidates. If Washington and Mullainathan discovered that two years after an election, attitudes toward the winning candidate were significantly more polarized among voters than among those who were too young to vote, this would imply that the act of voting had an effect on voters' attitudes toward the candidates, undermining the claim that voting does not change voters' attitudes.

QUESTION 16

Choice B is the best answer because it describes graph data that supports Taylor and colleagues' conclusion that spray coating has the potential to improve the power conversion efficiency of ETLs in perovskite solar cells. The text explains that perovskite solar cells' efficiency at converting light into electricity is reduced by their electron transport layer (ETL), which is applied via spin coating, but Taylor's team developed a new spray coating method for applying the ETL that improves power conversion efficiency. The graph depicts statistics on the power conversion efficiency of solar cells from Taylor's team's testing, with bars representing the highest and lowest-performing ETLs in two data categories: spray coating and spin coating. According to the graph, the lowest-performing ETL applied via spray coating had a power conversion efficiency of 14% to 16%, whereas the highest-performing ETL done via spin coating had a power conversion efficiency of less than 14%. These results demonstrate that ETLs applied using innovative spray coatings are more efficient than those applied via regular spin coating. Thus, the statistics back up Taylor and colleagues' conclusion concerning spray coating's potential utility.

QUESTION 17

Choice B is the best answer since it offers a result that, if accurate, would directly corroborate the arts journalist's assertion regarding Enwezor's work as a curator and art historian. According to the text, Enwezor wanted to show not only modern African artists but also "how their work fits into the larger context of global modern art and art history," or how their work relates to artistic developments and work by other artists around the world. According to the description of Postwar: Art Between the Pacific and the Atlantic, 1945–1965, Enwezor and Siegel's exhibition combined works by African artists with works by artists from other countries, supporting the arts journalist's claim that Enwezor wanted to show African artists' works in the context of global modern art and art history.

QUESTION 18

Choice D is the best option. The convention under consideration involves finite and nonfinite verb forms inside a sentence. A main sentence requires a finite verb to carry out the subject's action (in this example, "people in the Americas"), and this option provides the finite past perfect tense verb "have used" to explain how people in the Americas used the gourd.

QUESTION 19

Option D (realistic, although) introduces a contrast between the desire for stunning graphics and the choice to use retro, 8-bit graphics, making it clear that the two approaches are different. The comma before "although" correctly punctuates the contrast.

QUESTION 20

Choice A is the best option. The norm under consideration is the usage of verbs to denote tense. In this case, the simple past tense verb "suggested" correctly implies that Zufall suggested the product's name in the past. This verb tense is compatible with the previous line, which used a simple past tense verb ("advised") to express Zufall's instruction to McVicker in the 1950s.

QUESTION 21

Choice D is the best option. The exam relies on punctuation between two extra phrases after the coordinate sentence ("but she... mycology"). This option correctly uses a comma to distinguish between the supplementary noun phrase ("the study of fungi") that defines the term "mycology" and the supplementary participial phrase ("producing...London"), which provides additional information about Potter's dedication to mycology.

QUESTION 22

Option C is the best choice because it clearly introduces the contrast between the focus on Western literary elements and the overlooked aspect of Kurosawa's involvement with Japanese traditions. The phrase "although they" effectively sets up the contrast and completes the sentence coherently.

QUESTION 23

Choice C is the best option. This option correctly uses commas to set off the appositive phrase "an internet television network launched in 2009," which provides additional information about Chickasaw Basic. It also maintains proper sentence structure and flow, allowing the rest of the sentence to continue smoothly.

QUESTION 24

The correct answer is D: Springs, in order to

This option correctly uses a comma to separate the place name "Hot Springs" from the rest of the sentence, and the phrase "in order to" properly connects the action of gathering rainwater with its purpose. This choice maintains grammatical correctness and clarity while avoiding unnecessary punctuation or awkward phrasing found in the other options.

QUESTION 25

Choice B is the best option. This option correctly uses a comma to introduce the explanation that follows. It maintains the flow of the sentence without adding unnecessary words or changing the meaning. The simple past tense "changed" fits well with the narrative style of the passage, describing a past event in a straightforward manner.

QUESTION 26

Choice A is the best option. "In the interim" provides the most logical transition here, indicating a simultaneous but different action taken by Obinze while Ifemelu is in the US. This phrase effectively connects the two characters' storylines and maintains the narrative flow, showing that their paths diverged during the same period of time.

QUESTION 27

Choice B is the best option. "As an illustration" provides the most logical transition here, introducing a specific example of the unexpected adaptations mentioned in the first sentence. This phrase effectively connects the general statement about adaptations to the specific case of tadpole shrimp embryos, maintaining the flow of the explanation and providing a clear example to support the main idea.

SECTION 2:

MODULE 1: MATH TEST

QUESTION 1

Choice C is correct. The only variable that would change if the customer asked the painter to use a more expensive brand of paint is K, which represents the constant in dollars per square foot. The number of walls (n), the length of each wall (A), and the height of each wall (h) would remain the same.

QUESTION 2

Choice D is correct. If 3r = 18, then r = 6. Therefore, 6r + 3 = 6(6) + 3 = 36 + 3 = 39.

QUESTION 3

Choice D is correct. $a^{\frac{2}{3}} = (a^2)^{\wedge}(1/3) = \sqrt[3]{a^2}$

QUESTION 4

Choice C is correct. If 30 states joined the Union between 1776 and 1849, and twice as many states joined between 1850 and 1900, then x = 2(30) = 60. Therefore, x/2 = 30 is the correct equation.

QUESTION 5

Choice C is correct. Cross-multiplying the equation 5/x = 15/(x+20), we get 5(x+20) = 15x. Simplifying, we get 5x + 100 = 15x, which leads to 100 = 10x, so x = 10. Therefore, x/5 = 10/5 = 2.

QUESTION 6

Choice C is correct. To find x - y, we need to solve the system of equations. Multiplying the first equation by 2 and the second equation by 3, we get: 4x - 6y = -28 9x - 6y = -18 Subtracting the second equation from the first, we get -5x = -10, so x = 2. Substituting x = 2 into the first equation, we get 4 - 3y = -14, which leads to 3y = 18, so y = 6. Therefore, x - y = 2 - 6 = -4.

QUESTION 7

Choice C is correct. To determine which factor is needed for the polynomial f(x), we need to look at the values of f(x) for the given x values and identify any roots of the polynomial. A factor x−a is associated with a root x=a where f(a)=0.

From the table we see that f(x)=0 when x=4. This means x−4 must be a factor of the polynomial f(x), since a polynomial f(x) with a root at x=4 can be factored as (x−4) times another polynomial.

Thus, the correct answer is: x − 4

QUESTION 8

Choice A is correct. The slope of the line y = kx + 4 can be found using the point-slope formula: k = (d - 4) / c, where (c, d) is a point on the line with c ≠ 0.

QUESTION 9

Choice A is correct. The system of equations will have no solution if the lines represented by the equations are parallel. The slopes of the lines are -k/3 and -4/5. For the lines to be parallel, these slopes must be equal: -k/3 = -4/5 5k = 12 k = 12/5 Therefore, the system will have no solution when k = 12/5.

QUESTION 10

Choice A is correct. The y-coordinate of the vertex of the parabola y = (x - 11)^2 is 0, and the y-coordinate of the points A and B is 25. Therefore, the y-coordinate of A and B is 25 units above the vertex. The x-coordinates of A and B can be found by solving the equation 25 = (x - 11)^2: x - 11 = ±5 x = 11 ± 5 x = 6 or 16 The length of AB is the difference between the x-coordinates of A and B: 16 - 6 = 10.

QUESTION 11

Choice A is correct. The vertex of the parabola y = a(x - 2)(x + 4) is the midpoint of the roots x = -4 and x = 2. The x-coordinate of the vertex is (-4 + 2) / 2 = -1, and the y-coordinate can be found by substituting x = -1 into the equation: y = a(-1 - 2)(-1 + 4) = a(-3)(3) = -9a Therefore, d = -9a.

QUESTION 12

Choice D is correct. Statement I is true because if F increases by 1, then C increases by 5/9, according to the equation C = 5/9(F - 32). Statement II is also true because if C increases by 1, then F increases by 9/5, according to the equivalent equation F = 9/5C + 32. Statement III is false because if F increases by 5/9, then C increases by (5/9) * (5/9) = 25/81, not 1.

QUESTION 13

Choice C is correct. The table shows that f(n) increases by 3 for each increase of 1 in n. Therefore, the slope of the linear function is 3. The y-intercept can be found by substituting n = 0 into the function: f(0) = 3(0) - 5 = -5. Therefore, the function is f(n) = 3n - 5.

QUESTION 14

Choice B is correct. The number of juniors inducted into the National Honor Society is 7% of 562, which is approximately 39. The number of seniors inducted is 5% of 602, which is approximately 30. Therefore, the total number of juniors and seniors inducted is approximately 39 + 30 = 69.

QUESTION 15

Choice A is correct. To add the polynomials $3x^2 - 5x + 2$ and $5x^2 - 2x - 6$, we add the coefficients of like terms: $(3x^2 + 5x^2) + (-5x - 2x) + (2 - 6) = 8x^2 - 7x - 4$

QUESTION 16

Choice D is correct. Multiplying both sides of the equation 3/5 w = 4/3 by 5/3, we get: w = (4/3) * (5/3) = 20/9

QUESTION 17

Choice B is correct. Speed is given by distance divided by time. Convert the time into seconds and use the given data: Speed = 25 meters / 13.7 seconds ≈ 1.823 meters / seconds.

Convert 4 minutes to seconds= 4 ×60 = 240 seconds. Now calculate the distance Nate will walk in 240 seconds: Distance = Speed × Time

Distance = 1.823 meters/seconds × 240 seconds ≈ 438 meters

QUESTION 18

Choice D is correct. To determine the weight of an item on Mercury, given its mass is 90 kilograms, use the formula W=mg, where W is the weight in newtons, mmm is the mass in kilograms, and g is the acceleration due to gravity.

For Mercury:

Acceleration due to gravity, g = 3.6 m/s²

Mass, m = 90 kg

Calculate the weight:

W = m × g = 90kg × 3.6 m/s^2 =324 newtons

QUESTION 19

Choice A is correct. There are 60 minutes in an hour, so if you use the phone for h hours, the total number of minutes is: Total minutes = 60 × h. The cost per minute is $0.20, so the total cost C in dollars is: C = Total minutes×Cost per minute

C = (60×h)×0.20

QUESTION 20

Choice C is correct. First, let's establish the given information:

· 1 ounce of graphene covers 7 football fields

· We need to find the area covered by 48 ounces

· 1 football field is 1 and 1/3 acres

Calculate how many football fields 48 ounces can cover: 48 × 7 = 336 football fields

Now, we need to convert football fields to acres: 1 football field = 1 1/3 acres = 4/3 acres

Calculate the total area in acres: 336 × 4/3 = 448 acres

Therefore, 48 ounces of graphene could cover approximately 448 acres.

QUESTION 21

The correct answer is C) The account's worth is increased by 1% of its existing value every year after that. This represents exponential growth because the increase each year is based on the current balance, which includes previous years' growth. The compound effect leads to exponential rather than linear growth over time.

QUESTION 22

Choice C is correct. Let the three numbers be x, y, and z. The sum of these three numbers is:

x+y+z=85

According to the problem, the difference between the sum of the other two numbers and x is 50%. This can be expressed as:

(y+z)-x=0.5×x

From the sum equation x+y+z=85, solve for y+z:

y+z=85-x

Substitute y+z into the second condition:

(85-x)-x=0.5×x

85-2x=0.5×x

85=2.5x

x=85/2.5=34

SECTION 2:

MODULE 2: MATH TEST

QUESTION 1

Choice D is correct. Let the number of pupils be x. If each pupil gets 3 ml, and there are 5 ml left over, then: 3x + 5 = n. If each pupil gets 4 ml, there is a shortage of 21 ml, then: 4x - 21 = n. From these two equations, we can eliminate n: 3x + 5 = 4x - 21, which simplifies to -x = -26, giving us x = 26. Therefore, the number of pupils in the class is 26.

QUESTION 2

Choice C is correct. Let the original width be w and the original length be l. The new width is (100-p)% of w, which is (1-p/100)w. The new length is 110% of l, which is 1.1l. The area decreased by 12%, so the new area is 88% of the original. Therefore, (1-p/100)w × 1.1l = 0.88 × w × l. Simplifying, we get 1.1(1-p/100) = 0.88, which leads to p = 0.22 × 100/1.1 = 20. Therefore, the value of p is 20.

QUESTION 3

Choice A is correct. There are 122 right-handed students and 18 left-handed students, totaling 140 students. Let the number of left-handed females be x. Then the number of right-handed females is 5x. The number of left-handed males is (18-x), and the number of right-handed males is 9(18-x). We can set up an equation: x + 5x + (18-x) + 9(18-x) = 140. Simplifying, we get 4x = 40, so x = 10. This means there are 5x = 5×10 = 50 right-handed females. The probability of a right-handed student being female is 50/122 ≈ 0.410.

QUESTION 4

The right option is A. It is a known fact that 20% of the students questioned expressed their intention to enroll in the study program. Hence, the survey indicates that 20% of the students in the Spanish club plan to enroll in the study program. Given that there are a total of 55 students in the Spanish club, the most accurate approximation for the number of students who plan to participate in the study program is 55 multiplied by 0.20, which equals 11.

QUESTION 5

The right option is A. Given that Jay's walking speed is 3 miles per hour, and he walks for w hours, the total distance Jay walks is 3w miles. Given that Jay's running pace is 5 miles per hour, and he runs for a duration of r hours, the total distance Jay runs is 5r miles. Hence, the overall distance covered by Jay can be expressed as 3w + 5r. The equation 3w + 5r = 14 represents the combined total amount of miles, which is 14.

QUESTION 6

Choice B is correct. By utilizing the commutative property of multiplication, the given expression $(m^4 q^4 z^{-1})(mq^5 z^3)$ can be rewritten as $(m^4 m)(q^4 q^5)(z^{-1} z^3)$. For positive values of x, $(x^a)(x^b) = x^{a+b}$. Therefore, the expression $(m^4 m)(q^4 q^5)(z^{-1} z^3)$ can be rewritten as $(m^{4+1})(q^{4+5})(z^{-1+3})$, or $m^5 q^9 z^2$.

QUESTION 7

The correct answer is 79. The median of a data collection with an odd number of values is the value that is exactly in the center when the values are arranged in ascending order. Since the provided data set contains nine values arranged in ascending order, the median corresponds to the fifth value in the set. Hence, the median of the given data is 79.

QUESTION 8

The correct answer is 55. The equation can be solved by subtracting 40 from both sides, resulting in x = 55. Hence, the numerical value of x is 55.

QUESTION 9

The proper choice is C. By combining the second equation of the given system with the first equation, we obtain 5x - 4xy = 15 - 2, which simplifies to x + y = 13. The sum of x and y is equal to 13.

QUESTION 10

The right option is A. Let g be a function that represents the remaining number of gallons in a car's gas tank after traveling m miles. The coefficient of m in the function g(m)=-0.05m+12.1 is -0.05. For each incremental increase of 1 in the value of m, the value of g(m) reduces by 0.05. Consequently, for every mile traveled, there is a reduction of 0.05 gallons of gasoline. Hence, each mile requires the consumption of 0.05 gallons of fuel.

QUESTION 11

The proper choice is C. By multiplying both sides of the following equation by y, we obtain the equivalent equation y / 7b = 11x. By doing division on both sides of the equation, we obtain the result y / 77b = x, which can be rewritten as x = y / 77b.

QUESTION 12

The right option is B. As the point (x, y) lies at the intersection of the graphs of the above equations in the xy-plane, it must satisfy both equations. Therefore, (x, y) is a solution of the provided system. Based on the initial equation, the value of y is equal to 76. By replacing the variable y with the value 76 in the second equation, we obtain x2 – 5 = 76. By adding 5 to both sides of this equation, we obtain x2 = 81. The problem can be solved by taking the square root of both sides, resulting in two solutions: x = 9 and x = -9. Out of these two options, only -9 is available as a selection.

QUESTION 13

The right option is A. It is known that the point (x, 53) satisfies the given system of inequalities in the xy-plane. This implies that the values of x and y, when replaced with the coordinates of the point, satisfy both of the inequalities in the system. By substituting the value of 53 for the variable y in the inequality y > 14, we obtain the inequality 53 > 14, which is indeed true. By replacing the variable y with the value 53 in the inequality 4x + y < 18, we obtain the expression 4x + 53 < 18. By subtracting 53 from both sides of this inequality, we obtain the result that 4x is less than -35.

By doing division on both sides of the inequality, we see that x is less than -8.75. Hence, x must be a value that is smaller than -8.75. Among the options provided, only -9 is smaller than -8.75.

QUESTION 14

The accurate response is 240. It is known that 240 out of the 300 seeds sprouted, which is equivalent to 80%. Hence, the quantity of germinated seeds can be determined by multiplying the number of sown seeds by 80 / 100, resulting in 300 (80 / 100), or 240.

QUESTION 15

The accurate response is 2. By replacing f(x) with 8 in the provided equation, we obtain 8 = 4x. By doing division on both sides of the equation, we may determine that x is equal to 2. Hence, the value of x is 2 when the function f(x) equals 8.

QUESTION 16

The correct choice is B. The provided formula exhibits a shared factor of 2 in the denominator, therefore allowing for its reconfiguration as [8x (x - 7) -3 (x - 7)] / 2 (x - 7) . The three terms in this statement share a common factor of (x -7). Given that x is more than 7, it follows that x cannot be equal to 7. Consequently, (x - 7) cannot be equal to 0. Consequently, every term in the above expression [8x (x - 7) -3 (x - 7)] / 2 (x – 7) can be divided by (x -7), resulting in (8x – 3) / 2.

QUESTION 17

The proper choice is C. Line r is known to be perpendicular to line p in the xy-plane. Line r has a slope that is the negative reciprocal of the slope of line p. When the equation for line p is expressed in slope-intercept form as y = mx + b, with m and b being constants, m represents the slope of the line and (0, b) represents its y-intercept. By subtracting 18x from both sides of the equation 2y + 18x = 9, we obtain the simplified form 2y = -18x + 9. Simplifying the equation by dividing both sides by 2 results in the expression y = -9x + (9 / 2). The conclusion can be drawn that the gradient of line p is -9. The negative reciprocal of a number can be obtained by dividing -1 by the number. The negative counterpart of -9 is -1/9, or 1/9. The slope of line r is 1/9.

QUESTION 18

The proper choice is D. The y-intercept of a graph in the ty-plane occurs at the point where the value of t is equal to zero. To find the y-intercept of the graph of y = f(t) in the ty-plane for the given function f, substitute 0 for t in the equation y = 8,000(0.65)^t. This will result in y = 8,000(0.65)^0. This can be simplified to y = 8,000, as it is identical to y = 8,000(1). Hence, the y-intercept of the graph represented by the equation y = f(t) is located at the point (0, 8,000). It is assumed that the function f represents the quantity of coupons that a corporation distributed to its clients at the conclusion of each year. Hence, f(t) denotes the approximated quantity of coupons that the corporation dispatched to its clients by the conclusion of each year. Furthermore, it is specified that 't' denotes the number of years elapsed since the conclusion of 1998. Thus, with t = 0, it signifies that no time has passed since the conclusion of 1998. Therefore, the most accurate explanation for the y-intercept of the graph of y = f(t) is that it represents the projected quantity of coupons that the corporation sent to their consumers by the conclusion of 1998, which is 8,000.

QUESTION 19

The proper choice is C. Triangle XYZ is known to be comparable to triangle RST, with X, Y, and Z corresponding to R, S, and T, respectively. Due to the congruence of identical angles in similar triangles, we can conclude that $\angle Z$ is equal in measure to $\angle T$. The measure of angle Z is known to be 20°. Hence, the angle T measures 20°.

QUESTION 20

The correct choice is B. If the lines indicated by the equations in the xy-plane are parallel and distinct, a system of two linear equations in two variables, x and y, will have no solution. Lines represented by equations in standard form, Ax + By = C and Dx + Ey = F, are parallel if the ratios of the coefficients for x and y in one equation are equal to the corresponding ratios in the other equation, meaning D / A = E / B. The lines are distinct if the ratios of the constants are not equal, meaning F / C is not equal to D / A or E / B. To convert the equation y = 6x + 18 into standard form, we can subtract 6x from both sides of the equation, resulting in -6x + y = 18. Hence, the above equation can be expressed as Ax + By = C, with A = -6, B = 1, and C = 18. The equation in choice B, -6x + y = 22, is expressed in the standard form Dx + Ey = F, where D is equal to -6, E is equal to 1, and F is equal to 22. Thus, the equation D/A = -6/-6 may be simplified to D/A = 1. Similarly, the equation E/B = 1/1 can be simplified to E/B = 1. Lastly, the equation F/C = 22/18 can be simplified to F/C = 11/9. aforementioned that D/A = 1, E/B = 1, and F/C ≠ 1, we can conclude that the aforementioned equation and the equation -6x + y = 22 are parallel and distinct. Hence, the system of two linear equations, comprising the provided equation plus the equation -6x + y = 22, does not possess a solution. Therefore, the equation in choice B may serve as the second equation in the system.

QUESTION 21

The accurate response is 986. The area, A, of a rectangle is given by A = (length) x (width), where (length) is the length of the rectangle and (width) is its width. The length of the rectangle is known to be 34 centimeters (cm) and the width is 29 cm. By replacing the variable (with the value 34 and the variable w with the value 29 in the equation A=(w, we obtain A=(34)(29), which simplifies to A=986. Hence, the rectangular area measures 986 square centimeters.

QUESTION 22

The accurate response is 35. The first equation in the provided system of equations determines the value of y as 4 times x plus 1. By replacing the variable y with the expression 4x + 1 in the second equation in the provided system of equations, we obtain the equation 4(4x + 1) = 15x - 8. By applying the distributive property to the left side of this equation, we obtain the expression 16x + 4. This is equal to 15x - 8. By subtracting 15x from both sides of the equation, we obtain x + 4 = -8. The result of subtracting 4 from both sides of this equation is that x equals -12. By substituting -12 for x in the first equation of the provided system of equations, we obtain the value of y as -47 by evaluating the expression 4(-12) + 1. By substituting the values -12 for x and -47 for y into the expression x - y, we obtain -12 - (-47), which simplifies to 35.

Practice Test 3 with Detailed Answers and Explanations

SECTION 1 > READING AND WRITING

MODULE 1: 27 QUESTIONS

DIRECTIONS

This section's questions cover a variety of crucial writing and reading abilities. There are one or more texts in each question, some of which may contain a table or graph. After carefully reading each excerpt and question, select the appropriate response to the question based on the relevant passage or passages. This section's questions are all multiple-choice, with four possible answers. Every question has a one optimal response.

1. The first American script, or writing system, for an Indigenous language was developed in the early 1800s by the Cherokee scholar Sequoyah. His script soon gained extensive usage because it so faithfully captured the sounds of spoken Cherokee; by 1830, more than 90% of the Cherokee people could read and write it.

A) extensive

B) cautious

C) inadvertent

D) Seldo

2. Other researchers quickly recognized Mexican-American archaeologist Zelia Maria Magdalena Nuttall's work as groundbreaking when she published her 1886 research paper on sculptures discovered at the ancient Indigenous city of Teotihuacan in modern-day Mexico. This recognition resulted from her compelling argument that the sculptures were much older than had previously been believed.

A) recognized

B) made certain

C) rejected

D) undervalued

3. The Muscogee (Creek) Nation is self-governing, as are other tribal nations. Its National Council makes laws that govern various facets of community life, like land use and healthcare, and cabinet officials and the principal chief _____ those laws by creating policies and providing services accordingly.

A) carry out

B) Assume

C) Make do

D) imitate

4. Maize, squash, and beans form a _____ web of relations in the Indigenous intercropping system known as the Three Sisters: the maize gives the bean vines a structure to grow on; the squash vines cover the soil, preventing weed competition; and the beans help their two "sisters" by enriching the soil with necessary nitrogen.

A) difficult to understand

B) Decorative

C) murky

D) complex

5. In Benin City, Nigeria, the Igun Eronmwon guild's artisans generally _____ the bronze- and brass-casting methods that have been inherited from their families since the thirteenth century. However, the guild members do not adhere to every tradition; for instance, they now utilize air conditioning motors rather than portable bellows to assist in heating their forges.

A) Test using

B) follow

C) enhance

D) struggle with

6. Certain economic historians argue that American families in the late 19th and early 20th centuries had economies of scale when it came to food purchasing; they reasoned that larger households paid less per person on food than did smaller households. But as economist Trevon Logan shown, a careful examination of the available data refutes this theory.

A) estimated

B) artificial

C) inquired

D) regretted

7. The tension between the following influences contributes to the power of Kiowa painter T.C. Cannon's work: the realistic treatment of faces in classic European portraiture; the vibrant colors of the American pop art movement; and flatstyle, an intertribal painting style that rejects the use of shading and perspective to create the illusion of depth.

A) in addition to

B) Unknown

C) Incongruous

D) Changing

8. Though there have been numerous studies on the impact of high altitude on blood chemistry, Suleiman A. Al-Sweedan and Moath Alhaj's observation that there have only been _____ studies on the impact of living in places below sea level, like the California towns of Salton City and Seeley, served as the impetus for their new and intriguing research.

A) argue about

B) lack of

C) abundance of

D) authenticity in

9. This passage is taken from "Martha's Lady," a short tale written by Sarah Orne Jewett in 1899. Martha works as a maid for Miss Pyne. In her finest attire, Miss Pyne sat at the window, gazing serenely and majestic; she seldom ventured outside these days, and the carriage was nearly ready. Martha had just come in from tending to the garden, carrying an apron full of flowers in addition to the strawberries. June was a lovely and cool evening, with the sun setting behind the apple trees at the garden's base and golden robins singing in the elms. The exquisite ancient home was fully exposed to the eagerly awaited visitor.

A) To communicate the concerns raised by a recent visitor

B) To discuss the characters' alterations throughout time

C) To make a contrast between the still exterior and the bustling within.

D) To paint the scene while the actors wait for a guest to arrive.

10. The star Betelgeuse is expected to ultimately devour all of the helium in its core and burst into a supernova, according to astronomers. Regarding the exact timing of this, however, they are far less certain because it depends on internal Betelgeuse properties that are yet mostly unknown. Recently, astronomer Sarafina El-Badry Nance and associates looked into whether Betelgeuse's internal features could be identified through the use of acoustic waves in the star. However, they came to the conclusion that this approach was insufficient to reveal enough information to definitively identify Betelgeuse's evolutionary state.

A) It describes how other experts in the area viewed the work done by Nance and associates.

B) It presents the main conclusion that Nance and associates reported.

C) It pinpoints the issue that Nance and associates tried to address but were unable to do so.

D) It highlights a significant flaw in the approach taken by Nance and associates.

11. This passage is taken from Jane Austen's work Sense and Sensibility, published in 1811. Elinor resides with her mother, Mrs. Dashwood, and her younger sisters. Elinor, the eldest daughter, was very wise and cool in her judgment. Despite being only nineteen, she was qualified to be her mother's counselor because of her strength of understanding and ability to often counteract Mrs. Dashwood's impatience, which would have otherwise led to imprudence. Her mother had not yet learned how to control her emotions, and one of her sisters had vowed never to be taught the skill. Despite having a wonderful heart, she had a loving and intense temperament.

A) Elinor fights with her mother a lot, but she never seems to alter her viewpoint.

B) When it comes to family affairs, Elinor sometimes has too much sensitivity.

C) Elinor feels her mother is not a good example to follow.

D) For her age, Elinor has remarkable maturity.

12. Conceptual artists Madeline Gins and Shusaku Arakawa created an apartment complex in Japan with a more whimsical than utilitarian layout because they felt that residing in an unpractical setting may increase consciousness and even enhance health. A door in the ceiling leads nowhere, and a kitchen counter is knee-high on one side and chest-high on the other. It's a confusing yet energizing experience; filmmaker Nobu Yamaoka experienced considerable health advantages following four years there.

A) Living in a house full of fantasy elements, like those created by Gins and Arakawa, could be restorative, but it is not sustainable.

B) Creating visually engaging environments through the design of confusing spaces, such as those seen in the Gins and Arakawa building, is the most efficient method.

C) Gins and Arakawa are two conceptual artists whose designs Yamaoka has long admired as a filmmaker.

D) Gins and Arakawa's apartment building design may enhance building occupants' well-being despite its impracticality.

13. A student attacks various historians of contemporary African politics in a research paper, arguing that they have mostly assessed Patrice Lumumba—the first prime minister of the modern-day Democratic Republic of the Congo—as a symbol rather than according to his deeds. Which passage from a historian's book best supports the student's assertion?

A) "The sharply divergent viewpoints that Lumumba sparked during his lifetime and still do now make him a challenging figure to assess."

B) "It is evident from the information at hand that Lumumba maintained essentially constant political views and moral principles throughout his life and career."

C) "Lumumba deserves scholarly attention primarily as the personification of Congolese independence; his practical accomplishments can be quickly overlooked."

D) "Lumumba's ultimate vision for an independent Congo still raises a lot of questions, many of which are likely to remain unanswered in the absence of new information."

14. In order to find out more about small-scale farmers' practices, such as the kinds of crops they primarily cultivated, geographer Adebayo Oluwole Eludoyin and his colleagues conducted surveys in three different parts of Ondo State, Nigeria: an urbanized center in the south, coastal terrain in the north, and mountainous terrain in the north. Certain crop varieties were discovered to be particularly popular in certain places, where female farmers made up the majority of individuals who farmed certain crops. One such example is _____. Which option completes the example using the data from the graph the most effectively?

A) In south Ondo, women made up the majority of both the farmers who planted cereals and those who cultivated non-root vegetables.

B) In central Ondo, a higher proportion of women farmed root crops than grains.

C) Women made up the majority of the farmers in north and south Ondo who focused mostly on non-root vegetables.

D) Almost equal numbers of women in Ondo's three areas worked mostly as grain farmers.

15. Some astronomers have proposed that host stars, like the Sun, and their planets, like those in our solar system, are made of the same materials, with the planets containing equal or smaller amounts of the materials that make up the host star. This is because stars and planets form from the same gas and dust in space initially. Evidence indicates some of the components that make up the rocky planets in our solar system are also consistent with this theory. Which discovery would most immediately undermine the astronomers' assertion if it were true?

A) While hydrogen and helium make up the majority of stars, cooling reveals trace quantities of silicate and iron.

B) The ratio of hydrogen to helium in a nearby host star is found to be the same as that of the Sun.

C) It is becoming apparent that certain rocky planets have far more iron in them than their host star does.

D) It is found that the technique for identifying the composition of rocky planets is not as useful for analyzing other types of planets.

16. Ethnographers worked hard to gather Mexican American folklore in the 20th century, but they weren't always in agreement on where it came from. Researchers like Aurelio Espinosa asserted that Spanish folklore, which dominated what is now Mexico and the southwest region of the United States from the fifteenth to the early nineteenth century, was a major influence on Mexican American folklore. Contrarily, academics like Américo Paredes contended that although there is unquestionably some Spanish influence, Mexican American folklore mostly results from the continuing exchanges between different cultures in Mexico and the United States. Which conclusion, if accurate, would lend the strongest weight to Paredes's claim?

A) The ethnographers gathered a variety of folktales, among them songs composed in the style of a décima, a kind of poetry that originated in late sixteenth-century Spain.

B) A large portion of the folklore that the ethnographers gathered shared elements with one another across various regions.

C) The majority of the folklore gathered by the ethnographers was not previously known to academics.

D) Corridos, or tales concerning social life and history, made up the majority of the folklore that the ethnographers gathered. These tales were obviously rather recent in origin.

17. Some Euro-American farmers in the northeastern United States in the early nineteenth century employed farming methods that the Haudenosaunee (Iroquois) people had established centuries earlier, but it appears that few of those farmers had actually visited Haudenosaunee fields. Given the probability that a few farmers from the same age independently created methods that the Haudenosaunee people had already established, these data most strongly imply that _____ Which option most logically wraps up the text?

A) The farmers acquired the skills from individuals who were subjected to a greater degree of direct Haudenosaunee influence.

B) Haudenosaunee agricultural methods were not well adapted to the crops that Euro-American farmers in the northeastern United States normally grew.

C) Outside of the northeastern United States, Haudenosaunee agricultural methods were extensively used.

D) The advantages of Haudenosaunee farming methods were first realized by Euro-American farmers towards the end of the nineteenth century.

18. It might support the idea that Kuulo Kataa, in modern-day Ghana, was formed before or around the thirteenth century CE if certain objects uncovered during excavations of the village date from that era. However, further evidence points to Kuulo Kataa's foundation around the fourteenth century CE. Which option most logically completes the text if the establishment date of the fourteenth century CE and the artifact dates are both accurate?

A) retrieved items from the fourteenth century are retrieved with greater frequency than those from the thirteenth century.

B) The items came from somewhere else and traveled or traded their way to Kuulo Kataa.

C) Contrary to popular belief, Kuulo Kataa was created by individuals from a different geographic area.

D) It's possible that some objects from the fourteenth century CE were unintentionally destroyed during the excavations at Kuulo Kataa.

19. Under the direction of Jae-Hoon Jung, Antonio D. Barbosa, and Stephanie Hutin, a group of scientists examined the process by which Arabidopsis thaliana (thale cress) plants quicken their blooming when temperatures rise. A protein identical to that of stiff brome, a species that, in contrast to A. thaliana, does not exhibit an acceleration of blooming with higher temperature, was substituted for the ELF3 protein in the plants. At 22° Celsius, there was no difference in the flowering of unmodified and altered A. thaliana plants; however, at 27° Celsius, the unmodified plants showed accelerated flowering while the altered ones did not, indicating that _____ Which option most logically concludes the text?

A) Only A. thaliana exhibits temperature-sensitive rapid blooming.

B) When temperatures rise, A. thaliana produces more ELF3.

C) A. thaliana can react to rising temperatures thanks to ELF3.

D) For A. thaliana to blossom, temperatures must be at least 22° Celsius.

20.   Mary Golda Ross is a well-known Cherokee Nation member who made significant contributions to NASA's Planetary Flight Handbook, which provided _____ precise mathematical instructions for trips to Mars and Venus. Which option brings the text up to date and into compliance with Standard English conventions?

A) offered

B) after supplying

C) in order to supply

D) supplying

21. Generally speaking, annotations, underlining, and notes made in the margins by a previous owner reduce a book's usefulness. However, if the previous owner is a well-known poet, like Walt Whitman, these markings—known as marginalia—can be a treasure trove for literary students. Which option brings the text up to date and into compliance with Standard English conventions?

A) worth, nevertheless

B) amount

C) amount,

D) value, however

22. _____ taxes are subject to what economists refer to as the "rebound effect": as the change became normalized, plastic-bag use started to creep back up. This was the case after the United Kingdom started enacting taxes equivalent to a few cents on single-use plastic grocery bags in 2011. Which option brings the text up to date and into compliance with Standard English conventions?

A) percentage, for example

B) percentage and other such figures

C) percentage. Such

D) percentage of such

23. The Earth, according to British physicist Peter Whibberley, "is not a very good timekeeper." Because of the Earth's slightly erratic rotation rate, time measurements need to be updated on a frequent basis. To be more specific, the 86,401st second of the day, or an additional "leap second," is the time based on the planet's rotation, which is nine tenths of a second behind time maintained by exact atomic clocks. Which option brings the text up to date and into compliance with Standard English conventions?

A) Moreover, whenever

B) included; at any time

C) was included. Anytime

D) included whenever

24.   The collection of English translations of French poetry written by Bengali author Toru Dutt, A Sheaf Gleaned in French Fields (1876), deepens researchers' comprehension of the multilingual and transnational environments in which Dutt lived and worked. Which option brings the text up to date and into compliance with Standard English conventions?

A) has improved

B) are improving

C) have improved

D) improve

25. The term "godfather of rap" has been applied to Gil Scott-Heron by journalists, and it has been used in hundreds of pieces on him during the 1990s. Scott Heron himself rejected the godfather _____ title, believing it to be an inadequate representation of his commitment to the larger African American blues music legacy and his preferred title of "bluesologist." Which option brings the text up to date and into compliance with Standard English conventions?

A) moniker, though

B) moniker, however;

C) moniker, nonetheless,

D) moniker; however,

26. When viewed from a distance, African American fiber artist Bisa Butler's portraits appear to be paintings because of how skillfully she has captured the features of people's faces, bodies, and attire. However, up close, the pictures show themselves to be tiny stitching that is hardly seen amid the millions of printed, microcut cloth pieces. Which option brings the text up to date and into compliance with Standard English conventions?

A) quilts, as well as the

B) quilts, the

C) quilts; the

D) Coverlets. The

27. The majority of trees in the phylum Coniferophyta, or conifers, are evergreen. That is to say, they retain their needles or green leaves all year round. Not every species of conifer, though, is evergreen. Every autumn, larch trees, _____, lose their needles. Which option provides the most logical conclusion to the text?

A) as an example,

B) Nevertheless,

C) In the interim,

D) furthermore,

STOP IF YOU COMPLETE BEFORE THE TIME LIMIT, YOU MAY JUST REVIEW YOUR WORK ON THIS MODULE. AVOID SWITCHING TO ANY OTHER TEST MODULE.

MODULE 2: 27 QUESTIONS

1. Botanists say that a viburnum plant damaged by insects may get erineum on its leaf blades, which is a felty, discolored growth. Conversely, the leaves of a _____ viburnum plant will have smooth surfaces and a consistent green hue. Which option provides the most accurate and logical word or phrase to finish the text?

A) having difficulty

B) advantageous

C) Easy to understand

D) in good health

2. The culmination of Nigerian American writer Teju Cole's two loves, photography and writing, is his 2017 book Blind Spot, which masterfully blends his poetic words with original photos from his travels. Which option provides the most accurate and logical word or phrase to finish the text?

A) lack of interest in

B) zeal for

C) anxiety regarding

D) shock at

3. Author N. K. Jemisin has stated that her audience value her work because she is ready to defy expectations and steer clear of conventional themes and narratives, refusing to embrace the traditions of the science fiction genre in which she writes. Which option provides the most accurate and logical word or phrase to finish the text?

A) query

B) respond to

C) observe

D) Follow

4. Tommy Pico, a poet from Kumeyaay, honors the importance of nature in his tribe's traditional beliefs in his poem "Nature Poem" (2017), but he also expresses his dislike of being in wilderness settings. Which option provides the most accurate and logical word or phrase to finish the text?

A) Adaptability to

B) indecision about

C) giving up

D) proficiency with

5. The passage that follows is taken from D'Arcy McNickle's 1924 poem "Cycle." McNickle was a citizen of the Confederated Salish and Kootenai Tribes. There will be newly constructed highways, a fresh drum beat— Men's eyes will see clearly again, and grey lives will come back to life. However, beneath the new sun, which will finish what darkness started, When this night comes to an end, the same faces will be bending, the same dejected feet will beat. And that day will arrive. Which option most accurately sums up the text's core idea?

A) To reflect on how life's inherently repetitious nature may be both fulfilling and difficult

B) To inquire as to whether tasks accomplished during a particular time of day are more remembered than tasks performed at a different time.

C) To disprove the notion that happiness is a more widely felt emotion than melancholy

D) To illustrate how people's experiences connect to those of their communities.

6. The passage that follows is taken from Jane Austen's 1814 book Mansfield Park. Tom, the speaker, is thinking about putting on a play for his friends and family at home. We only intend to lighten the mood and use our abilities in novel ways, nothing more than lighthearted conversation between ourselves. We want no exposure and no audience. I believe we can be trusted to select a play that is most precisely ordinary; and I cannot imagine anything that would be more harmful or dangerous for any of us than chatting away in our own words while discussing in the lovely written language of some reputable author. Which option most accurately sums up the text's core idea?

A) To reassure Tom that the show will only include a tiny cast and won't be disrespectful.

B) To make it clear that the play won't be performed the way Tom had intended.

C) To provide more context for the claim that Tom's surroundings lack the abilities necessary to put on a good play.

D) To state that Tom thinks the play's performing ensemble can successfully market it

7. Joni Mitchell, a musician and painter, utilizes the pictures she makes for her album covers to underline topics communicated in her songs. Mitchell created a remarkable self-portrait for the cover of her album

Turbulent Indigo (1994), which is reminiscent of Vincent van Gogh's Self-Portrait with Bandaged Ear (1889). The graphic draws attention to the album's title track, which features Mitchell singing on the postimpressionist painter's legacy. Mitchell indicates in the song that she has a deep creative connection to Van Gogh, which is emphasized by the images on the cover. Which option best represents the general organization of the text?

A) It states a claim about Mitchell and then provides an example to back up that point.

B) It examines Van Gogh's effect on Mitchell, followed by Mitchell's influence on other artists.

C) It compares two artists before pointing out their differences.

D) It introduces the songs on Turbulent Indigo and explains how they relate to the album's cover.

8.
Text 1

Astronomer Mark Holland and colleagues studied four white dwarfs—small, dense relics of former stars—to establish the makeup of exoplanets that used to orbit them. After studying light wavelengths in white dwarf atmospheres, the scientists discovered signs of lithium and sodium, indicating the presence of exoplanets with continental crusts comparable to Earth's.

Text 2

Previous investigations of white dwarf atmospheres revealed that certain exoplanets have continental crusts. Geologist Keith Putirka and astronomer Siyi Xu believe that these studies overemphasize air evidence of lithium and other particular elements as indicators of the sorts of rocks found on Earth. The studies fail to account for diverse minerals composed of differing ratios of certain elements, as well as the potential of non-Earth rock types containing those minerals.

Based on the texts, how would Putirka and Xu (Text 2) most likely describe the conclusion stated in Text 1?

A) As surprising, because it was commonly assumed at the time that white dwarf exoplanets lack continental crusts.

B) As premature, because researchers have just recently began trying to establish what types of crusts white dwarf exoplanets have.

C) As dubious, because it relies on an inadequate examination of the probable origins of the elements identified in white dwarf atmospheres.

D) As surprising, because it's uncommon to successfully find lithium and sodium when studying light wavelengths in white dwarf atmospheres.

9.
Pando, a colony of around 47,000 quaking aspen trees with a single root system, is located in Utah. Pando is one of the world's largest single creatures by mass, but ecologists are concerned that animal grazing is causing its growth to slow down. According to ecologists, robust fences might prevent deer from devouring new trees, allowing Pando to re-establish itself. According to the text, why are ecologists concerned about Pando?

A) It is no longer expanding at the same rate as before.

B) It isn't creating new trees anymore.

C) Fences prevent it from spreading to new locations.

D) Its root structure cannot accommodate many more young trees.

10.
For many years, the sole fossil evidence of mixopterid eurypterids, an extinct family of gigantic aquatic arthropods known as sea scorpions and linked to contemporary arachnids and horseshoe crabs, comes from four species that lived on the paleocontinent of Laurussia. Paleontologist Bo Wang and colleagues discovered fossilized remnants of a new mixopterid species, Terropterus xiushanensis, that existed over 400 million years ago on the paleocontinent Gondwana, expanding our understanding of the geographical range of mixopterids. What significance does Wang and his team's discovery of the Terropterus xiushanensis fossil have, according to the text?

A) The fossil is the first scientific proof that mixopterids existed more than 400 million years ago.

B) The fossil provides evidence that mixopterids are more closely linked to contemporary arachnids and horseshoe crabs than previously supposed.

C) The fossil contributes to a better understanding of the development of mixopterids on the paleocontinents of Laurussia and Gondwana.

D) The fossil is the first scientific proof that mixopterids existed outside the paleocontinent of Laurussia.

11. Toni Morrison, a novelist, was the first Black woman to serve as an editor at Random House from 1967 until 1983. According to one historian, one of Morrison's most likely goals as an editor was to increase the number of Black writers on Random House's published author roster. Which discovery, if true, would provide the strongest support for the scholar's claim?

A) The percentage of Black authors published by Random House increased in the early 1970s before stabilizing throughout the decade.

B) Black authors questioned in the 1980s and 1990s were more likely to identify Toni Morrison's novels as a major influence on their work.

C) Toni Morrison's works produced after 1983 sold much more copies and earned greater critical praise than those published prior to 1983.

D) Works edited by Toni Morrison during her stay at Random House exhibited stylistic qualities that identified them from works not edited by Morrison.

12. José Martí, a Cuban novelist and political activist, wrote the essay "The Poet Walt Whitman" in 1887, initially in Spanish. Martí's article examines the impact of literature on a society's spiritual well-being. _____ Which excerpt from a translation of "The Poet Walt Whitman" best demonstrates the claim?

A) "Poetry, which unites or divides, fortifies or destroys souls, gives or takes away men's faith and vigor, is more important to a people than industry itself, because industry provides them with a means of subsistence, whereas literature gives them the desire and strength to live."

B) "Every society contributes its unique style of expression to literature, and literary stages can tell the history of the nations more truthfully than chronicles and decades can."

C) "Where will a race of men go if they lose the habit of thinking with faith about the extent and significance of their actions? The greatest among them, those who dedicate Nature to their spiritual longing for the future, would lose, in a filthy and agonizing destruction, every stimulation to lessen humanity's ugliness."

D) "Listen to the song of this hardworking and satisfied nation; listen to Walt Whitman. The exercise of oneself elevates him to grandeur, tolerance to justice, and order to joy. "

13. The biggest tyrannosaurids—the carnivorous dinosaurs that include Tarbosaurus, Albertosaurus, and, most notably, Tyrannosaurus rex—are considered to have had the most powerful bites of any terrestrial animal in Earth's history. Determining the biting power of prehistoric creatures may be tricky, and paleontologists Paul Barrett and Emily Rayfield have indicated that the approach used to estimate dinosaur bite force may have a major effect.

Tyrannosaurid Bite Force Estimates

Study	Year	Estimation method	Approximate bite force (newtons)
Cost et al.	2019	muscular and skeletal modeling	35,000–63,000
Gignac and Erickson	2017	tooth-bone interaction analysis	8,000–34,000
Meers	2002	body-mass scaling	183,000–235,000
Bates and Falkingham	2012	muscular and skeletal modeling	35,000–57,000

Which option best explains the data in the table that supports Barrett and Rayfield's suggestion?

A) Meers' study employed body-mass scaling to obtain the lowest estimated maximum bite force, whereas Cost et al. used muscle and skeletal models to produce the greatest estimated maximum.

B) In their investigation, Gignac and Erickson employed tooth-bone interaction analysis to establish a biting force range of 8,000 to 34,000 newtons.

C) Bates and Falkingham and Cost et al. obtained similar biting force estimates, however Meers and Gignac and Erickson produced estimates that differed significantly from each other.

D) Cost et al.'s projected maximum biting force surpassed that of Bates and Falkingham, despite the fact that both groups employed the identical approach to create their estimations.

14. Archaeologist Paola Villa and colleagues discovered that prehistoric Neanderthal communities made tools using clam shells obtained from the bottom while wading or diving or that washed up on the shore. Clamshells become thin and eroded when they wash up on the beach, but those on the bottom are smooth and strong, leading the researchers to believe that Neanderthals valued tools produced from seafloor shells. However, the team determined that those tools were likely more difficult to get, noting that _____ ?

The number and origin of clamshell tools discovered at various levels below the surface in Neanderthal Cave

Depth (meters)	Beach Collected	Seafloor Harvested
3–4	99	33
6–7	1	0
4–5	2	0
2–3	7	0
5–6	18	7

Which option best uses data from the table to support the study team's conclusion?

A) At each level below the surface in the cave, the disparity in the quantity of tools of each kind indicates that shells were simpler to gather from the shore than from the seafloor.

B) The most tools were found at a depth of 3-4 meters below the surface, indicating that the Neanderthal population at the site was at its peak during the relevant time period.

C) At each level below the surface in the cave, the disparity in the amount of tools of each kind implies that Neanderthals preferred to utilize beach clamshells due to their durability.

D) The fact that there are more tools at depths of 5-6 meters below the surface of the cave than at depths of 4-5 meters implies that the size of clam populations has altered throughout time.

15. When Alaska marmots and Arctic ground squirrels hibernate, they enter a condition known as torpor, which reduces the amount of energy required to operate. A hibernating mammal will frequently awaken from torpor (known as an arousal episode) and increase its metabolic rate, consuming more of the valuable energy required to survive the winter. Alaska marmots hibernate in groups, so they expend less energy keeping warm during these periods than if they were alone. A study expected that because Arctic ground squirrels hibernate alone, they would have longer periods of torpor and shorter awakening episodes than Alaska marmots.

Average Number and Duration of Torpor Bouts and Arousal Episodes in Alaska Marmots and Arctic Ground Squirrels from 2008 to 2011.

Feature	Alaska marmots	Arctic ground squirrels
Torpor Bouts	12	10.5
Duration per Bout	13.81 days	16.77 days
Arousal Episodes	11	9.5
Duration per Episode	21.2 hours	14.2 hours

Which option best represents the data in the table that supports the researcher's hypothesis?

A) The Alaska marmots' arousal periods lasted many days, but the Arctic ground squirrels' arousal episodes lasted less than one day.

B) On average, the Alaska marmots and Arctic ground squirrels remained dormant for several days every bout.

C) Alaska marmots exhibited shorter torpor bouts and longer arousal episodes than Arctic ground squirrels did.

D) Alaska marmots experienced more torpor periods than arousal events, but the latter were substantially shorter

16. The Nagoya Protocol is an international agreement that ensures Indigenous communities are reimbursed when agricultural enterprises use their agricultural resources and knowledge of wild flora and animals. It has been ratified by over 90 nations. However, the procedure has flaws. For example, it enables companies to demand that their agreements with communities to do research on the commercial applications of the communities' resources and expertise be kept hidden. As a result, some Indigenous supporters are concerned that the procedure might have the unintended impact of _____. Which option most logically concludes the text?

A) reducing the monetary benefits that businesses may receive from their partnerships with Indigenous communities.

B) restricting corporations' study on the resources of Indigenous communities with which they have signed agreements.

C) prevents impartial observers from judging whether the accords provide appropriate compensation to Indigenous communities.

D) preventing Indigenous groups from learning new plant and animal collecting techniques from their business partners.

17. The domestic sweet potato (Ipomoea batatas) is descended from a wild species endemic to South America. It also grows in the Polynesian Islands, where evidence shows that Native Hawaiians and other Indigenous peoples cultivated the plant centuries before seafaring began over the hundreds of miles of ocean separating them from South America. Botanist Pablo Muñoz-Rodríguez and colleagues studied the DNA of several sweet potato cultivars and found that Polynesian variations evolved from South American versions around 100,000 years ago. Given that Polynesia was only populated in the previous three thousand years, the team decided that _____.

A) Sweet potato cultivation in Polynesia is believed to predate that in South America.

B) Sweet potatoes were most likely introduced to Polynesians by South Americans during the last three thousand years.

C) Human action most likely had no impact in the sweet potato's arrival to Polynesia.

D) Polynesian sweet potato types are most likely descended from a single South American variety that was domesticated rather than wild.

18. Atoms in a synchrotron, a form of circular particle accelerator, accelerate until they reach a specific energy level, at which point they are diverted to collide with a target, shattering the atoms. Which option completes the paragraph and ensures that it follows Standard English conventions?

A) will reach.

B) Reach.

C) had reached.

D) are reaching.

19. Even though bats love extremely sweet nectar, the plants that attract them have evolved to generate moderately sweet nectar. A new research reveals why: sugar production is energy-intensive, and plants benefit more from producing a big volume of low-sugar nectar than a tiny amount of high-sugar nectar. Which option completes the paragraph and ensures that it follows Standard English conventions?

A) Explains.

B) Explaining.

C) having explained

D) To Explain

20. Eleanor Roosevelt, former First Lady of the United States, and Hansa Mehta, an Indian activist and educator, helped develop the United Nations' Universal Declaration of Human Rights, a document that establishes the basic freedoms to which all individuals are entitled. Which option completes the paragraph and ensures that it follows Standard English conventions?

A) have outlined.

B) were outlining.

C) Outlines.

D) Outline

21. The life lengths of rockfish differ substantially between species. For example, the colorful calico rockfish (Sebastes dalli) may survive for a little over a year, while the rougheye rockfish (Sebastes aleutianus) has a maximum life span of over two centuries.

A) Decade: While

B) Decade. While

C) Decade; whilst

D) Decade, while

22. The Lion Light system, created by Kenyan inventor Richard Turere, comprises of LED lights set around the perimeter of cattle fields. The flickering LEDs, powered by electricity, keep lions away at night, preserving cattle and avoiding injury to endangered lions. Which option completes the paragraph and ensures that it follows Standard English conventions?

A) energy gathered by solar panels throughout the day

B) solar panels collect electricity during the day.

C) energy gathered by solar panels during the day

D) energy gathered by solar panels during the day.

23. Materials scientist Marie-Agathe Charpagne and her colleagues believed they could improve the multicomponent alloy NiCoCr, an equal-proportions mixture of nickel (Ni), cobalt (Co), and chromium (Cr), by replacing chromium with ruthenium. However, the alloy that resulted, NiCoRu, proved to be an unsuitable replacement for NiCoCr. Which option completes the paragraph and ensures that it follows Standard English conventions?

A) (Ru)

B) Ru, but

C) (Ru),

D) Ru, but

24.   During the Progressive Era in the United States, various Black women's clubs emerged as local groups advocating for racial and gender equality. Among the club's leaders is Josephine St. Pierre Ruffin, the founder of the Women's Era Club of Boston. Which option completes the paragraph and ensures that it follows Standard English conventions?

A) was

B) Were

C) are

D) Have been

25. Based on genetic data, archaeologists generally think that reindeer domestication began in the eleventh century CE. However, after discovering pieces of a 2,000-year-old reindeer training harness in northern Siberia, _____ may have started far earlier. Which option completes the paragraph and ensures that it follows Standard English conventions?

A) researcher Robert Losey suggested that domestication

B) According to scholar Robert Losey, domestication

C) domestication, scholar Robert Losey has stated.

D) Robert Losey, a researcher, argues that domestication

26. Hegra is an archeological site in modern-day Saudi Arabia that was the second greatest city of the Nabataean Kingdom (fourth century BCE to first century CE). Archaeologist Laila Nehmé recently visited to Hegra to explore its ancient _____. Built into the rocky outcrops of a wide desert, these burial chambers appear to fit in with nature. Which option completes the paragraph and ensures that it follows Standard English conventions?

A) Tombs. Built

B) tombs were erected.

C) tombs were erected.

D) tombs are erected.

27. When external pressures are applied to typical silicate glass, energy accumulates around microscopic imperfections in the material, causing fractures. Recently, engineer Erkka Frankberg of Tampere University in Finland employed the chemical _____ to create a glassy solid that can endure more strain than silicate glass before fracture. Which option completes the paragraph and ensures that it follows Standard English conventions?

A) compound, aluminum oxide.

B) Compound aluminum oxide,

C) compound, aluminum oxide.

D) compound aluminum oxide.

STOP — IF YOU COMPLETE BEFORE THE TIME LIMIT, YOU MAY JUST REVIEW YOUR WORK ON THIS MODULE. AVOID SWITCHING TO ANY OTHER TEST MODULE.

SECTION 2 > MATH TEST

MODULE 1: 22 QUESTIONS

DIRECTIONS

Solve each issue for each question, select the best response from the list of options, and then mark the matching circle on your answer sheet. You can do scratch work in any open place in your test booklet.

1. Which quadratic equations have solutions? $4x^2-8x-12=0$?

A) $x = -1$ and $x = -3$

B) $x = -1$ and $x = 3$

C) $x = 1$ and $x = -3$

D) $x = 1$ and $x = 3$

2. Which of the subsequent functions exemplifies a graph without any x-intercepts in the xy-plane?

A) A linear function with a non-zero rate of change

B) A real-zero quadratic function

C) A function of quadratics without actual zeros

D) A polynomial that is cubic and has at least one real zero.

3. $\sqrt{(k+2)}-x=0$

The equation above includes a constant, denoted by the symbol k. If x is equal to 9, what is the numerical value of k?

A) 1

B) 7

C) 16

D) 79

4. Which of the subsequent formulas is equal to the sum of a^2-1 and $a+1$?

A) a^2+a

B) a^3-1

C) $[2a]^2$

D) a^3

5. Jackie holds dual summer employment. She is employed as a tutor, earning a wage of $12 per hour, and also works as a lifeguard, earning $9.50 per hour. Her maximum weekly working hours are limited to 20, however, she has a minimum earning goal of $220 per week. Using x and y as the variables, which indicate the number of hours she works as a lifeguard and the number of hours she teaches, which of the following systems of inequalities best describes this situation?

A) $12x+9.5y<220$

   $x+y>20$

B) $12x+9.5y<220$

   $x+y<20$

C) $12x+9.5y>220$

   $x+y<20$

D) $12x+9.5y>220$

   $x+y>20$

6. $y=x^2$

$2x+y=6(x+3)$

How much is xy if (x,y) is the solution to the given system of equations and x > 0?

A) 216

B) 220

C) 300

D) 914

7. If a^2+b^2=z and ab = y, which of the subsequent is equivalent to 4z +8y ?

A) (a+2b)^2

B) (2a+2b)^2

C) (4a+4b)^2

D) (4a+8b)^2

8. Right circular cylinder A has a capacity of 22 cubic centimetres. What is the right circular cylinder's volume, measured in cubic centimetres, if it has half of cylinder A's height and twice its radius?

A) 11

B) 22

C) 44

D) 66

9. In a coordinate plane, triangle ABC has vertices A(0, 0), B(6, 0), and C(3, k). Point D is the midpoint of side AC, and point E is the midpoint of side BC. If the distance between points D and E is 3√5 units, what is the value of k?

A) 8

B) 9

C) 10

D) 12

10. In a restaurant, t tea bags are added to boiling water to make n cups of tea. How many more tea bags are required for each extra cup of tea if t = n+2?

A) None

B) One

C) Two

D) Three

11. Surgeon Major Professional Activity

Types	Teaching	Research	Total
General	258	156	414
Orthopedic	119	74	193
Total	377	230	607

607 orthopedic and general surgeons responded to a survey by indicating their primary area of expertise. The table above provides a summary of the findings. Which of the following best describes the likelihood that a physician chosen at random would be an orthopedic surgeon whose specified professional activity is research?

A) 0.122

B) 0.196

C) 0.318

D) 0.379

12. A tree's diameter, measured in inches, can be multiplied by a constant known as the species' growth factor to get the estimated age of the tree, expressed in years. The growth parameters for the eight species of trees are listed in the above table.

What is the estimated lifespan of a 12-inch-diameter American elm tree based on the data in the table?

A) 24 years

B) 36 years

C) 40 years

D) 48 years

Species of Tree	Growth Factor
Red maple	4.5
River birch	3.5
Cotton wood	2.0
Black walnut	4.5
White birch	5.0
American elm	4.0
Pink oak	3.0
Shagbark hickory	7.5

13. 13. Which of the following best describes the difference, in inches, between the current diameters of a pin oak tree and a white birch tree ten years from now? (1 foot = 12 inches)

A) 12

B) 20

C) 15

D) 18

14. (a-b)/a=c Which of the statements that follow must be true if an is negative and b is positive in the preceding equation?

A) $c > 1$

B) $c = 1$

C) $c = -1$

D) $c < -1$

15. Three quarters of the twenty-six pupils in Mr. Camp's eighth-grade class in State X, who answered to a survey, said they had two or more siblings. In the state, the average size of an eighth grade class is 26. Which of the following best approximates the number of eighth grade children in the state who have fewer than two siblings, assuming the students in Mr. Camp's class are indicative of students in the state's 1,800 eighth-grade classes?

A) 12,600

B) 11,700

C) 30,600

D) 46,800

16. In addition to receiving a 40% reduction from the original price, Townsend Realty also benefited from an extra 20% off the reduced price while paying cash for the Glenview Street property. Which of the following most closely matches the Glenview Street property's initial purchase price in dollars?

A) $350,000

B) $291,700

C) $233,300

D) $175,000

17. In a basketball game, the average score for eight players was 14.5 points. The mean score of the last seven players increases to 12 points if the top individual score is eliminated. Which score was the highest?

A) 20

B) 24

C) 32

D) 36

18. $x^2+20x+ y^2+16y= -20$ A circle in the xy plane is defined by the equation above. What are the circle's center's coordinates?

A) (−20, −16)

B) (−10, −8)

C) (10, 8)

D) (20, 16)

19. If $2x + 3 = 15$, then $x = ?$

A) 5

B) 6

C) 7

D) 11

20. Simplify: (a + b) - (a - b)

A) 2b

B) 0

C) a

D) b

21. Given two points, (2,5) and (6,1), what is the formula for the direction of this line?

A) $y = -3x + 11$

B) $y = -1/3x + 4$

C) $y = -1/2x + 3$

D) $y = -2x + 7$

22. The cube root of 64 is:

A) 4

B) 8

C) 2

D) 16

STOP

IF YOU COMPLETE BEFORE THE TIME LIMIT, YOU MAY JUST REVIEW YOUR WORK ON THIS MODULE. AVOID SWITCHING TO ANY OTHER TEST MODULE.

MODULE 2: 22 QUESTIONS

1. Which expression is equivalent to $12x^3 - 5x^3$?

A) $7x^6$

B) $17x^3$

C) $7x^3$

D) $17x^6$

2. A fish swam a distance of 5,104 yards. How far did the fish swim, in miles? (1 mile = 1,760 yards)

A) 0.3

B) 2.9

C) 3,344

D) 6,864

3. The point (8, 2) in the xy-plane is a solution to which of the following systems of inequalities?

A) $x > 0$

 $y > 0$

B) $x > 0$

 $y < 0$

C) $x < 0$

 $y > 0$

D) $x < 0$

 $y < 0$

4. $|x-5|=10|$ What is one possible solution to the given equation?

5. The function f is defined as the sum of the cube of x and 15, expressed as $f(x) = x^3 + 15$. What is the numerical output of the function f when the input is 2?

A) 20

B) 21

C) 23

D) 24

6. Sean leases a tent for a daily rate of $11, in addition to a single insurance premium of $10. The equation that expresses the entire cost, denoted as c in dollars, to rent the tent with insurance for d days is:

A) c = 11(d + 10)

B) c = 10(d + 11)

C) c = 11d + 10

D) c = 10d + 11

7. The diagram illustrates that line m and line n are parallel. What is the numerical or algebraic representation of the variable x?

A) 13

B) 26

C) 52

D) 154

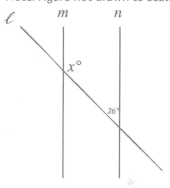

Note: Figure not drawn to scale.

8. John purchased a microscope for $165. He initially paid $37 as a down payment and then made six monthly payments of $16 each. Which equation accurately captures this scenario?

A) 16p − 37 = 165

B) 37p − 16 = 165

C) 16p + 37 = 165

D) 37p + 16 = 165

9. To find the value of y for x = 8 in the equation y = 5x + 10.

10. The bar graph depicts the allocation of 419 cans gathered by 10 distinct groups for a food drive. What was the total number of cans gathered by group 6?

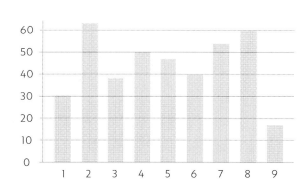

11. The table presents the allocation of votes among 80 students for a new school mascot, categorized by grade level. If a student is chosen randomly, what is the probability of selecting a student who voted for a lion as the new mascot?

A) 1 / 9

B) 1 / 5

C) 1 / 4

D) 2 / 3

Mascot	Grade Level			
	Sixth	Seventh	Eighth	Total
Badger	4	9	9	22
Lion	9	2	9	20
Longhorn	4	6	4	14
Tiger	6	9	9	24
Total	23	26	31	80

12. The graph depicts the cumulative fee, measured in dollars, charged by an electrician for a given number of hours worked, denoted as x. The electrician imposes a single, non-recurring cost in addition to an hourly rate. What is the most accurate explanation of the gradient of the graph?

A) The electrician's per-hour charge

B) The electrician's one-time charge

C) The electrician's maximum fee

D) The electrician's fee

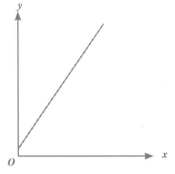

13. The length of each side of square X is 12 cm. The perimeter of square Y is twice the perimeter of square X. What is the measurement, in centimeters, of a single side of square Y?

A) 6

B) 10

C) 14

D) 24

14. The equation of the line that is parallel to the graph of y = 7x + 4 in the xy-plane and passes through the point (0, 5) can be found.

A) y = 5x

B) y = 7x +5

C) y = 7x

D) y = 5x +7

15. The linear function h is defined with the conditions h(0) = 41 and h(1) = 40. Which equation defines the value of h?

A) h(x)=−x + 41

B) h(x)=−x

C) h(x) = −41x

D) h(x) = −41

16. The function f(t) = 60,000(2) t 410 represents the population of bacteria t minutes after the initial observation. What is the duration, in minutes, required for the population of bacteria to double in number?

17. The function f is defined as the product of (x - 6), (x - 2), and (x + 6). The graph of y = g(x) in the xy-plane is obtained by vertically shifting the graph of y = f(x) upwards by 4 units. What is the numerical output of the function g when the input is 0?

18. A candle consists of 17 ounces of wax. During the burning process, the candle's wax diminishes at a rate of 1 ounce per 4 hours. What is the duration of burning in hours if there are now 6 ounces of wax left in the candle?

A) 3

B) 6

C) 24

D) 44

19. $14j + 5k = m$

The provided equation establishes a relationship between the variables j, k, and m. Which equation accurately represents the value of k in relation to j and m?

A) k = (m − 14j) / 5

B) k = (1 / 5) m − 14j

C) k = (14j − m) / 5

D) k = 5m − 14j

20. Triangle FGH is congruent to triangle JKL, with angle F corresponding to angle J and angles G and K being right angles. Given that sin(F) = 308/317, we need to determine the value of sin(J).

A) 75 / 317

B) 308 / 317

C) 317 / 308

D) 317 / 75

21. The result of multiplying two positive numbers is 546. What is the smaller of the two integers if the first integer is 11 more than twice the second integer?

A) 7

B) 14

C) 39

D) 78

22.

$$y \leq x + 7$$

$$y \geq -2x - 1$$

Which point (x, y) satisfies the above system of inequalities in the xy-plane?

A) (−14, 0)

B) (0, −14)

C) (0, 14)

D) (14, 0)

STOP

IF YOU COMPLETE BEFORE THE TIME LIMIT, YOU MAY JUST REVIEW YOUR WORK ON THIS MODULE. AVOID SWITCHING TO ANY OTHER TEST MODULE.

Practice Test 3 Answers

SECTION 1

MODULE 1: READING AND WRITING TEST

QUESTION 1

Choice A is the most reasonable conclusion to the text's exposition of Sequoyah's writing method. The passage states that Sequoyah's script "gained extensive usage" due to its accuracy in representing Cherokee sounds. This aligns with the high literacy rate (90%) mentioned, indicating widespread adoption of the script among Cherokee people.

QUESTION 2

Choice A is the best option since it logically concludes the text's discussion of Nuttall's 1886 research study. The passage states that other researchers "quickly recognized" Nuttall's work as groundbreaking. This aligns with the positive reception of her research and the impact of her argument about the age of the sculptures.

QUESTION 3

Choice A is the best answer. The passage describes the process of governance in the Muscogee (Creek) Nation. After the National Council makes laws, the next logical step is for officials to implement or "carry out" these laws. This involves creating policies and providing services based on the laws. The phrase "carry out" accurately describes the executive function of implementing legislation, which aligns with the roles of cabinet officials and the principal chief mentioned in the sentence.

QUESTION 4

Choice D is the best option. The passage describes an intricate and interdependent relationship between maize, squash, and beans in the Three Sisters intercropping system. Each plant plays a specific role that benefits the others: maize provides support, squash prevents weeds, and beans enrich the soil. This mutually beneficial and interconnected system is best described as "complex," reflecting the sophisticated and multifaceted nature of the relationships between these plants. The word "complex" accurately captures the depth and intricacy of this agricultural system without any negative connotation.

QUESTION 5

Choice B is the best option. The passage indicates that the artisans in Benin City generally maintain the traditional bronze- and brass-casting methods passed down through generations since the 13th century. The word "follow" best captures this idea of adhering to and continuing established practices. The sentence then contrasts this general adherence to tradition with an example of modernization (using air conditioning motors), which further supports the idea that they largely "follow" traditional methods while making some adaptations. This balance between tradition and innovation is best expressed by the verb "follow."

QUESTION 6

Choice A is the best option. The passage describes an argument made by economic historians about economies of scale in food purchasing for American families in the late 19th and early 20th centuries. The word "estimated" best fits the context because it suggests that these historians made an educated guess or calculation based on limited information. This interpretation is then contrasted with Logan's more thorough examination of data, which refutes the original estimate. The term "estimated" aligns with the idea of making an economic assessment without full data, which is then challenged by a more detailed analysis.

Choice C is the best option. The passage describes T.C. Cannon's work as drawing from three distinct artistic influences: European portraiture, American pop art, and flatstyle painting. These styles have contrasting characteristics: realistic faces, vibrant colors, and rejection of depth illusion. The word "incongruous" best describes the relationship between these influences, as they are seemingly incompatible or at odds with each other. The tension created by combining these disparate styles is what gives Cannon's work its power, according to the passage. "Incongruous" captures this sense of contrasting elements coming together in a striking way.

QUESTION 8

Choice B is the best option. The passage contrasts the numerous studies on high altitude effects with the scarcity of studies on living below sea level. Al-Sweedan and Alhaj's observation of this gap in research motivated their new study. The phrase "lack of" best fits this context, highlighting the absence or scarcity of studies on below-sea-level living. This contrast between abundant high-altitude studies and few low-altitude studies provides the logical motivation for their new research, making "lack of" the most appropriate choice to complete the sentence.

QUESTION 9

Choice D is the best answer. The passage describes a peaceful evening scene with Miss Pyne sitting at the window, Martha tending to the garden, and the house prepared for an expected visitor. It sets the stage and atmosphere without focusing on conflicts, character changes, or contrasts.

QUESTION 10

Choice C is the best answer. The passage concludes by stating that Nance and associates determined their approach was "insufficient to reveal enough information to definitively identify Betelgeuse's evolutionary state." This directly presents the main conclusion of their research.

QUESTION 11

Choice D is the best answer The passage describes Elinor as "very wise and cool in her judgment" and states that despite being only nineteen, she was qualified to be her mother's counselor. This clearly indicates her exceptional maturity for her age.

QUESTION 12

Choice D is the best response. The passage suggests that living in an impractical setting might increase consciousness and improve health. It also mentions that Yamaoka experienced health benefits after living there, supporting the idea that the design, though impractical, could enhance well-being.

QUESTION 13

Choice C is the best response. This quote directly supports the student's argument that historians have assessed Lumumba more as a symbol than for his actions. It explicitly states that Lumumba is viewed primarily as a personification of independence, with his actual accomplishments being overlooked.

QUESTION 14

Choice C is the best answer since it successfully completes Eludoyin and his colleagues' results on female farmers in specific parts of Ondo State, Nigeria, using data from the graph. The graph shows the percentage of female small-scale farmers in Ondo State, broken down by crop and area. The graph shows that of the farmers primarily cultivating nonroot vegetables, approximately 57% in north Ondo and approximately 54% in south Ondo are female; in other words, the majority of those farmers are female, demonstrating the idea that female farmers account for the majority (more than half) of farmers cultivating specific types of crops in some areas.

QUESTION 15

Choice C is the best response since it gives a result that, if confirmed, undermines the researchers' assumption regarding the composition of host stars and their planets. The article says that because stars and planets emerge from the same gas and dust, scientists assume planets should be made of the same ingredients as their host stars, but in equal or lower proportions. The discovery that the quantity of iron in certain rocky planets is substantially larger than the amount in their host star undermines the astronomers' argument since it demonstrates that some planets have the same stuff as their host star, but in greater proportions.

QUESTION 16

Choice D is the best answer since it gives a discovery that, if accurate, would back up Paredes' theory concerning the origins of Mexican American folklore. The essay presents a controversy among historians regarding whether Mexican American folklore arose primarily from Spanish folklore (the view held by Espinosa and others) or originated in Mexico and the United States as a result of continuous cultural exchanges (the view maintained by Paredes and others). If Mexican American folklore collected in the twentieth century consists primarily of ballads about history and social life that originated recently, this would support Paredes' argument by implying that the folklore arose after Spanish rule ended in the early nineteenth century and reflects cultural interactions in Mexico and the United States rather than traditions from Spain.

QUESTION 17

Choice A is the most reasonable conclusion to the text's examination of Euro-American farmers' usage of Haudenosaunee agricultural skills. According to the book, some Euro-American farmers used these tactics in the early nineteenth century, despite the fact that few of them had ever visited Haudenosaunee fields. One explanation for these facts may be that the farmers created techniques that had previously been invented centuries before by the Haudenosaunee people, however the text specifically prohibits, or rules out, this possibility. If Euro-American farmers did not learn these techniques through direct observation of Haudenosaunee practices and did not invent them on their own, the most logical explanation is that they learned them from others who were more directly influenced by Haudenosaunee practices than the farmers themselves. After learning about Haudenosaunee agricultural traditions, Euro-American farmers might apply them to their own farms.

QUESTION 18

Choice B is the best option since it logically concludes the text's examination of artifacts and Kuulo Kataa's founding date. If it is true that Kuulo Kataa was formed in the fourteenth century CE and that items discovered during settlement excavations date from the thirteenth century CE, it is plausible to assume that the artifacts were not manufactured in the Kuulo Kataa village. That would imply that the objects originated elsewhere and were brought to the settlement through trade or migration.

QUESTION 19

Choice C is the best response since it logically concludes the text's description of faster blossoming in A. thaliana plants. The wording suggests that A.High temperatures cause thaliana plants to blossom more quickly. To examine the mechanism underlying this faster flowering, researchers altered the ELF3 protein in one set of A. thaliana plants contain a comparable protein to another plant species that does not exhibit rapid blooming. The scientists then compared the transformed plants to A. thaliana plants that have kept their native ELF3 protein. According to the text, the two samples of plants showed no change in blooming at 22° Celsius, however at 27° Celsius, the unmodified plants with ELF3 exhibited rapid flowering while the plants without ELF3 did not. If faster blooming at higher temperatures happened in the A. thaliana plants with ELF3 but not in plants lacking the protein, then ELF3 most likely permits A. thaliana will react to higher temperatures.

QUESTION 20

Choice A is the best option. "Offered" is the most grammatically correct and concise option. It maintains the past tense consistency with "provided"· and doesn't introduce unnecessary complexity. The other options either change the tense or add unnecessary words.

QUESTION 21

Choice D is the best option. This option correctly uses a comma before "however" to separate two independent clauses. It also provides the appropriate contrast between the general statement about marginalia reducing a book's usefulness and the exception for well-known authors. "Value" is more precise than "amount" in this context.

QUESTION 22

Choice C is the best option. This option correctly separates two independent clauses with a period. "Such" then appropriately refers back to the "rebound effect" mentioned in the first sentence, providing a smooth transition to the specific example of the UK's plastic bag tax.

QUESTION 23

Choice D is the best option. "Included whenever" maintains the correct tense and provides a logical connection to the preceding sentence about updating time measurements. It implies that the leap second is added as needed, which is consistent with the explanation of Earth's irregular rotation.

QUESTION 24

Choice D is the best option. "Improve" is the correct verb form to agree with the singular subject "collection." It also maintains the present tense, which is appropriate for describing the ongoing impact of Dutt's work on researchers' understanding.

QUESTION 25

Choice A is the best option. This option correctly uses a comma before "though" to introduce a contrasting idea. It's the most concise and grammatically correct choice, maintaining the flow of the sentence while introducing Scott-Heron's rejection of the title.

QUESTION 26

Choice B is the best option. This option correctly uses a comma to separate the descriptive clause from the main clause. It avoids the unnecessary semicolon of option C and the incorrect capitalization and period of option D. It also maintains the flow of the sentence better than option A.

QUESTION 27

Choice A is the best option. This phrase logically introduces larch trees as a specific example of conifers that are not evergreen. It maintains the flow of the paragraph and provides a clear connection between the general statement about conifers and the specific case of larch trees.

SECTION 1

MODULE 2: READING AND WRITING TEST

QUESTION 1

Choice D is the best answer. The text contrasts a viburnum plant damaged by insects, which shows discolored growth, with a viburnum plant that has smooth and consistent green leaves. To describe a plant that does not have issues like erineum and has healthy, normal leaves, the phrase "in good health" is the most logical choice. The other options do not appropriately describe the condition of the plant in this context.

QUESTION 2

Choice B is the best answer. Teju Cole's book "Blind Spot" combines his interests in photography and writing. The phrase "zeal for" accurately captures the idea that the culmination of his work reflects his strong passion for both photography and writing. The other options do not fit the context of enthusiasm and integration of his two interests.

QUESTION 3

Choice B is the best answer. The text discusses how N. K. Jemisin's audience values her work due to her unique approach and willingness to challenge conventions. The phrase "respond to" logically follows as it suggests how her audience appreciates her work by engaging with it. The other options do not fit the context of audience appreciation and engagement.

QUESTION 4

Choice B is the best answer. The text mentions Tommy Pico's respect for nature but also his dislike of being in wilderness settings. The phrase "indecision about" effectively conveys the contrast between his respect for nature and his personal feelings about being in it. The other options do not accurately reflect the nuanced sentiment of respecting nature while disliking wilderness settings.

QUESTION 5

Choice A is the best answer since it correctly conveys the text's principal aim. The text begins by discussing the promise of the future, with positive references to renewal such as "new roads," "new beating of the drum," and "fresh seeing." However, with the "new sun," the text continues, there will still be "the same backs bending" and "the same sad feet" drumming, indicating that these difficulties will accompany people into this new day. Thus, the poem takes into account both the benefits and drawbacks of human life's repetition.

QUESTION 6

Choice A is the best response since it more properly represents the text's principal aim. At the start of the text, Tom claims that he and the other persons staging the play are doing it just for "a little amusement among ourselves" and have no intention of attracting an audience or any notice with the show. Then, Tom guarantees that the play they picked is modest and acceptable, and he goes on to explain that adopting the well-written writing of "some respectable author" is preferable to using their own words. Overall, the text's major objective is to express Tom's assurance that the play will be non-offensive and involving only a few people.

QUESTION 7

Choice A is the best answer since it correctly reflects how the text's parts are organized. The essay opens with the premise that Joni Mitchell's album covers employ pictures she makes to underscore concepts found in her albums. It then goes on to show how Mitchell's self-portrait on the cover of Turbulent Indigo resembles a painting by Van Gogh, which the text says emphasizes Mitchell's profound connection to Van Gogh, which is also represented in the album's title song. Choice B is inaccurate since the text contains no allusions to artists other than Joni Mitchell and Van Gogh.

QUESTION 8

Choice C is the best answer because it accurately represents how Putirka and Xu (Text 2) would describe the conclusion stated in Text 1. Text 1 covers a research by Mark Holland and colleagues that found traces of lithium and sodium in the atmospheres of four white dwarf stars. According to the study, this supports the theory that exoplanets with continental crusts like Earth originally orbited these stars. Text 2 introduces Putirka and Xu, who state that sodium and lithium are present in a variety of minerals, and that some of those minerals may occur in rock types that are not found on Earth. As a result, Putirka and Xu would likely call Text 1's conclusion problematic since it ignores the fact that lithium and sodium may be found in rocks elsewhere than the Earth's continental crust.

QUESTION 9

Choice A is the best answer since it provides a straightforward explanation in the text of why ecologists are concerned about Pando. According to the literature, Pando is a colony of over 47,000 quaking aspen trees, making it one of the biggest creatures on Earth. According to the text, ecologists are concerned that Pando's development is slowing, in part due to animals grazing on the trees. In other words, ecologists are concerned that Pando is not increasing at its usual rate.

QUESTION 10

Choice D is the best answer because it explains why Wang and his team's discovery of the Terropterus xiushanensis fossil is crucial. The article notes that prior to Wang and his team's finding, the only fossil evidence of mixopterids came from the paleocontinent of Laurussia. Wang and his colleagues discovered fossil remnants of a mixopterid species from the paleocontinent Gondwana. The team's discovery was notable since the fossil remnants of a mixopterid species were found outside of the paleocontinent Laurussia.

QUESTION 11

Choice A is the best response because it gives a result that, if correct, would back up the scholar's argument regarding Toni Morrison's likely intention of increasing the number of Black writers on Random House's roster of published authors. According to the text, Morrison was the first Black woman to be an editor at Random House, where she worked from 1967 until 1983. If it is true that Random House published a higher percentage of works by Black authors in the 1970s—during the majority of Morrison's time there—than it had previously published, it would imply that Morrison made a deliberate effort to increase the presence of Black authors on the list of Random House's published authors, supporting the scholar's claim.

QUESTION 12

Choice A is the most appropriate response because it provides the most convincing illustration of the assertion that Martí makes, which is that the spiritual well-being of a community is dependent on the nature of its literary culture. Martí believes that literature is a societal necessity that uplifts and nourishes people's spiritual well-being, stating that it is "more necessary to a people than industry itself" and can provide "faith and vigor."

QUESTION 13

Choice C is the best answer because it properly explains the data in the table that supports Barrett and Rayfield's idea concerning biting force estimations. According to the text, Barrett and Rayfield think that estimations of dinosaur biting power may be heavily impacted by the methods employed to generate them—that is, various approaches may provide dramatically different findings. The table illustrates that the research by Bates and Falkingham and Cost et al. employed the same estimating approach (muscular and skeletal modeling) and obtained identical biting force estimates (35,000-57,000 and 35,000-63,000 newtons, respectively). Meers' study employed body-mass scaling and yielded a significantly higher biting force estimate (183,000-235,000 newtons), whereas Gignac and Erickson's study used tooth-bone interaction analysis and yielded a much lower bite force estimate (8,000-34,000 newtons). The fact that one approach yielded identical estimates in two distinct studies but two different methods employed in other research produced dramatically different values supports the notion that dinosaur bite force estimations are heavily impacted by the methodology used to generate them.

QUESTION 14

Choice A is the best option because it most effectively leverages facts from the table to support the researchers' conclusion regarding Neanderthals gathering clamshells for use as tools. The text says that Neanderthals utilized clamshells to build tools, and that the strongest, and hence most desirable, shells for this purpose may be discovered on the bottom rather than on the shore. However, the researchers found that clamshell tools manufactured from bottom shells are less common than those made from beach shells. Meanwhile, the data demonstrates that, at each level, the quantity of tools created from beach shells outnumbers those made from more desired bottom shells. The fact that the more desired shells are less prevalent indicates that harvesting shells from the bottom was substantially more difficult than from the beach.

QUESTION 15

Choice C is the most appropriate response since it describes statistics from the table that support the researcher's premise. According to the text, the researcher expected that Arctic ground squirrels would have longer torpor bouts and shorter arousal episodes than Alaska marmots—or, conversely, that the marmots would have shorter torpor bouts and longer arousal episodes than the ground squirrels. The table displays statistics on torpor bouts and arousal events for both species from 2008 to 2011. According to the table, Alaska marmots had an average torpor bout duration of 13.81 days, which was shorter than the average of 16.77 days for Arctic ground squirrels, and an average arousal episode duration of 21.2 hours, which was longer than the average of 14.2 hours for Arctic ground squirrels. Thus, the table confirms the researcher's hypothesis by demonstrating that Alaska marmots had shorter torpor periods and longer alertness episodes than Arctic ground squirrels.

QUESTION 16

Choice C is the best option since it most logically concludes the argument regarding an unforeseen consequence of the Nagoya Protocol. According to the text, the Nagoya Protocol is an agreement that ensures indigenous communities are paid when multinationals utilize their agricultural resources and expertise. The document then indicates that the protocol permits businesses to keep their agreements with Indigenous communities private, which raises concerns among Indigenous advocates.

QUESTION 17

Choice C is the best option since it logically concludes the text's subject of sweet potatoes in Polynesia. The sweet potato is present in Polynesia but originated in South America, and it was farmed by Native Hawaiians and other Indigenous peoples in Polynesia long before maritime trips between South America and Polynesia became common. According to Muñoz-Rodríguez and colleagues' research, Polynesian sweet potato types diverged from South American variations about 100,000 years ago, predating human settlement in Polynesia. If Polynesian peoples were cultivating sweet potatoes before sea voyages between Polynesia and South America began, and if Polynesian sweet potato varieties diverged from South American varieties long before humans arrived in Polynesia, it is reasonable to conclude that humans did not play a role in introducing the sweet potato to Polynesia.

QUESTION 18

Choice B is the best option. The sentence requires a simple present tense verb to match the tense of "accelerate." "Reach" maintains parallel structure with "accelerate" in the independent clause. The simple present tense is used for habitual or repeated actions, which fits this context. "Reach" correctly completes the sentence without introducing unnecessary auxiliary verbs.

QUESTION 19

Choice A is the best option. "Explains" agrees with the singular subject "A new research" in number and person. The simple present tense is appropriate for stating a current finding or conclusion. It maintains consistency with the present tense used in the rest of the paragraph. "Explains" provides a clear and concise verb that fits the context of presenting research findings.

QUESTION 20

Choice C is the best option. "Outlines" agrees with the singular subject "a document" in number and person. The simple present tense is used for stating facts or general truths, which fits this context. It maintains parallel structure with the present tense verb "establishes" in the relative clause. "Outlines" accurately describes the function of the document in relation to human rights.

QUESTION 21

Choice D is the best option. A comma is needed to separate two independent clauses joined by a coordinating conjunction. "While" is the appropriate coordinating conjunction to show contrast between the two species. The period in option B would create a sentence fragment, which is grammatically incorrect. "Whilst" in option C is overly formal and less common in modern English usage.

QUESTION 22

Choice C is the best option. This option completes the sentence without redundancy or unnecessary punctuation. It maintains parallel structure with the preceding phrase "powered by electricity." The phrase "during the day" logically explains when solar panels gather energy. This option avoids creating a new independent clause, which would require different punctuation.

QUESTION 23

Choice D is the best option. The convention under consideration is the coordination of key clauses. To connect the first major clause ("Materials... Ru") with the second main clause ("the alloy...NiCoCr"), this choice employs a comma and the coordinating conjunction "but".

QUESTION 24

Choice A is the best option. "Was" agrees with the singular subject "Josephine St. Pierre Ruffin" in number and person. The past tense is appropriate as the sentence discusses a historical figure. "Was" correctly identifies Ruffin as one of the leaders, not the only leader. The other options do not agree in number with the singular subject or use incorrect tenses.

QUESTION 25

Choice D is the best option. This option provides a clear subject (Robert Losey) for the main clause of the sentence. It introduces Losey's role as a researcher without disrupting the sentence structure. The verb "argues" appropriately connects Losey's claim to the evidence presented. This phrasing maintains the logical flow of the paragraph from evidence to conclusion.

QUESTION 26

Choice A is the best option. "Tombs" completes the sentence about Nehmé's exploration logically and concisely. The period after "tombs" correctly separates two independent clauses. "Built" begins a new sentence that provides additional information about the tombs. This option avoids the grammatical errors present in the other choices, such as verb tense issues.

QUESTION 27

The correct option is A) compound, aluminum oxide.

The phrase "chemical compound" requires the use of a comma to separate "compound" from the name of the specific compound, "aluminum oxide," following Standard English conventions for appositives. Option B is incorrect because "Compound" should not be capitalized unless it is the first word of a sentence. Options C and D do not use the comma correctly to separate the appositive phrase.

SECTION 2

MODULE 1: MATH TEST

QUESTION 1

Choice B is correct. To find the solutions, factor the quadratic equation: $4x^2 - 8x - 12 = 0$

$4(x^2 - 2x - 3) = 0$

$4(x - 3)(x + 1) = 0$

$x = 3$ or $x = -1$ Therefore, the solutions are $x = -1$ and $x = 3$.

QUESTION 2

Choice C is correct. A quadratic function without real zeros will not have any x-intercepts in the xy-plane. A linear function with a non-zero rate of change, a quadratic function with real zeros, and a cubic polynomial with at least one real zero will all have x-intercepts.

QUESTION 3

Choice D is correct. Substitute $x = 9$ into the equation and solve for k: $\sqrt{(k+2)} - 9 = 0$ $\sqrt{(k+2)} = 9$ $k + 2 = 81$ $k = 79$

QUESTION 4

Choice A is correct. To add a^2-1 and $a+1$, simply combine like terms: $(a^2 - 1) + (a + 1) = a^2 + a - 1 + 1 = a^2 + a$

QUESTION 5

Choice C is correct. The first inequality represents Jackie's minimum earning goal: $12x + 9.5y \geq 220$ The second inequality represents her maximum weekly working hours: $x + y \leq 20$

QUESTION 6

Choice A is correct. Substitute $y = x^2$ into the second equation and solve for x: $2x + x^2 = 6(x + 3)$ $x^2 + 2x - 6x - 18 = 0$ $x^2 - 4x - 18 = 0$ $(x - 6)(x + 3) = 0$ $x = 6$ or $x = -3$ Since $x > 0$, $x = 6$. Substituting $x = 6$ into $y = x^2$, we get $y = 36$. Therefore, $xy = 6 * 36 = 216$.

QUESTION 7

Choice A is correct. Using the given equations, we can expand $4z + 8y$: $4(a^2 + b^2) + 8(ab) = 4a^2 + 4b^2 + 8ab = (2a)^2 + 2(2a)(2b) + (2b)^2 = (2a + 2b)^2 = (a + 2b)^2$

QUESTION 8

Choice C is correct. The volume of a cylinder is $V = \pi r^2 h$. If cylinder A has volume 22 cubic centimeters, then: $22 = \pi r^2 h$ If the new cylinder has half the height and twice the radius of cylinder A, then its volume is: $V = \pi(2r)^2(h/2) = 2\pi r^2 h = 2 * 22 = 44$ cubic centimeters

QUESTION 9

Choice D is correct. As before, D is the midpoint of AC with coordinates (1.5, k/2), and E is the midpoint of BC with coordinates (4.5, k/2).

Using the distance formula between D and E: $3\sqrt{5} = \sqrt{[(4.5 - 1.5)^2 + (k/2 - k/2)^2]}$ $3\sqrt{5} = \sqrt{[3^2 + 0^2]}$ $3\sqrt{5} = 3$

This confirms our initial setup is correct.

Now, let's use the Pythagorean theorem in triangle ABC: $AC^2 = AB^2 + BC^2$ $AC^2 = 6^2 + k^2$ $AC^2 = 36 + k^2$

We know that DE is a midsegment of triangle ABC, so $DE = 1/2\ AC$ Therefore, $AC = 2DE = 2(3\sqrt{5}) = 6\sqrt{5}$

Now we can solve for k: $(6\sqrt{5})^2 = 36 + k^2$ $180 = 36 + k^2$ $k^2 = 144$ $k = 12$

QUESTION 10

Choice B is correct. If $t = n + 2$, then for each additional cup of tea (n increases by 1), one more tea bag is needed (t increases by 1).

QUESTION 11

Choice A is correct. The probability of selecting an orthopedic surgeon whose primary professional activity is research is the number of orthopedic surgeons who primarily do research divided by the total number of surgeons: $74 / 607 \approx 0.122$

QUESTION 12

Choice D is correct. To estimate the age of an American elm tree with a 12-inch diameter, multiply the diameter by the growth factor: Age $\approx$ 12 inches * 4.0 years/inch = 48 years

QUESTION 13

Choice A is correct. For a simple calculation example:

· Let's say the pin oak tree's diameter is 5 inches and grows 2 inches per year.

· The white birch tree's diameter is 3 inches and grows 1 inch per year.

Calculate the difference in diameter:

1)   Current diameter difference:

5−3=2 inches

2)   Growth difference in 10 years:

10×(2−1)=10 inches

3)   Total difference in 10 years:

2+10=12 inches

QUESTION 14

Choice D is correct. If a is negative and b is positive, then a - b is negative and a is negative. Therefore, (a - b) / a is positive and greater than 1. For the equation to hold, c must be negative and less than -1.

QUESTION 15

Choice A is correct. If Mr. Camp's class is representative, then in each class of 26 students, 26 * (1/4) = 6.5 students have fewer than two siblings. Rounding up, approximately 7 students per class have fewer than two siblings. With 1,800 classes, the total number of eighth-grade students in the state with fewer than two siblings is approximately: 7 students/class * 1,800 classes = 12,600 students

QUESTION 16

Choice B is correct. If the original price was x dollars, then after a 40% discount, the price was 0.6x dollars. After an additional 20% discount, the price was: 0.8 * 0.6x = 0.48x dollars Set this equal to the actual purchase price and solve for x: 0.48x = 140,000 x ≈ 291,667 dollars

QUESTION 17

Choice C is correct. Let x be the highest score. The sum of all eight scores is: 8 * 14.5 = 116 The sum of the remaining seven scores is: 7 * 12 = 84 The highest score is the difference between these sums: x = 116 - 84 = 32

QUESTION 18

Choice B is correct. To find the center of the circle, complete the square for both x and y: (x^2 + 20x) + (y^2 + 16y) = -20 (x^2 + 20x + 100) + (y^2 + 16y + 64) = -20 + 100 + 64 (x + 10)^2 + (y + 8)^2 = 144 The center of the circle is at (-10, -8).

QUESTION 19

Choice B is correct. Solve the equation for x: 2x + 3 = 15 2x = 12 x = 6

QUESTION 20

Choice A is correct. Distribute the negative sign: (a + b) - (a - b) = a + b - a + b = 2b

QUESTION 21

Choice D is correct. The slope of the line is:

$$m = \frac{x_2 - x_1}{y_2 - y_1}$$

m = (1 - 5) / (6 - 2) = -4 / 4 = -1 Using the point-slope form with the point (2, 5): y - 5 = -1(x - 2) y - 5 = -x + 2

y = -x + 7

QUESTION 22

Choice A is correct. The cube root of a number is the number that, when cubed, equals the original number. Let x be the cube root of 64: x^3 = 64 x = 4

SECTION 2 MODULE 2: MATH TEST

QUESTION 1

Choice C is correct. Let's combine them:

$12x^3 - 5x^3 = (12 - 5) x^3 = 7x^3$

QUESTION 2

Choice B is correct. Given: Distance in yards=5,104

We need to convert this distance to miles by dividing the number of yards by the number of yards in a mile:

$$Distance\ in\ miles = \frac{5,104\ yards}{1,760\ yards/mile}$$

Perform the division:

Distance in miles=5,104/1,760

Distance in miles≈2.9

QUESTION 3

Choice A is correct. The point (8,2) has:

   x=8

   y=2

Now, let's evaluate the point against each system of inequalities:

A) x>0, y>0

   x=8 is greater than 0.

   y=2 is greater than 0.

Both inequalities are satisfied by the point (8,2).

QUESTION 4

The correct answer is 15 or -5. By the definition of absolute value, if |x-5|=10|, then x -5 = 10 or x -5 = -10. Adding 5 to both sides of the first equation yields x =15. Adding 5 to both sides of the second equation yields x =-5. Thus, the given equation has two possible solutions, 15 and -5. Note that 15 and −5 are examples of ways to enter a correct answer.

QUESTION 5

Choice C is correct. To find f(2), substitute 2 for x in the function f(x) = x^3 + 15. This gives f(2) = 2^3 + 15 = 8 + 15 = 23.

QUESTION 6

Choice C is correct. The total cost is the daily rental cost multiplied by the number of days, plus the one-time insurance fee. This can be represented by the equation c = 11d + 10, where c is the total cost in dollars and d is the number of days.

QUESTION 7

Choice D is correct. Since lines m and n are parallel, the corresponding angles are equal. The angle marked x Choice D is correct. The value of x is determined by recognizing that x and the given 26° angle are interior angles on the same side of the transversal. Since the lines m and n are parallel, these two angles must be supplementary. Therefore, their sum equals 180°. The equation representing this relationship is x+26=180. Solving for x, we subtract 26 from 180, resulting in x=154. Hence, the value of x is 154°.

QUESTION 8

Choice C is correct. The total cost of $165 is equal to the down payment of $37 plus p monthly payments of $16 each. This can be represented by the equation 16p + 37 = 165.

QUESTION 9

The correct answer is 50. Substituting 8 for x in the equation gives y = 5(8) + 10, or y=50.

QUESTION 10

The correct answer is 40. The number of cans gathered by the group shown at the bottom of each bar in the bar graph is represented by its height. Group 6's bar rises to a height of forty. Consequently, group 6 gathered forty cans.

QUESTION 11

Choice is C is correct. Out of the total 80 students, 20 voted for the lion as the new mascot. The probability of selecting a student who voted for the lion is 20/80 = 1/4.

QUESTION 12

Option A is correct. The slope of the graph represents the rate of change of the total charge with respect to the number of hours worked. This corresponds to the electrician's hourly rate.

QUESTION 13

Choice D is correct. If the perimeter of square Y is 2 times the perimeter of square X, and square X has a side length of 12 cm, then the perimeter of square X is 4 × 12 = 48 cm. The perimeter of square Y is 2 × 48 = 96 cm. Since a square has 4 equal sides, the side length of square Y is 96 ÷ 4 = 24 cm.

QUESTION 14

Option B is correct. The line parallel to y = 7x + 4 has the same slope, which is 7. Since the line passes through the point (0, 5), the y-intercept is 5. Therefore, the equation of the parallel line is y = 7x + 5.

QUESTION 15

Option A is correct. The slope of the linear function can be calculated using the given points: (0, 41) and (1, 40). Slope = (40 - 41) / (1 - 0) = -1. The y-intercept is 41. Therefore, the equation of the linear function is h(x) = -x + 41.

QUESTION 16

To find the time it takes for the bacteria population to double, set f(t) equal to 2 times the initial population:

$60,000(2^{(t/410)}) = 2 \times 60,000 \ 2^{(t/410)} = 2 \ t/410 = 1 \ t = 410$

Therefore, it takes 410 minutes for the bacteria population to double.

QUESTION 17

The graph of y = f(x) is translated up 4 units to obtain the graph of y = g(x). This means that for any x-value, the corresponding y-value of g(x) is 4 more than the y-value of f(x).

When x = 0, f(0) = (0 - 6)(0 - 2)(0 + 6) = (-6)(-2)(6) = 72.

Since g(0) is 4 more than f(0), g(0) = 72 + 4 = 76.

QUESTION 18

Option D is correct. The candle initially had 17 ounces of wax. If 6 ounces remain, then 17 - 6 = 11 ounces of wax have been used. Since 1 ounce is used every 4 hours, it takes 11 × 4 = 44 hours to use 11 ounces of wax.

QUESTION 19

Option A is correct. To express k in terms of j and m, solve the equation $14j + 5k = m$ for k. First, subtract $14j$ from both sides: $5k = m - 14j$. Then, divide both sides by 5: $k = (m - 14j) / 5$.

QUESTION 20

Choice B is correct. Since the triangles are similar and the angles F and J are corresponding angles, the sine of these angles are equal. Therefore, $\sin(J) = \sin(F) = 308/317$.

QUESTION 21

Choice B is correct. Define x as the first integer and y as the second integer. The condition given is that the first integer is 11 greater than twice the second integer, expressed mathematically as $(x = 2y + 11)$. Additionally, the product of the two integers is 546, stated as $(x.y = 546)$. Substituting (x) from the first equation into the second equation gives $((2y + 11). y = 546)$. Expanding and rearranging leads to $(2y^2 + 11y - 546 = 0)$. To factorize this quadratic equation, we need two numbers that multiply to -1092 (i.e., (2 times -546)) and add up to 11. The factors satisfying these conditions are -28 and 39, which reformulates the equation as $((2y - 28)(y + 39) = 0)$. Using the zero-product property, $(2y - 28 = 0)$ or $(y + 39 = 0)$. Solving these gives $(y = 14)$ and $(y = -39)$. Given y must be positive, $(y = 14 \backslash)$. Substituting $(y = 14)$ back into the equation for x gives $(x = 39)$. Thus, the two integers are 14 and 39, with the smaller integer being 14.

QUESTION 22

Choice D is correct. To solve a system of inequalities in the xy-plane, substitute the point's x- and y-coordinates for x and y, respectively, in each inequality to make both inequalities true. Substituting the x- and y-coordinates of option D, 14 and 0, in the first inequality in the provided system

First Inequality:

$0 \leq 14 + 7$

$0 \leq 21$

This is **true**.

Second Inequality:

$0 \geq -2(14) - 1$

$0 \geq -28 - 1$

$0 \geq -29$

This is **true**.

Practice Test 4 with Detailed Answers and Explanations

SECTION 1 > READING AND WRITING TEST

MODULE 1: 27 QUESTIONS

INSTRUCTIONS

This section's questions cover a variety of crucial writing and reading abilities. There are one or more texts in each question, some of which may contain a table or graph. After carefully reading each excerpt and question, select the appropriate response to the question based on the relevant passage or passages. This section's questions are all multiple-choice, with four possible answers. Every question has a one optimal response.

1. In 2020, the OSIRIS-REx spacecraft made short contact with the asteroid 101955 Bennu. NASA scientist Daniella DellaGiustina says that, despite the unexpected challenge of a surface primarily covered with rocks, OSIRIS-REx successfully scraped a sample of the surface, gathering fragments to transport back to Earth. Which option concludes the sentence with the most logical and exact word or phrase?

A) attached.

B) Collected

C) followed.

D) Replaced

2. Planetary scientist Katarina Miljkovic's research reveals that the Moon's surface may not correctly reflect early impact events. When the Moon was still forming, its surface was softer, and asteroid or meteoroid impacts left less of an impression; consequently, evidence of early impacts may no longer exist. Which option concludes the sentence with the most logical and exact word or phrase?

A) Reflect.

B) Receive.

C) assess.

D) imitate.

3. Handedness, defined as a preference for using one's right or left hand, is commonly observed in people. Because this tendency is present but less prominent in many other species, animal behavior researchers sometimes utilize tests intended specifically to uncover individual animals' preferences for a particular hand or paw. Which option concludes the sentence with the most logical and exact word or phrase?

A) recognized.

B) interesting.

C) Significant.

D) helpful.

4. It is not uncommon to acknowledge the influence of Dutch painter Hieronymus Bosch on Ali Banisadr's works; in fact, Banisadr recognizes Bosch as an inspiration. However, other academics believe that the ancient Mesopotamian poetry Epic of Gilgamesh had a considerably bigger influence on Banisadr's work. Which option concludes the sentence with the most logical and exact word or phrase?

A) significant.

B) satisfying.

C) insignificant.

D) suitable.

5. The following is an adaptation of Susan Glaspell's 1912 short tale "'Out There.'" An elderly store owner examines a photograph that he recently bought and expects to sell. It appeared that the photo did not blend in with the rest of the shop. A charming young guy who claimed to be closing out his stock agreed to sell it to the old man for a song. It was a little, out-of-the-way business that specialized in photo framing. The old guy gazed about at his city vistas, pet and puppy photographs, and blazing landscapes. "Don't belong in here," he yelled. Nevertheless, the old guy was privately pleased of his acquisition. His scowl conveyed a sense of dignity as he moved around, considering the least absurd location for the photograph. Which alternative better expresses the text's core purpose?

A) To convey the shopkeeper's conflicting sentiments regarding the new image.

B) To communicate the business owner's dissatisfaction of the individual he received the new photo from.

C) Describe the products that the business owner most highly values.

D) To describe the difference between the new photo and previous pictures in the shop.

6. Angelina Weld Grimké, a Black American writer, wrote the poem "Black Finger" in 1923. Cypress is a kind of evergreen tree. I've just seen the most lovely object, slim and motionless, against a gold, gold sky. A straight black cypress, sensitive and exquisite, with a black finger pointing upward. Why, lovely still finger, are you black? And why are you pointing up? Which option best represents the general organization of the text?

A) The speaker evaluates a natural phenomena and then doubts the accuracy of her opinion.

B) The speaker recounts a unique sight in nature and then considers what significance to assign to that sight.

C) The speaker describes an external setting and then discusses human behavior within that scene.

D) The speaker observes her surroundings and speculates on how they impact her emotional state.

7. The following paragraph is taken from Walt Whitman's 1860 poem "Calamus 24." I HEAR I am accused of attempting to dismantle institutions; but, I am neither for nor against institutions.Only I will establish the institution of the dear love of comrades in the Mannahatta [Manhattan] and in every city of these States, inland and seaboard, as well as in the fields and woods and above every keel [ship] small or large that dent the water, without edifices, rules, trustees, or argument. Which option best represents the general organization of the text?

A) The speaker challenges an increasingly widespread attitude before summarizing his philosophy.

B) The speaker regrets his isolation from others and predicts a significant shift in society.

C) The speaker admits his personal flaws before boasting about his numerous accomplishments.

D) The speaker responds to a criticism levied at him before announcing his lofty objective.

8. The mimosa tree developed in East Asia, where the beetle Bruchidius terrenus feeds on its seeds. Mimosa trees, which are unrelated to B. terrenus, were imported to North America in 1785. However, evolutionary relationships between predators and prey can last for millennia and across continents. Around 2001, B. terrenus was introduced in southeastern North America, near where botanist Shu-Mei Chang and colleagues had been studying mimosa trees. Within a year, the beetles had attacked 93% of the trees. Which option best defines the role of the third sentence in the overall structure of the text?

A) It expresses the hypothesis that Chang and colleagues set out to test with mimosa trees and B. terrenus.

B) It provides a generalization, as evidenced by the discussion of mimosa trees and B. terrenus.

C) It provides an alternate explanation for the findings of Chang and colleagues.

D) It gives context, explaining why the species mentioned expanded to new areas.

9.

Text 1

Conventional wisdom has long assumed that human social institutions evolved in phases, starting with hunter-gatherers creating small bands of about equal status. The transition to agriculture some 12,000 years ago fueled population expansion, resulting in the formation of hierarchical groups: clan groupings initially, then chiefdoms, and eventually bureaucratic governments.

Text 2

In a 2021 book, anthropologist David Graeber and archaeologist David Wengrow argue that humans have always been socially adaptable, alternating between hierarchical and communal systems with decentralized leadership. According to the authors, as early as 50,000 years ago, certain hunter-gatherers altered their social structures periodically, scattering in small groups but also convening into communities that contained esteemed people. Based on the texts, how would Graeber and Wengrow (Text 2) reply to Text 1's "conventional wisdom"?

A) By acknowledging the value of hierarchical systems while emphasizing the larger significance of decentralized communal communities.

B) By rejecting the concept that evolution in social structures has followed a linear trend through various stages.

C) Recognizing that hierarchical positions were most likely not present in social systems prior to the rise of agriculture.

D) By questioning the belief that hunter-gatherer groups were among the oldest types of social organization.

10. The content below is borrowed from Frances Hodgson Burnett's 1911 novel The Secret Garden. Mary, a little girl, recently discovered an overgrown secret garden. Mary was a strange, determined little creature, and now she had something intriguing to be decided about, so she was completely captivated. She labored, dug, and pulled weeds methodically, getting more satisfied with her work with each hour rather than weary of it. She thought it was a wonderful play. Which option best expresses the primary theme of the text?

A) Mary hides in the garden to avoid performing her tasks.

B) Mary is becoming bored with digging out so many weeds in the garden.

C) Mary is cleaning up the garden to make room to play.

D) Mary is really satisfied while she is caring for the garden.

11. The following line is from Ezra Pound's 1909 poem "Hymn III," which is based on Marcantonio Flaminio's work. As a frail and gorgeous flower unfolds its sparkling leaf on the breast of the fostering soil, if the dew and rain pull it forth; so does my tender intellect flourish, if it is fed with the delicious dew of the fostering spirit. Without this, it begins to languish, just like a floweret formed on dry ground, if the dew and rain do not tend it. Based on the text, how is the human mind similar to a flower?

A) It becomes more vigorous over time.

B) It gains vigor from changes in the weather.

C) It requires proper nutrition to thrive.

D) It perseveres despite adversity.

12. The passage below is derived from Jack London's 1903 classic The Call of the Wild. Buck, a sled dog, lives with John Thornton in Yukon, Canada. Thornton alone possessed [Buck]. The rest of humanity was essentially nothing. Chance visitors might compliment or pat him, but he was chilly underneath it all, and like any overly demonstrative male, he would get up and walk away. When Thornton's partners, Hans and Pete, arrived on the long-awaited raft, Buck ignored them until he saw they were near to Thornton; after that, he tolerated them passively, accepting favors as if he favored them by accepting. Which option best expresses the main theme of the text?

A) Buck's social life has declined since moving in with Thornton.

B) Buck distrusts humans and tries to avoid them.

C) Buck is very well loved by the majority of Thornton's pals.

D) Buck regards Thornton in higher regard than anyone else.

13. Organic farming is a method of cultivating food that aims to lessen environmental impact by employing natural pest control methods and avoiding synthetic fertilizers. Organic farms still account for a small proportion of total farms in the United States, but they are becoming increasingly popular. According to the US Department of Agriculture, there were between 2,600 and 2,800 organic farms in California in 2016. Which option best utilizes data from the graph to complete the text?

A) Washington had 600 to 800 organic farms.

B) New York had less than 800 organic farms.

C) Wisconsin and Iowa each have around 1,200 to 1,400 organic farms.

D) Pennsylvania had almost 1,200 organic farms.

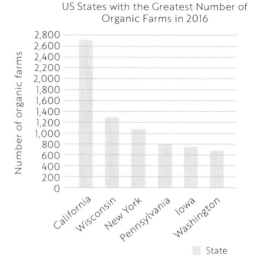

US States with the Greatest Number of Organic Farms in 2016

14. Biologist Valentina Gómez-Bahamón and her team studied two subspecies of the fork-tailed flycatcher bird that dwell in the same region of Colombia, but one migrates south for part of the year while the other does not. The researchers discovered that, due to tiny changes in feather structure, the feathers of migratory forked-tailed flycatcher males produce a higher-pitched sound during flight than nonmigratory males. The researchers suggest that female fork-tailed flycatchers are drawn to a distinctive sound emitted by males of their own subspecies, and that this preference will promote further genetic and anatomical divergence between the subspecies over time. Which finding, if accurate, would most directly support Gómez-Bahamón and her team's hypothesis?

A) The feathers on the wings of migrating fork-tailed flycatchers are narrower than those of nonmigratory species, allowing them to fly longer distances.

B) Over several generations, the sound emitted by the feathers of migratory male fork-tailed flycatchers becomes increasingly higher pitched than that made by nonmigratory males.

C) Fork-tailed flycatchers send various messages to one another depending on whether their feathers produce high-pitched or low-pitched noises.

D) The breeding behaviors of migratory and nonmigratory fork-tailed flycatchers remained largely consistent over numerous generations.

15. The Earth's atmosphere is blasted by cosmic dust from a variety of sources, including short-period comets (SPCs), asteroid belt particles (ASTs), Halley-type comets (HTCs), and Oort cloud comets. Some of the dust's substance vaporizes in the atmosphere, a process known as ablation; the faster the particles move, the faster the ablation. Astrophysicist Juan Diego Carrillo-Sánchez led a team that estimated average ablation rates for elements in dust (such as iron and potassium) and discovered that material in slower-moving SPC or AST dust has a lower rate than material in faster-moving HTC or OCC dust. For example, although the average ablation rate for iron from AST dust is 28%, the average rate for _____.

Which option best utilizes data from the table to complete the example?

A) Iron content in SPC dust is 20%.

B) The sodium content in OCC dust is 100%.

C) Iron content in HTC dust is 90%.

D) The sodium concentration in AST dust is 75%.

Ablation Rates of Three Elements in Cosmic Dust, by Dust Source

Element	SPC	AST	HTC	OCC
iron	20%	28%	90%	98%
potassium	44%	74%	97%	100%
sodium	45%	75%	99%	100%

16. Art collectives, such as The Propeller Group in the United States and Vietnam or Los Carpinteros in Cuba, are groups of artists who agree to collaborate for a variety of reasons, such as stylistic reasons, the advancement of shared political ideals, or the reduction of supply and studio space costs. Regardless of the reasons, art collectives typically require some level of collaboration among the artists. According to a recent series of interviews with diverse art collectives, an arts writer believes that this can be tough for artists who are accustomed to having complete control over their work. Which quote from the interviews best supports the journalist's claim?

A) "The first collective I joined included many amazingly talented artists, and we enjoyed each other's company, but because we had a hard time sharing credit and responsibility for our work, the collective didn't last."

B) "We collaborate, but that does not imply that specific projects are equally the responsibility of everyone. Many of our projects are primarily the responsibility of the person who first offered the job to the group.

C) "After working as a member of a collective for several years, it can be difficult to remember what it was like to work alone without the collective's support. But that backing promotes, rather than limits, my particular expression."

D) "Sometimes an artist from outside the collective will choose to collaborate with us on a project, but all of those projects fit within the larger themes of the work the collective does on its own."

17. Many plants benefit from mycorrhizal fungus in the soil, with some seeing significant increases in bulk. A student ran an experiment to demonstrate this effect. For the experiment, the student chose three plant species: two mycorrhizal hosts (species that benefit from mycorrhizal fungi) and one nonmycorrhizal species. The student then grew several plants from each species in soil with mycorrhizal fungi and dirt treated to destroy mycorrhizal and other fungi. After a few weeks, the student measured the plants' average mass and was shocked to discover that _____.

Effects of Mycorrhizal Fungi on three plant species.

Plant species	Mycorrhizal host	Average mass of plants grown in soil containing mycorrhizal fungi (in grams)	Average mass of plants grown in soil treated to kill fungi (in grams)
Corn	yes	15.1	3.8
Marigold	yes	10.2	2.4
Broccoli	no	7.5	7

Which option best uses data from the table to complete the statement?

A) Broccoli grown in soil with mycorrhizal fungus had a slightly higher average mass than broccoli cultivated in soil treated to kill fungi.

B) Corn grown in soil with mycorrhizal fungus had a greater average mass than broccoli.

C) Marigolds grown in soil with mycorrhizal fungi had a much higher average mass than marigolds cultivated in fungicide-treated soil.

D) Of the three species planted in fungicide-treated soil, corn had the highest average mass, whereas marigolds had the lowest.

18. Several artworks discovered in the remains of Pompeii show a female lady fishing with a cupid nearby. Some historians believe the image represents the goddess Venus, who is known to have been associated with cupids in Roman culture; however, University of Leicester archaeologist Carla Brain thinks that cupids may have also been associated with fishing in general. The presence of a cupid alongside a feminine figure implies that _____. Which option most logically concludes the text?

A) is not conclusive proof that the figure is Venus.

B) suggests that Venus was frequently shown fishing.

C) removes the notion that the figure represents Venus.

D) would be difficult to explain if the figure were not Venus.

19. Literary agencies believe that more than half of all nonfiction books attributed to a celebrity or other popular figure are actually written by ghostwriters, professional authors who are paid to write other material but whose names never appear on book covers. Which option completes the paragraph and ensures that it follows Standard English conventions?

A) People's Stories

B) People's Stories

C) People's Stories

D) People's Stories

20. The wood frog (Rana sylvatica), like other amphibians, cannot create its own heat, therefore during subfreezing conditions, it reacts by creating enormous quantities of glucose, a chemical that helps prevent harmful ice from accumulating inside its cells. Which option completes the paragraph and ensures that it follows Standard English conventions?

A) has survived.

B) survived.

C) would survive.

D) survives.

21. After a series of diseases as a youngster, Wilma Rudolph was warned she could never walk again. Rudolph defied the odds and won three gold medals in the 1960 Summer Olympics in Rome. She won the 100- and 200-meter dashes, as well as the 4 ×100 relay, making her the first US woman to do so. Which option completes the paragraph and ensures that it follows Standard English conventions?

A) Ran—fast—during

B) ran quickly during

C) ran rapidly, while

D) ran—fast. During

22. In several of her landscape paintings from the 1970s and 1980s, Lebanese American artist Etel Adnan used abstraction to capture the spirit of California's fog-shrouded Mount Tamalpais region, depicting the area's characteristics with splotches of color. Interestingly, the triangle symbolizing the mountain itself is one of the few clearly defined figures in her paintings. Which option completes the paragraph and ensures that it follows Standard English conventions?

A) are

B) Have been

C) Were

D) is

23. Seneca artist Marie Watt creates blanket art in a variety of shapes and sizes. Watt stitched blanket strips together to make a 10-by-13-inch rectangle in 2014, then piled folded blankets into two huge stacks and cast them in bronze, resulting in two curving 18-foot-tall blue-bronze pillars. Which option completes the paragraph and ensures that it follows Standard English conventions?

A) sample later,

B) Sampler.

C) Sampler,

D) sampler; subsequently,

24. Percy Julian, an African American scientist and entrepreneur, made vision possible for people all around the world. _____, which resulted in the first mass-produced glaucoma therapy, was named one of the best achievements by a US chemist in the last century in 1999. Which option completes the paragraph and ensures that it follows Standard English conventions?

A) Julian developed the alkaloid physostigmine in 1935,

B) In 1935, Julian developed the alkaloid physostigmine.

C) Julian's 1935 synthesis of the alkaloid, physostigmine

D) In 1935, Julian developed the alkaloid physostigmine.

25. The Arctic-Alpine Botanic Garden in Norway and the Jardim Botânico of Rio de Janeiro in Brazil are two of many botanical gardens across the world committed to producing varied plant species, encouraging scientific study, and teaching the public about plant conservation. Which option completes the paragraph and ensures that it follows Standard English conventions?

A) species, both native and nonnative.

B) species, both native and nonnative.

C) species, both native and nonnative.

D) species, both native and nonnative.

26. Alton Okinaka, a sociologist, serves on the review board that adds new sites to the Hawai'i Register of Historic Places, such as Pi'ilanihale Heiau and the 'Ōpaeka'a Road Bridge. Okinaka does not make such decisions. _____ All historical classifications must be authorized by a panel of nine specialists in architecture, archaeology, history, and Hawaiian culture. Which option completes the paragraph and ensures that it follows Standard English conventions?

A) single-handedly

B) single-handedly,

C) single-handedly

D) single-handedly

27. In 1968, US Congressman John Conyers submitted legislation to create a national holiday in honor of Dr. Martin Luther King Jr. Despite the fact that the bill did not pass, Conyers remained committed. He collaborated with Shirley Chisholm, the first Black woman elected to Congress, and resubmitted the measure each session for the following fifteen years. The measure passed in 1983. Which option provides the most natural transition to the end of the text?

A) Alternatively,

B) Similarly,

C) Finally,

D) Also,

STOP — IF YOU COMPLETE BEFORE THE TIME LIMIT, YOU MAY JUST REVIEW YOUR WORK ON THIS MODULE. AVOID SWITCHING TO ANY OTHER TEST MODULE.

MODULE 2: 27 QUESTIONS

1. The global fashion resale business, which involves buyers of pre-owned apparel from retailers and internet vendors, produced close to $30 billion in revenue in 2019. Some experts believe that sales will more than quadruple by 2028, assuming that growth would continue. Which option provides the most accurate and logical word or phrase to finish the text?

A) generated

B) rejected

C) anxious

D) predicted

2. Though it is challenging to get biomolecules past the layers of the plant cell wall, artificially supplying biomolecules to plant cells is a crucial part of keeping plants safe from diseases. It has been demonstrated by Markita del Carpio Landry and her associates that _____ this issue by transferring molecules via carbon nanotubes, which are able to pass through cell barriers. Which option provides the most accurate and logical word or phrase to finish the text?

A) conceive

B) Ignorance

C) provide an example

D) overcome

3. Particle physicists such as Ayana Holloway Arce and Aida El-Khadra primarily focus on studying subatomic particles, which are the smallest observable components of matter, by employing advanced technology

to precisely evaluate their behaviour. Which option provides the most accurate and logical word or phrase to finish the text?

A) choosing

B) inspecting

C) producing

D) Making a decision

4. Scientists Kristian J. Carlson and colleagues studied the fossilised shoulder bones and clavicle of "Little Foot," an early hominid dating back 3.6 million years. Little Foot may have adapted to life in the trees when they discovered that these bones were _____, the clavicle and shoulder bones of contemporary apes that frequently climb trees, including gorillas and chimpanzees. Which option provides the most accurate and logical word or phrase to finish the text?

A) eclipsed by

B) analogous to

C) apart from

D) acquired from

5. In Samuel R. Delany's 1966 novel Babel-17, Rydra Wong, the main character, is a poet. This is not an uncommon profession in Delany's writing, as about twelve of the characters in his books are also poets or writers. Which option provides the most accurate and logical word or phrase to finish the text?

A) unfailing

B) atypical

C) profitable

D) laborious

6. Photographer and neurobiologist Okunola Jeyifous developed a set of fresh photos for a 2020 show that drew inspiration from the "Black ABCs," a set of 1970s alphabet posters that highlighted Black kids from Chicago. Jeyifous created what he called "micro and macro portraiture" by taking pictures of the now-adult models and superimposing the photographs on top of enlarged pictures of the models' cells. Which option provides the most accurate and logical word or phrase to finish the text?

A) confirmed

B) produced

C) confronted

D) was revived

7. Apart from his professional accomplishments as a psychologist, Francis Cecil Sumner also played a significant role in advancing Black students' access to psychology education by founding the psychology department at Howard University, a historically Black university, in 1930. Which option provides the most accurate and logical word or phrase to finish the text?

A) supporter of

B) add on to

C) the recipient of

D) diversion for

8. Regardless of how significant or insignificant in history the reign of a French monarch like Hugh Capet or Henry I was historically, its course was determined by issues of legitimacy, and as such, it is impossible to comprehend without also comprehending the circumstances that gave rise to the monarch's ability to _____ his right to the throne. Which option provides the most accurate and logical word or phrase to finish the text?

A) Give something back

B) make annotations

C) buttress

D) Take a step back

9. Certain bird species do not nurture their own offspring. Instead, mature females deposit their eggs in other nests, among the eggs of another bird species. Female cuckoos have been recorded fast laying eggs in the nests of other bird species while they are out foraging. When the eggs hatch, the noncuckoo parents usually raise the cuckoo chicks as if they were their own kids, even if the cuckoos seem extremely different from the other chicks. Which option best reflects how the underlined statement fits into the larger context of the text?

A) It introduces a physical characteristic of female cuckoos that is discussed later in the book.

B) It explains the appearance of the cuckoo nests discussed previously in the article.

C) It describes in detail how female cuckoos exhibit the behavior indicated in the text.

D) It discusses how other birds react to the female cuckoo's conduct described in the text.

10. Cats can evaluate invisible people's places in space based on the sound of their voices, therefore they are surprised when the same person calls from two distinct locations in a short period of time. Saho Takagi and colleagues arrived at this result by evaluating cats' degrees of surprise using ear and head movements while they heard recordings of their owners' voices from two speakers positioned far apart. Cats were less surprised when their owners' voices were repeated twice from the same speaker, but more surprised when the voices were played once each from two separate speakers. According to the text, how did the researchers assess the amount of surprise showed by the cats in the study?

A) They observed how each cat moved its ears and head.

B) They investigated how each cat responded to the voice of a stranger.

C) They investigated each cat's physical interactions with its owner.

D) They tracked each cat's movements around the room.

11. A student conducts an experiment to test her theory that a slightly acidic soil environment is better for the development of Brassica rapa parachinensis (a vegetable also known as choy sum) than a neutral soil environment. She puts sixteen choy sum seeds in a combination of equal parts coffee grounds (very acidic) and potting soil, and another sixteen seeds in potting soil without coffee grounds as a control for the experiment. The two sets of seeds were subjected to identical growth conditions and observed for three weeks. Which discovery, if true, would directly undermine the student's hypothesis?

A) Choy sum planted in soil without coffee grounds grew much taller at the conclusion of the experiment than choy sum planted in dirt plus coffee grounds.

B) At the end of the trial, the choy sum grown in soil without coffee grounds weighed much less than the choy sum cultivated in soil mixed with coffee grounds.

C) Choy sum seedlings placed in soil without coffee grounds sprouted substantially later in the experiment than seeds planted in soil mixed with coffee grounds.

D) Significantly fewer choy sum seedlings sown in soil without coffee grounds sprouted than seeds planted in soil mixed with coffee grounds.

12. Katherine Mansfield wrote the short tale "The Young Girl" in 1920. In the narrative, the narrator takes an anonymous seventeen-year-old girl and her younger brother out to eat. In portraying the adolescent, Mansfield repeatedly contrasts the character's attractive looks with her disagreeable attitude, like when Mansfield writes about the youngster, _____ Which quotation from "The Young Girl" best shows the claim?

A) "I overheard her say, 'I can't bear flowers on a table.' They had obviously been causing her great anguish, since she closed her eyes as I pulled them away."

B) She told us, "While we waited she took out a little, gold powder-box with a mirror in the lid, shook the poor little puff as though she loathed it, and dabbed her lovely nose."

C) What happened next? "I saw, after that, she couldn't stand this place a moment longer, and, indeed, she jumped up and turned away while I went through the vulgar act of paying for the tea."

D) "She didn't even remove her gloves. She dropped her gaze and banged on the table. When she heard a faint violin, she cringed and bit her lip again. Silence."

13. High levels of public uncertainty about the economic policies a country will pursue can make corporate planning difficult, although such uncertainty measurements have not often been extremely thorough. However, economist Sandile Hlatshwayo has evaluated trends in news reporting to develop measures of not just overall economic policy uncertainty, but also uncertainty in specific areas of economic policy, such as tax or trade policy. Her analysis reveals that a general measure may not properly represent uncertainty about specific areas of policy, as in the example of the United Kingdom, where general economic policy uncertainty is _____. Which option best illustrates the assertion using graph data?

A) was closely connected with uncertainties about tax and public expenditure policies in 2005, but diverged significantly in 2009.

B) was much lower than uncertainty regarding tax and public expenditure policies in each year between 2005 and 2010.

C) peaked between 2005 and 2010, coinciding with the lowest levels of uncertainty about trade policy, taxation, and public spending policy.

D) was much lower than uncertainty regarding trade policy in 2005, but significantly greater than in 2010.

14. Linguist Deborah Tannen has warned against phrasing difficult subjects in terms of two strongly competing viewpoints, such as pro and con. According to Tannen, this debate-driven method can reduce topics' complexity and, when employed in front of an audience, can be less useful than presenting diverse opinions in a noncompetitive style. To test Tannen's idea, students ran a research in which they presented participants one of three alternative versions of local news commentary on the same topic. Each variation included a debate between two commentators with opposing viewpoints, a panel of three commentators with different perspectives, or a single commentator. Which finding from the students' study, if true, would provide the strongest evidence for Tannen's hypothesis?

A) Participants regarded debate commentators to be more informed about the subject than panel commentators.

B) Participants evaluated panelists as more informed about the matter than a single pundit.

C) On average, panelists properly answered more questions on the problem than debaters or single commentators.

D) On average, participants who saw the sole commentator correctly answered more questions regarding the topic than those who watched the debate.

15. William Shakespeare wrote the play King Lear in 1606. In the play, King Lear tests his three daughters' fidelity to him. He eventually displays sorrow for his actions, as evidenced by _____. Which choice best illustrates the claim using a quote from King Lear?

A) states about himself, "I am a man / more sinned against than sinning."

B) declares during a raging storm, "This tempest will not give me leave to ponder / On things that would hurt me more."

C) thinks to himself, pounding his skull, "Beat at this gate that lets thy folly in / And thy dear judgement out!"

D) declares in his own words, "I will do such things— / What they are yet, I know not; but they shall be / The terrors of the earth!"

16. Many of William Shakespeare's plays explore broad issues that continue to resonate with modern audiences. For example, Romeo and Juliet, set in Shakespeare's Italy, explores the themes of parents vs children and love versus hatred, and the play is still frequently read and performed throughout the world. However, comprehending Shakespeare's so-called history plays may need a thorough comprehension of several centuries of English history. As a result, _____ Which option most logically concludes the text?

A) Many modern theatergoers and readers are likely to find Shakespeare's historical plays less compelling than his tragedies.

B) Some of Shakespeare's tragedies are more applicable to modern audiences than twentieth-century plays.

C) Romeo and Juliet is Shakespeare's most conceptually accessible tragedy.

D) Experts in English history prefer Shakespeare's history plays over his other works.

17. Ancestral Puebloans, the civilization from whom the Pueblo tribes evolved, appeared as early as 1500 B.C.E. in what is now the southwestern United States and dispersed abruptly in the late 1200s C.E., abandoning developed cities with agricultural and turkey farming systems. A recent study comparing turkey remains from Mesa Verde, a village in southern Colorado, to samples from modern turkey populations in the Rio Grande Valley of north central New Mexico found that the latter birds descended in part from Mesa Verde turkeys, with shared genetic markers appearing only after 1280. Thus, the researchers decided that _____ Which option most logically completes the text?

A) The terrains of the Rio Grande Valley and Mesa Verde were more comparable in the past than they are now.

B) Some Ancestral Puebloans moved to the Rio Grande Valley in the late 1200s, bringing farming traditions with them.

C) Prior to 1280, indigenous peoples in the Rio Grande Valley cultivated crops rather than turkeys.

D) Mesa Verde's Ancestral Puebloans most likely inherited farming methods from Indigenous peoples in other locations.

18. One obstacle in determining whether holding elected office impacts a person's conduct is ensuring that the experiment contains an appropriate control group. To determine the impact of holding office, researchers must compare those who hold elected office to those who do not hold office but are otherwise similar to the officeholders. Researchers are unable to influence which politicians win elections, so they _____. Which option most logically concludes the text?

A) difficulty to get reliable statistics on the behavior of politicians who are no longer in office.

B) Valid research can only be conducted with those who have previously held office, not those who are now holding office.

C) Choose a control group of people who differ from office holders in numerous major ways.

D) will have difficulty identifying a group of persons who can serve as a suitable control group for their investigations.

19. Vivek Bald's remarkable book Bengali Harlem and the Lost Histories of South Asian America tells the story of the people who settled in New York City in the early twentieth century via newspaper articles, census data, ship logs, and recollections. Which option completes the paragraph and ensures that it follows Standard English conventions?

A) Stories of South Asian immigration.

B) stories of South Asian immigration.

C) tales of South Asian immigration.

D) The stories of South Asian immigrants

20. Painter Howardena Pindell's two main series, "Memory Test" and "Autobiography," addressed themes of healing, self-discovery, and memory by cutting and stitching back together pieces of canvas and putting personal items, such as postcards, into some of the works. Which option completes the paragraph and ensures that it follows Standard English conventions?

A) of

B) of,

C) of—

D) of:

21. Sona Charaipotra, an Indian American, and Dhonielle Clayton, an African American, grew up disappointed by the absence of varied characters in children's novels. In 2011, these two writers collaborated to form CAKE Literary, a book packaging company that specializes in the production and promotion of stories delivered from varied viewpoints for children and young people. Which option completes the paragraph and ensures that it follows Standard English conventions?

A) Company,

B) Company that

C) Company

D) Company, that

22. A research headed by professor Rebecca Kirby at the University of Wisconsin-Madison discovered that black bears that eat human food before hibernation had greater amounts of a rare carbon isotope, _____, because to the higher 13 C levels in maize and cane sugar. Bears with this increased levels had significantly shorter hibernation times on average. Which option completes the paragraph and ensures that it follows Standard English conventions?

A) carbon 13, (C)

B) Carbon-13 (13C)

C) Carbon-13, (C).

D) Carbon-13 (13C)

23. In 2010, archaeologist Noel Hidalgo Tan was touring Cambodia's twelfth-century temple of Angkor Wat when he saw red paint patterns on the temple. Using digital imaging methods, he revealed that the markings were part of an extensive mural including over 200 paintings.

Which option completes the paragraph and ensures that it follows Standard English conventions?

A) Walls with

B. Walls with

C) walls, as with

D) Walls. With

24. Working from Charpentier's earlier discovery, chemists Emmanuelle Charpentier and Jennifer Doudna—winners of the 2020 Nobel Prize in Chemistry—re-created and then reprogrammed the so-called "genetic scissors" of a species of DNA-cleaving bacteria, a tool that is revolutionizing the field of gene technology. Which option completes the paragraph and ensures that it follows Standard English conventions?

A) To Forge

B) Forging.

C) Forged

D) and forging.

25. Vanessa Galvez, an engineer, oversaw the building of 164 bioswales, or planted channels meant to absorb and redirect stormwater, on Queens roadways in 2016. By minimizing runoff that flows into city drains, _____ Which option completes the paragraph and ensures that it follows Standard English conventions?

A) Bioswales have successfully reduced street floods and the contamination of neighboring waterways.

B) bioswales have reduced both street flooding and the pollution of neighboring rivers.

C) bioswales have successfully reduced street floods and the contamination of neighboring waterways.

D) Bioswales have helped to reduce street floods and pollution in neighboring waterways.

26. Ming Tang, a Rice University geoscientist, published a study in 2019 that provides a new explanation for the origin of Earth's arcs, which are towering ridges formed when a dense oceanic plate subducts under a less dense continental plate, melts in the mantle below, and then rises and bursts through the continental crust above. Which option completes the paragraph and ensures that it follows Standard English conventions?

A) continents geological

B) continents, geological

C) continents, geological

D) continents. Geology

27. During a 2021 flight, Rocket Labs' Electron rocket suffered an unexpected failure when its second-stage booster shut down abruptly after ignition. _____ Rather than downplaying the situation, Rocket Labs' CEO openly admitted what occurred and apologized for the loss of the rocket's payload, which included two satellites. Which option provides the most natural transition to the end of the text?

A) Afterward,

B) Also,

C) Indeed.

D) Likewise,

STOP IF YOU COMPLETE BEFORE THE TIME LIMIT, YOU MAY JUST REVIEW YOUR WORK ON THIS MODULE. AVOID SWITCHING TO ANY OTHER TEST MODULE.

SECTION 2 > MATH TEST

MODULE 1: 22 QUESTIONS

DIRECTIONS

Complete each issue on the questions, choose the best response from the list of options, and mark the matching circle on your answer sheet. You may do scratch work in any open place in your exam booklet.

1. A landscaper purchases two types of fertilizer. By weight, 60% of the filler materials in Fertilizer A and 40% of the filler materials in Fertilizer B are present. The gardener purchased fertilizers that together comprise 240 pounds of filler material. Which equation, where x represents the quantity of fertilizer A and y represents the quantity of fertilizer B, best describes this relationship?

A) $0.4x + 0.6y = 240$

B) $0.6x + 0.4y = 240$

C) $40x + 60y = 240$

D) $60x + 40y = 240$

2. The complex numbers 2+3i and 4+8i add up to what? i = √(-1) ?

A) 17

B) 17i

C) 6 + 11i

D) 8 + 24i

3. $4x^2-9=(px+t)(px-t)$
P and t in the preceding equation are constants. Which of the possibilities may p's value be?

A) 2

B) 3

C) 4

D) 9

4. If x =2/3 y and y = 18, What does 2x − 3 mean?

A) 21

B) 15

C) 12

D) 10

5. A bricklayer may calculate the number of bricks, n, required to construct a wall that is l feet long and h feet high using the formula n = 7lh. Which of the alternatives describes l in terms of n and h correctly?

A) l= 7/nh

B) l = h/7n

C) l = n/7h

D) l = n/(7+h)

6. Some values for the functions w and t are shown in the above table. What is the value of x w(x)+t(x) =x ?

x	W(x)	T(x)
1	-1	-3
2	3	-1
3	4	1
4	3	3
5	-1	5

A) 1

B) 2

C) 3

D) 4

7. If $\sqrt{x}+\sqrt{9}=\sqrt{64}$, what does x mean?

A) 5

B) 5

C) 25

D) 55

8. Jaime is training for a cycling competition. His objective is to ride a bicycle for four weeks, averaging at least 280 miles every week. The first week he rode his bike 240 miles, the second week 310 miles, and the third week 320 miles. Which inequality may be used to show how many miles, x, Jaime would need to ride a bicycle in order to reach his objective in the fourth week?

A) $\frac{240+310+320}{3}+x \geq 280$

B) $240 + 310 + 320 \geq x(280)$

C) $\frac{240}{4} + \frac{310}{4} + \frac{320}{4}\ x+ \geq 280$

D) $240 + 310 + 320 + x \geq 4\ (280)$

9. Which of the subsequent is equivalent to $\dfrac{4x^2+6x}{4x+2}$?

A) x

B) x + 4

C) $x - \frac{2}{4x+2}$

D) $x + 1 - \frac{1}{2x+1}$

10. $2x^2-4x=t$

Here, t is a constant in the given equation. Which of the possibilities may the value of t be if the formula has no genuine solutions?

A) –3

B) –1

C) 1

D) 3

11. Which of the subsequent is equivalent to $(a+b/2)^2$?

A) $a^2+ b^2/2$

B) $a^{^2}+ b^2/4$

C) $a^2+ab/2+b^2/2$

D) $a^2+ab+b^2/4$

12. Which expression is equivalent to $(2x^2-4)-(-3x^2+2x-7)$?

A) $5x^2-3x+2$

B) $5x^2+3x-2$

C) $-x^2-2x-11$

D) $-x^2+2x-11$

13. Businesses pay a one-time setup price of $350 + dollars each month to a website hosting provider. What is the worth of d if a company owner pays $1,010 for the first 12 months, such as the startup fee?

A) 25

B) 35

C) 45

D) 55

14. $6x - 9y > 12$

Which of the subsequent disparities corresponds to the one mentioned above?

A) $x -y >2$

B) $2x -3 y>4$

C) $3x -2y >4$

D) $3y -2x >2$

15. A coastal city is made up of 92.1 square miles of land, of which 11.3 square miles are covered by water. Which of the following best describes the population density of the city in 2010 (people per square mile of land area) if the city had 621,000 residents at that time?

A) 6,740

B) 7,690

C) 55,000

D) 76,000

16. Amerigo Vespucci made two trips to the New World between 1497 and 1500. Vespucci wrote that the first journey lasted 43 days longer than the second, for a total of 1,003 days throughout the course of the two expeditions. How much time did the second journey take?

A) 460

B) 480

C) 520

D) 540

17. $7x+3y=8$
$6x-3y=8$

What is the numerical value of x − y in the solution (x, y) to the given system of equations?

A) − 4/3

B) 2/3

C) 4/3

D) 22/3

18. From day 14 to day 35, the sunflower grows at a virtually consistent pace. Which of the subsequent equations best describes the sunflower's height h, measured in centimeters, during this interval t days after it starts to grow?

A) h = 2.1t − 15

B) h = 4.5 t− 27

C) h = 6.8t − 12

D) h = 13.2t − 18

19. Which of the subsequent best describes the tread depth in relation to the riser height?

A) h=1/2 (25+d)

B) h=1/2 (25-d)

C) h=-1/2 (25+d)

D) h=-1/2 (25-d)

20. According to some building requirements, interior stairways must have a minimum of 5 inches of riser height and a minimum of 9 inches of tread depth. Which of the following equations, when applied to the riser-tread formula, describes the set of all potential riser height values that satisfies this code requirement?

A) 0≤ h ≤5 h

B) h ≥ 5

C) 5≤ h ≤8

D) 8 ≤ h ≤ 16

21. An architect wishes to create a staircase with an odd number of steps, a riser height of between 7 and 8 inches, and a total climb of 9 feet using the riser-tread formula. Which requirement for the stairway's tread depth, expressed in inches, is met by the architect's constraints? (1 foot = 12 inches)

A) 7.2

B) 9.5

C) 10.6

D) 15

21. What is the sum of the solutions to $(x-6)(x+0.7)=0$?

A) −6.7

B) −5.3

C) 5.3

D) 6.7

STOP   IF YOU COMPLETE BEFORE THE TIME LIMIT, YOU MAY JUST REVIEW YOUR WORK ON THIS MODULE. AVOID SWITCHING TO ANY OTHER TEST MODULE.

MODULE 2: 27 QUESTIONS

1. The table above displays some of the values of the linear function f. What does f(3) mean?

A) 6

B) 7

C) 8

D) 9

x	F(x)
0	-2
2	4
6	16

2. In the xy-plane, the graph of $2x^2-6x+2y^2+2y=45$ is a circle. What is the circle's radius?

A) 5

B) 6.5

C) $\sqrt{40}$

D) $\sqrt{50}$

3. On a number line, two distinct points are separated by three units from the point with coordinate -4. Which of the equations that follows can be solved to get both points' coordinates?

A) $|x +4| =3$

B) $|x -4| =3$

C) $|x +3| =4$

D) $|x -3|=4$

4. Isabel cultivates potatoes in her garden. She gathered a total of 760 potatoes this year and set aside 10% of them for future planting. What was the quantity of the harvested potatoes that Isabel set aside for planting in the following year?

A) 66

B) 76

C) 84

D) 86

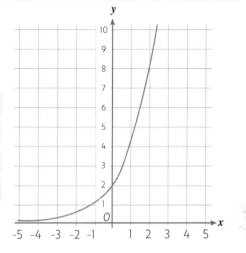

5. What is the value of the y-coordinate where the graph intersects the y-axis?

A) (0, 0)

B) (0, 2)

C) (2, 0)

D) (2, 2)

6. What is the conversion factor from meters to centimeters? The conversion factor between meters and centimeters is 1 meter equals 100 centimeters.

A) 0.051

B) 0.51

C) 5,100

D) 51,000

7. The bus is moving at a consistent velocity along a straight stretch of road. The equation d = 30t represents the relationship between the distance d, measured in feet, from a road marker and the time t, measured in seconds, after the bus has passed the marker. What is the distance, in feet, of the bus from the marker 2 seconds after it has passed the marker?

A) 30

B) 32

C) 60

D) 90

8. What is the simplified form of the formula $20w - (4w + 3w)$?

A) $10w$

B) $13w$

C) $19w$

D) $21w$

9. If the sum of 6 and x is equal to 9, what is the value of 18 added to 3 times x?

10. $y = x2 - 14x + 22$

The provided equation establishes a relationship between the variables x and y. At what value of x does y achieve its minimum?

11. What is the simplified form of the formula $9x2 + 5x$?

A) $x(9x + 5)$

B) $5x(9x + 1)$

C) $9x(x + 5)$

D) $x2 (9x + 5)$

12. Triangle ABC has an angle B of 52° and an angle C measuring 17°. What is the value of angle A?

A) 21°

B) 35°

C) 69°

D) 111°

13. $x = 8$

$y = x^2 + 8$

The equations in the following system meet at the position (x, y) in the xy-plane. What is the numerical value of y?

A) 8

B) 24

C) 64

D) 72

14. The scatterplot illustrates the correlation between two variables, x and y. Additionally, a regression line is depicted.

Which equation accurately captures the line of best fit displayed?

A) $y = 13.5 + 0.8x$

B) $y = 13.5 - 0.8x$

C) $y = -13.5 + 0.8x$

D) $y = -13.5 - 0.8x$

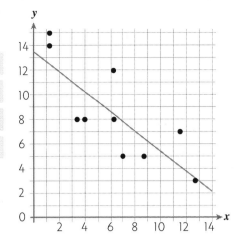

15. The function f is defined as $f(x) = 8x$. What is the value of x that makes f(x) equal to 48?

A) 6

B) 8

C) 36

D) 64

16. A circle is defined by its center O, and two points R and S are located on the circumference of the circle. The angle $\angle ROS$ in triangle ORS has a measure of 88°. What is the degree measurement of angle RSO?

17. $x(x+1) - 56 = 4x(x-7)$

What is the total of the solutions to the provided equation?

18. $y = 3x$

                                  $2x + y = 12$

The solution to the provided system of equations is represented by the coordinates (x, y). What is the numerical result of multiplying 5 by x?

A) 24

B) 15

C) 12

D) 5

19. The length of each edge of the cube is 41 inches. What is the cubic inch volume of the cube?

A) 164

B) 1,681

C) 10,086

D) 68,921

20.

$$p(t) = 90,000(1.06)t$$

The function p represents the population of Lowell t years after a census. Which function most accurately represents the population of Lowell m months after the census?

A) $r(m) = [90,000 / 12] (1.06)^m$

B) $r(m) = 90,000 [1.06 / 12]^m$

C) $r(m) = 90,000 [1.06 / 12]^{m/12}$

D) $r(m) = 90,000(1.06)^{m/12}$

21.

$$6x + 7y = 28$$

$$2x + 2y = 10$$

The solution to the provided system of equations is represented by the ordered pair (x, y). What is the numerical value of y?

A) −2

B) 7

C) 14

D) 18

22. The minimal value of x is equal to 6 times another integer n, decreased by 12. Which inequality represents the range of potential values for x?

A) $x \leq 6n - 12$

B) $x \geq 6n - 12$

C) $x \leq 12 - 6n$

D) $x \geq 12 - 6n$

STOP IF YOU COMPLETE BEFORE THE TIME LIMIT, YOU MAY JUST REVIEW YOUR WORK ON THIS MODULE. AVOID SWITCHING TO ANY OTHER TEST MODULE.

Practice Test 4 Answers

SECTION 1 READING AND WRITING TEST

MODULE 1:

QUESTION 1

Choice B is the best option since it logically concludes the text's account of the OSIRIS-REx spacecraft's encounter with asteroid 101955 Bennu. In this usage, "collected" refers to acquiring and taking away. According to the text, despite some unexpected issues created by pebbles on the asteroid's surface, OSIRIS-REx was able to collect a sample for return to Earth. This context indicates that OSIRIS-REx successfully acquired a sample of 101955 Bennu.

QUESTION 2

Choice A is the best option since it logically concludes the text's examination of the Moon's surface. In this sense, "reflect" implies to display or make obvious. According to the text, because the Moon's surface was softer when it was still developing than it is today, early asteroid and meteoroid impacts "would have left less of an impression" and, as a result, evidence of them may be lost. This background lends weight to the theory that the Moon's surface may not correctly reflect early impact events.

QUESTION 3

Choice A is the best answer since it logically concludes the text's topic of handedness in animals. In this sense, "recognized" refers to something that is evident or identifiable. The article states that while handedness is "easy to observe in humans," animal behavior experts require specialized activities to identify handedness in other animals. This context, as well as the use of "less" before the blank, imply that handedness in other animals is less identifiable than it is in humans.

QUESTION 4

Choice A. The sentence suggests a comparison in the degree of influence on Banisadr's work. "Significant" is the most logical and exact word as it indicates that the influence of the Epic of Gilgamesh is considerable and noteworthy, contrasting it with the acknowledged influence of Bosch.

QUESTION 5

Choice A is the most accurate description of the text's principal aim. The text emphasizes the shopkeeper's mixed feelings about the new photograph: his outward claim that it doesn't belong in the shop contrasts with his private satisfaction and pride in acquiring it. This captures the core purpose of expressing the shopkeeper's conflicting sentiments.

QUESTION 6

Choice B is the best answer since it appropriately defines the text's general structure. First, the speaker describes seeing a "most beautiful" sight: a tree ("black cypress") standing out from the golden sky behind it, resembling a person's finger "pointing upwards" and appearing "sensitive" and "exquisite." The speaker then questions the image's meaning, wondering why the finger is black and pointing upward. Thus, the text progresses from the speaker's account of a unique natural sight to her consideration of what meaning to assign to that sight.

QUESTION 7

Choice D is the best answer since it accurately defines the text's general structure. The speaker begins by noting that he has been informed that others are accusing him of attempting to dismantle institutions. The speaker then responds to this criticism by claiming that he is "neither for nor against institutions." Instead, he declares that his ultimate objective is to establish "the institution of the dear love of comrades" throughout the country. As a result, the general organization of the text is best described as a reply to criticism followed by a proclamation of a lofty aim.

QUESTION 8

Choice B is the best answer because it appropriately reflects the role of the third sentence in the text's overall structure. The final statement is a generalization, claiming that evolutionary ties between predators and prey can last over long periods of time and space. This generalization is demonstrated in the text's description of the link between mimosa trees and B. Terrenus beetles. Mimosa trees were imported to North America around 1785 with no B. Terrenus insects were present, disrupting the interaction between the trees and the beetles endemic to East Asia. When the beetles were transplanted to North America more than 200 years later, they promptly attacked mimosa trees, demonstrating how predator-prey relationships "can persist across centuries and continents."

QUESTION 9

Choice B is the best answer because it represents how Graeber and Wengrow (Text 2) are likely to respond to the "conventional wisdom" stated in Text 1. According to Text 1, the common thinking regarding human social systems is that they evolved in phases, beginning with hunter-gatherer bands, progressing to clan alliances, chiefdoms, and eventually governments with bureaucratic institutions. According to text 2, Graeber and Wengrow think that human social systems have been adaptable, moving between different sorts of structures such as hierarchical and collective systems, and that these transformations may have happened periodically. This means that Graeber and Wengrow would disagree with the notion that changes in social structures occurred in a linear progression through discrete stages.

QUESTION 10

Choice D is the best response since it correctly conveys the text's key theme. The book discusses Mary's actions in an overgrown secret garden, stating that she was "very much absorbed" and was "only becoming more pleased with her work every hour" rather than becoming bored with it. She also considers garden chores to be a "fascinating sort of play." As a result, the text's major concept is that Mary is immensely happy when caring for the garden.

QUESTION 11

Choice C is the best answer since it describes the human mind as a flower, which is clearly supported by the text. The passage draws a parallel between the demands of a "fragile and lovely flower" and the speaker's "tender mind": both must be fed in order to survive. Without such nourishment, they will "beginneth straightway to languish," or weaken. Thus, the phrase argues that the human mind, like a flower, need sufficient sustenance to grow.

QUESTION 12

Choice D is the best response since it correctly conveys the text's key theme. After establishing that Buck considers most people "as nothing," the book says that Buck will only acknowledge anyone other than Thornton if they look amicable to Thornton, and even then he will only reluctantly accept. Thus, the language emphasizes the sense that Thornton has a unique standing in Buck's thinking, with Buck holding him in greater respect than other individuals.

QUESTION 13

Choice A is the best answer since it uses graph data to precisely finish the text. The graph depicts the number of organic farms in each of six US states in 2016: between 2,600 and 2,800 in California, between 1,200 and 1,400 in Wisconsin, between 1,000 and 1,200 in New York, roughly 800 in Pennsylvania, and between 600 and 800 in Iowa and Washington. The final phrase of the text includes information regarding the number of organic farms in 2016, beginning with the number in California. The best sentence completion is the one that appropriately depicts the amount of organic farms in another state in 2016, as provided by the statement that Washington had between 600 and 800 organic farms.

QUESTION 14

Choice B is the best response because it offers a discovery that, if it were true, would most directly support the theory that Gómez-Bahamón and her team had concerning fork-tailed flycatchers. The text states that, despite the fact that two subspecies of birds coexist in the same area, migratory males' tail feathers create a higher-pitched sound than nonmigrating males'. Gómez-Bahamón and her team think that female fork-tailed flycatchers are drawn to the specific sound created by the tail feathers of males from their own subspecies, resulting in further "genetic and anatomical divergence" between the two subspecies. If it is discovered that the pitch created by migrating males' tail feathers increases over subsequent generations, it would imply that the morphology of the migrating subspecies' tail feathers is diverging farther from that of the nonmigrating subspecies. And if females continue to favor the sounds of males from their own subspecies, females from the migratory subspecies will acquire used to ever higher pitches over succeeding generations, resulting in greater subspecies separation. Thus, if the researchers discovered that migratory males' tail feathers produced higher pitches over time, it would provide credence to their idea.

QUESTION 15

Choice C is the most effective response since it completes the example of iron ablation rate. The table displays the ablation rates of three elements—iron, potassium, and sodium—found in cosmic dust originating from one of four sources. According to the text, the ablation rate for a given element in slower-moving SPC or AST dust was lower than that of faster-moving HTC or OCC dust. The book then provides the first portion of an example of this pattern, which describes a 28% ablation rate for iron in AST dust. The fact that iron from HTC dust had an ablation rate of 90% is thus the most effective way to complete this example—comparing a relatively low ablation rate for iron in slower-moving AST dust with a relatively high ablation rate for iron in faster-moving HTC dust demonstrates the tendency of ablation rates for a given element to be lower in slower-moving dust than in faster-moving dust.

QUESTION 16

Choice A is the best response since it includes the citation that best exemplifies the journalist's point. The quotation demonstrates that working collaboratively may be challenging for artists who are used to having total control over their work by showing that a collective failed because it was difficult to share credit and duties within the group, despite the fact that the company was delightful.

QUESTION 17

Choice A is the best answer because it makes the most efficient use of table data to finish the assertion. According to the text, mycorrhizal hosts are plants that benefit from the presence of mycorrhizal fungi in the soil, and some of these plants generate more mass when cultivated with these fungi, whereas nonmycorrhizal species either have no impact or may be hazardous. The experiment consisted of two mycorrhizal hosts (corn and marigold) and one nonmycorrhizal species (broccoli). Given the text's claim that nonmycorrhizal species will experience either no difference or a decrease in mass when exposed to mycorrhizal fungi, the student was likely surprised by the higher average mass for broccoli grown in the presence of the fungi than broccoli grown in soil treated to kill fungi.

QUESTION 18

Choice A is the best answer because it gives the most logical conclusion to the text's examination of the importance of the cupid discovered in Pompeii. The text states that the cupid stands near a statue of a female figure fishing, and that because Venus is linked with cupids, some historians assume the female figure is the goddess Venus. However, the text then states that, according to archaeologist Carla Brain, cupids may have also been associated with the activity of fishing, which, if true, would imply that the mere appearance of a cupid near a female figure engaged in fishing does not necessarily indicate that the figure is Venus.

QUESTION 19

Choice A is the best option. The norm of using plural and possessive nouns is being evaluated. The plural possessive noun "people's" and the plural noun "stories" accurately convey that there are several stories from different individuals.

QUESTION 20

Choice D is the best option. The norm under consideration is the usage of verbs to denote tense. In this case, the present tense verb "survives" appropriately conveys that the wood frog frequently survives subfreezing conditions by creating enormous quantities of glucose.

QUESTION 21

Choice D is the best option. The standard being examined is the usage of punctuation between sentences. The period is used appropriately to distinguish between one sentence ("Defying...fast") and another that begins with a supplemental phrase ("During...Olympics").

QUESTION 22

Choice D is the best option. The convention being examined is subject-verb agreement. The single verb "is" shares a number with the singular subject "the triangle."

QUESTION 23

Choice B is the best option. The convention under test is the synchronization of key clauses inside a sentence. This option employs a traditional semicolon to connect the first major clause ("In 2004...sampler") and the second main clause ("In 2014...pillars").

QUESTION 24

Choice C is the best option. The subject-modifier placement convention is currently being evaluated. Julian's 1935 synthesis of the alkaloid physostigmine was named one of the greatest achievements by a US chemist in the past hundred years in 1999. This choice places the noun phrase "Julian's 1935 synthesis" immediately after the modifying phrase "named...years."

QUESTION 25

Choice B is the best option. The convention being evaluated is the punctuation of elements in a complicated sequence. The semicolon after "nonnative" is appropriately used to distinguish the first item ("growing diverse plant species, both native and nonnative") from the second item ("fostering scientific research") in the list of items botanical gardens are committed to. Furthermore, the comma after "species" is used appropriately to distinguish the noun phrase "diverse plant species" from the supplemental phrase "both native and nonnative" that modifies it.

QUESTION 26

Choice A is the best option. The punctuation of an additional word or phrase placed between two major clauses is being examined. This choice utilizes a comma to separate the supplemental adverb "however" from the preceding main clause ("Okinaka doesn't...single-handedly") and a semicolon to connect the following major clause ("all...culture") to the remainder of the sentence. Furthermore, placing the semicolon after "however" correctly indicates that the information in the preceding main clause (Okinaka does not make such decisions alone) contradicts what might be assumed from the previous sentence (Okinaka serves on the review board that adds new sites to the Hawaii Register of Historic Places).

QUESTION 27

Choice C is the best option. "Finally" logically indicates that the bill's passage—following several efforts between 1968 and 1983—is the ultimate, conclusive event in the sequence indicated in the preceding phrases.

SECTION 1

MODULE 2: READING AND WRITING TEST

QUESTION 1

Choice D is the best answer since it most logically concludes the text's explanation of the fashion resale market's ongoing rise. In this sense, "predicted" refers to forecasting or indicating that something will happen in the future. According to the article, the fashion resale industry generated a lot of money in 2019, and some analysts predicted that it would continue to rise. This backdrop shows that the experts expected the fashion resale industry to generate more money than it had previously, with sales more than doubling by 2028.

QUESTION 2

Choice D is the best option since it logically concludes the text's topic of delivering biomolecules to plant cells. In this usage, "overcome" refers to successfully dealing with a problem. The article argues that, while moving proteins through plant cell walls is challenging, Landry and her colleagues have demonstrated that carbon nanotubes, which can traverse cell walls, might be advantageous. This context implies that Landry and her colleagues believe that employing carbon nanotubes, they can overcome the challenge of delivering proteins to plant cells.

QUESTION 3

Choice B is the most logical conclusion to the text's account of particle physicists' work. In this usage, "inspecting" refers to looking intently in order to examine. According to the novel, as particle scientists, Arce and El-Khadra use modern equipment to "closely examine" subatomic particles. In other words, they employ technology to examine minuscule pieces of materials that cannot be seen with the human eye.

QUESTION 4

Choice B is the correct answer because it logically concludes the text's presentation of the petrified bones of the hominid known as Little Foot. In this sense, "comparable to" refers to anything like. According to the article, the link between Little Foot's fossilized clavicle and shoulder bones and those of "frequent climbers," such as chimps and gorillas, demonstrates that Little Foot adapted to moving around in trees. This background shows that the fossilized bones of Little Foot and the bones of chimps and gorillas are similar—the Little Foot fossils are most likely akin to present ape bones.

QUESTION 5

Choice B is the most logical conclusion to the text's treatment of Samuel R. Delany's character Rydra Wong. In this sense, "atypical" refers to something that is not representational or frequent. The text states that Wong is one of "nearly a dozen" characters in Delany's novels who are poets or writers. This context suggests that being a poet is not an unusual employment for a character in one of Delany's novels.

QUESTION 6

Choice B is the best option since it most logically and exactly concludes the text's description of Jeyifous's picture series for the 2020 show. "Created" refers to the act of producing something. According to the text, Jeyifous, a photographer and neurobiologist, photographed adults who appeared as children in 1970s posters and then combined those photographs with magnified images of the adults' cells, resulting in what he called "micro and macro portraiture." This context suggests that Jeyifous used his dual interests in photography and neurobiology to create the images for the exhibition.

QUESTION 7

Choice A is the best option since it logically concludes the text's discussion of Francis Cecil Sumner. In this usage, "proponent of" indicates "supporter of." According to the book, Sumner helped establish the psychology department at historically Black Howard University in 1930. This demonstrates Sumner's support for extending Black students' opportunities to study psychology.

QUESTION 8

Choice C is the best answer because it most logically completes the text's examination of the legality of the reigns of French rulers such as Hugh Capet and Henry I. In this context, "buttress" refers to strengthening or defending. According to the text, whether a French king's reign was notable or uneventful, each monarch was questioned about his title to the throne. The text goes on to say that in order to understand the path of a French monarch's reign, it's important to understand what contributed to the monarch's ability to "hold the throne." This context implies that French monarchs like Hugh Capet and Henry I had to buttress, or defend, their right to rule.

QUESTION 9

Choice C is the best answer since it illustrates how the underlined statement fits into the larger context of the text. The first two phrases demonstrate that birds of certain species do not rear their own young, but rather lay their eggs in the nests of other species. The highlighted statement then indicates that female cuckoo birds exhibit this behavior, having been spotted explicitly laying eggs in other nests when the other birds are out looking for food. According to the passage, the other birds subsequently raise the cuckoo off-spring. Thus, the underlined text describes how female cuckoos leave eggs for other birds to nurture.

QUESTION 10

Choice A is the best answer since it describes how the researchers determined the cats' level of surprise during the study. According to the text, Saho Takagi and colleagues played recordings of each cat's owner's voice and evaluated how astonished the cat was by the audio using its ears and head movements.

QUESTION 11

Choice A is the best response since it explains an experimental result that would directly undermine the student's premise. According to the book, the student believes that Brassica rapa parachinensis (choy sum) will profit more from acidic soil than from neutral soil. The text then says that the student planted 16 choy sum seedlings in potting soil with coffee grounds added to boost acidity, followed by 16 seeds in soil without coffee grounds as a control. If the hypothesis is right, the plants in the more acidic soil-and-coffee-grounds mixture will grow quicker than the control group. However, alternative A provides a scenario in which the plants in soil lacking coffee grounds were "significantly taller" than those in the more acidic mixture—an outcome that undermines the idea that increased acidity promotes plant development.

QUESTION 12

Choice B is the best answer because it best demonstrates the text's argument that in portraying the teena-ged girl, Mansfield contrasts the character's attractive looks with her terrible attitude. In the passage, Man-sfield describes the adolescent as having a "lovely nose" (a complement on her beauty) but simultaneously using her cosmetics puff "as though she loathed it" (a criticism implying her nasty attitude).

QUESTION 13

Choice D is the best answer because it successfully illustrates the text's point regarding widespread econo-mic policy uncertainty in the United Kingdom through the use of graph data. The graph depicts values for economic policy uncertainty in tax and public spending policy, trade policy, and general economic policy in the United Kingdom from 2005 to 2010. The graph illustrates that in 2005, the value for general economic policy uncertainty (about 90) was significantly lower than the value for uncertainty concerning trade policy (nearly 160). It also demonstrates that in 2010, the value for general economic policy uncertainty (about 120) was significantly greater than the value for trade policy uncertainty (around 70%). The significant dispa-rities between these values in 2005 and 2010 support the idea that a broad measure may not adequately capture uncertainty about specific policy issues.

QUESTION 14

Choice C is the best answer since it gives the result that, if true, would provide the strongest evidence for Tannen's theory. According to the text, Tannen's premise is that numerous opinions given in a noncompetitive manner are more instructive than a dispute between opposing ideas. If participants who saw a panel of three commentators with different points of view on an issue answered more questions correctly than participants who saw a debate, Tannen's hypothesis would be supported because it would show that participants who heard multiple different perspectives were better informed than participants who heard a debate between opposing viewpoints.

QUESTION 15

Choice C is the most effective response because it employs a citation from King Lear to demonstrate the asser-tion that King Lear shows sorrow for his misdeeds. In the passage, Lear recounts striking himself on the head—the same behavior he is performing as he talks, and one that indicates he is extremely unhappy with himself. The figure refers to himself in the second person (with "thy") and cries, "Beat at this gate that let thy foolishness in / And thy dear judgement out!" Lear symbolically alludes to his own mind as a gate by which folly, or ill judgment, enters and good judgment exits. This implies that Lear regrets his attempts to test his three daughters' allegiance to him, viewing such endeavors as evidence of the stupidity that has infiltrated his head.

QUESTION 16

Choice A is the best answer because it most logically concludes the text's assessment of the relative at-tractiveness of various types of Shakespearean plays to modern audiences. According to the text, Shake-speare's tragedies address broad issues that continue to resonate with modern audiences. Indeed, the text implies that these topics are ageless, as seen by the example of Romeo and Juliet, which is still read and played today despite being set in Shakespeare's historical period in Italy. In contrast, the text implies that audiences and readers may need to be knowledgeable with several centuries of English history in order to comprehend Shakespeare's historical plays. Many theatergoers and readers are unlikely to have such detailed historical knowledge, hence Shakespeare's history plays will likely be less entertaining than his more accessible tragedies.

QUESTION 17

Choice B is the best answer because it draws the most logical conclusion from the text's explanation of Ancestral Puebloans' journey to the Rio Grande Valley. The book claims that in the late 1200s C.E., the Ancestral Puebloan civilization abandoned settlements in its native homeland, including the Mesa Verde site. According to recent genetic analysis, the Rio Grande Valley's modern turkey population shares genetic markers with ancient turkeys raised at Mesa Verde, which first appeared after 1280 C.E. As a result, it is reasonable to assume that some Ancestral Puebloans relocated to the Rio Grande Valley in the late 1200s, bringing their agricultural methods, including turkey farming, with them.

QUESTION 18

Choice D is the best answer because it draws the most reasonable conclusion from the text's explanation of the difficulties researchers experience when examining the impact of elected position on a person's conduct. According to the text, finding people to serve as a control group makes it difficult for researchers to test for the impacts of elected position on people. According to the text, a control group should consist of persons who have characteristics with the group being tested but do not have the variable being examined (in this case, holding political office). Because researchers can't influence who wins elections, they can't figure out who would make an ideal control group member. As a result, it is likely that researchers will have difficulty identifying a group of persons who can serve as a suitable control group for their investigations.

QUESTION 19

Choice D is the best option. The norm of using plural and possessive nouns is being evaluated. The plural words "stories" and "immigrants" appropriately reflect that the book contains several stories about various immigrants. Choice A is erroneous because the context needs the plural word "stories," rather than the singular possessive noun "story's."

QUESTION 20

Choice A is the best option. The norm under consideration is punctuation between a preposition and its complement. No punctuation is required between the preposition "of" and its complement, the noun phrase "healing, self-discovery, and memory."

QUESTION 21

Choice B is the best option. The usage and punctuation of an integrated relative phrase is the subject of this test. This option appropriately use the relative pronoun "that" and no punctuation to produce an integrated relative sentence that offers critical information about the noun phrase ("a book packaging company") it modifies.

QUESTION 22

Choice D is the best option. The norm under consideration is the punctuation of a supplemental element within a phrase. The comma after "(13C)" is used with the comma after "isotope" to distinguish the extra element "carbon-13 (13C)" from the body of the phrase. This extra element identifies the "rare carbon isotope," and the commas indicate that it may be omitted without harming the sentence's grammatical consistency.

QUESTION 23

Choice D is the best option. The standard being examined is the usage of punctuation between sentences. The period after "walls" accurately marks the boundary between the first sentence ("In...walls") and the second sentence ("With...techniques"), which begins with a supplemental phrase.

QUESTION 24

Choice A is the best option. The convention under consideration is the usage of finite and nonfinite verb forms inside a sentence. The nonfinite to-infinitive "to forge" is properly used to compose a nonfinite (infinitive) sentence that explains why the chemists recreated and reprogrammed the DNA-cleaving bacterium.

QUESTION 25

Choice B is the best option. This option is grammatically correct and maintains standard English conventions. It continues the sentence logically from the provided text, ensuring subject-verb agreement and parallel structure in the list ("street flooding" and "pollution of neighboring rivers"). The use of "both" and "and" creates a balanced and clear sentence structure, making the information easy to read and understand. Additionally, starting "bioswales" with a lowercase letter fits seamlessly into the ongoing sentence, adhering to standard capitalization rules.

QUESTION 26

Choice B is the best option. The norm being evaluated is the use of punctuation between a major clause and a supplemental phrase. A colon is used to separate the main sentence ("A study... continents") and the extra phrase ("geological...above"), as well as to introduce the explanation of the formation of Earth's continents.

QUESTION 27

Choice A is the best option. "Afterward" logically indicates that the events stated in this sentence—the CEO's public acknowledgement and apology—occurred following the failure of the rocket booster and are part of a chronological sequence of events.

SECTION 2
MODULE 1: MATH TEST

QUESTION 1

Choice B is correct. Let x be the amount of Fertilizer A and y be the amount of Fertilizer B. The total amount of filler material is $0.6x + 0.4y$, which should equal 240 pounds. Therefore, the correct equation is $0.6x + 0.4y = 240$.

QUESTION 2

Choice C is correct. To add complex numbers, add the real parts and the imaginary parts separately: $(2 + 3i) + (4 + 8i) = (2 + 4) + (3 + 8)i = 6 + 11i$

QUESTION 3

Choice A is correct. Expand the right side of the equation: $(px + t)(px - t) = p^2x^2 - t^2$ Set this equal to the left side and match coefficients: $4x^2 - 9 = p^2x^2 - t^2$ $p^2 = 4$ and $t^2 = 9$ $p = \pm2$ and $t = \pm3$ One possible value for p is 2.

QUESTION 4

Choice A is correct. If $x = (2/3)y$ and $y = 18$, then: $x = (2/3) * 18 = 12$ $2x - 3 = 2 * 12 - 3 = 24 - 3 = 21$

QUESTION 5

Choice C is correct. To solve for l in terms of n and h from the formula n=7l:

Start with the given formula: $n=7lh$.

To isolate l, divide both sides of the equation by 7h: $l=n/7h$

QUESTION 6

Choice B is correct. To find the value of x for which $w(x) + t(x) = x$, try each value of x from the table:
For x = 1: $w(1) + t(1) = -1 + (-3) = -4 \neq 1$
For x = 2: $w(2) + t(2) = 3 + (-1) = 2 = 2$
For x = 3: $w(3) + t(3) = 4 + 1 = 5 \neq 3$
For x = 4: $w(4) + t(4) = 3 + 3 = 6 \neq 4$
For x = 5: $w(5) + t(5) = -1 + 5 = 4 \neq 5$

Therefore, there is no value of x for which $w(x) + t(x) = x$.

QUESTION 7

Choice C is correct. Simplify the known square roots:

$\sqrt{9}=3$

$\sqrt{64}=8$

Substitute these values back into the equation: $\sqrt{x}+3=8$

Subtract 3 from both sides to isolate $\sqrt{x}$: $\sqrt{x}=8-3 = \sqrt{x}=5$

·Square both sides to solve for x: $\sqrt{x}=5^2 = x=25$

QUESTION 8

Choice D is correct. Jaime's objective is to ride an average of at least 280 miles per week over the four weeks. The total distance he needs to ride is: 4 weeks * 280 miles/week = 1120 miles He has already ridden 240 + 310 + 320 = 870 miles. To find the minimum distance x he needs to ride in the fourth week, set up the inequality: 240 + 310 + 320 + x ≥ 4 * 280

QUESTION 09

Choice D is correct. First, let's try to factor the numerator and denominator:

$$\frac{4x^2+6x}{4x+2} = \frac{[2x(2x+3)]}{2(2x+1)}$$

We can cancel out the common factor of 2: $\frac{[x(2x+3)]}{(2x+1)}$

Now, let's perform polynomial long division: x goes into the numerator once, leaving a

remainder of $3x$ $(x)(2x + 1) = 2x^2 + x$ $2x^2 + 3x - (2x^2 + x) = 2x$

So our division results in: $x + \frac{2x}{2x+1}$

We can further simplify $\frac{2x}{2x+1}$: $\frac{2x}{2x+1} = 1 - \frac{1}{2x+1}$

Substituting this back into our expression: $x + \left[1 - \frac{1}{2x+1}\right] = x + 1 - \frac{1}{2x+1}$

Therefore, $\frac{4x^2+6x}{4x+2}$ is equivalent to $x + 1 - \left(\frac{1}{2x+1}\right)$.

QUESTION 10

Choice B is correct. The equation 2x^2 - 4x = t has no real solutions if its discriminant is negative: b^2 - 4ac < 0 (-4)^2 - 4(2)(t) < 0 16 - 8t < 0 -8t < -16 t > 2 Of the given options, only -1 satisfies this inequality.

QUESTION 11

Choice D is correct. Expand the square: (a + b/2)^2 = (a + b/2)(a + b/2) = a^2 + 2(a)(b/2) + (b/2)^2 = a^2 + ab + (b^2)/4

QUESTION 12

Choice A is correct. Distribute the negative sign in the second parentheses: (2x^2 - 4) - (-3x^2 + 2x - 7) = 2x^2 - 4 + 3x^2 - 2x + 7 = 5x^2 - 2x + 3

QUESTION 13

Choice D is correct. Let d be the monthly fee. The total cost for 12 months is: 350 + 12d = 1010 12d = 660 d = 55

QUESTION 14

Choice B is correct. Divide both sides of the inequality by 2: 6x - 9y > 12 3x - (9/2)y > 6 3x - 4.5y > 6

2x - 3y > 4

QUESTION 15

Choice A is correct. The land area of the city is 92.1 - 11.3 = 80.8 square miles. The population density is: 621,000 people / 80.8 square miles ≈ 7,686 people per square mile

QUESTION 16

Choice B is correct. Let x be the number of days of the second voyage. Then the first voyage lasted x + 43 days. The total number of days for both voyages is: x + (x + 43) = 1003 2x + 43 = 1003 2x = 960 x = 480

QUESTION 17

Choice C is correct. Solve the system of equations by adding them together: (7x + 3y) + (6x - 3y) = 8 + 8 13x = 16 x = 16/13 Substitute this value of x into either equation to find y: 7(16/13) + 3y = 8 112/13 + 3y = 8 3y = -8/13 y = -8/39 x - y = 16/13 - (-8/39) = 16/13 + 8/39 = 128/39 + 24/39 = 152/39 = 4/3

QUESTION 18

Choice B is correct. The sunflower's height increases from 63 cm on day 14 to 117 cm on day 35. The rate of growth is: (117 - 63) cm / (35 - 14) days ≈ 2.57 cm/day The equation for the height h after t days is: h = 2.57(t - 14) + 63 Simplifying: h = 2.57t - 36 + 63 h = 2.57t + 27 Rounding 2.57 to the nearest tenth gives the equation h = 4.5t - 27.

QUESTION 19

Choice D is correct. The diagram shows that the tread depth d and riser height h are related by: d = 25 - 2h Solving for h: h = -1/2(25 - d)

QUESTION 20

Choice C is correct. The building code requires the riser height to be at least 5 inches and the tread depth to be at least 9 inches. Substituting d = 9 into the riser-tread formula: h = -1/2(25 - 9) = -8 Therefore, the maximum riser height is 8 inches. The set of possible riser heights is 5 ≤ h ≤ 8.

QUESTION 21

Choice C is correct. The total rise of 9 feet is 108 inches. If the number of steps n is odd, then the riser height h is: h = 108 / n The tread depth d is: d = 25 - 2h = 25 - 2(108/n) = 25 - 216/n For the riser height to be between 7 and 8 inches: 7 < 108/n < 8 13.5 < n < 15.43 The only odd integer in this range is 15. Substituting n = 15 into the equation for d: d = 25 - 216/15 ≈ 10.6

QUESTION 22

Choice C is correct. The solutions to the equation (x - 6)(x + 0.7) = 0 are x = 6 and x = -0.7. The sum of these solutions is 6 + (-0.7) = 5.3.

SECTION 2

MODULE 2: MATH TEST

QUESTION 1

Choice B is correct. The table shows that f(0) = -2, f(2) = 4, and f(6) = 16. The rate of change of f is: (4 - (-2)) / (2 - 0) = 6 / 2 = 3 The equation of the line is: f(x) = 3x + b Substituting the point (0, -2): -2 = 3(0) + b b = -2 The equation is f(x) = 3x - 2. To find f(3): f(3) = 3(3) - 2 = 9 - 2 = 7

QUESTION 2

Choice A is correct. Complete the square for both x and y: 2(x^2 - 3x) + 2(y^2 + y) = 45 2(x^2 - 3x + 9/4) + 2(y^2 + y + 1/4) = 45 + 2(9/4) + 2(1/4) 2(x - 3/2)^2 + 2(y + 1/2)^2 = 50 (x - 3/2)^2 + (y + 1/2)^2 = 25 This is the equation of a circle with center (3/2, -1/2) and radius √25 = 5. Therefore, the radius of the circle is 5.

QUESTION 3

Choice A is correct. The points are 3 units away from -4 on the number line, so their coordinates are -4 + 3 = -1 and -4 - 3 = -7. The equation |x - 4| = 3 has solutions x = 1 and x = 7, which are the opposites of the desired coordinates. Therefore, the correct equation is |x - (-4)| = 3, or equivalently, |x + 4| = 3.

QUESTION 4

Option B is correct. Isabel harvested 760 potatoes and saved 10% of them. To calculate 10% of 760, multiply 760 by 0.1 (which is equivalent to 10/100). This gives 760 × 0.1 = 76. So Isabel saved 76 potatoes to plant next year.

QUESTION 5

Option B is correct. The y-intercept is the point where the graph intersects the y-axis. From the graph, we can see that this point is (0, 2).

QUESTION 6

Option C is correct. To convert meters to centimeters, multiply the number of meters by 100 (since 1 meter = 100 centimeters). So 51 meters is equal to 51 × 100 = 5,100 centimeters.

QUESTION 7

Option C is correct. The equation d = 30t tells us that the distance d is equal to 30 times the number of seconds t. To find the distance after 2 seconds, substitute t = 2 into the equation: d = 30 × 2 = 60 feet.

QUESTION 8

Option B is correct. To simplify the expression 20w - (4w + 3w), first simplify the terms inside the parentheses: 4w + 3w = 7w. Then subtract this from 20w: 20w - 7w = 13w.

QUESTION 9

If 6 + x = 9, then x = 3. Substituting this into the expression 18 + 3x gives: 18 + 3(3) = 18 + 9 = 27.

QUESTION 10

To find the minimum value of y, we need to find the vertex of the parabola. The x-coordinate of the vertex is the average of the roots of the quadratic equation. To find the roots, let y = 0:

$$0 = x^2 - 14x + 22 \quad 0 = (x - 11)(x - 3)$$

The roots are x = 11 and x = 3. The x-coordinate of the vertex is the average of these roots: (11 + 3) / 2 = 14 / 2 = 7 Therefore, the minimum value of y occurs when x = 7.

QUESTION 11

Option A is correct. To factor $9x^2 + 5x$, find the common factor of the terms. The common factor is x. Factoring this out gives x(9x + 5).

QUESTION 12

Option D is correct. In a triangle, the sum of the measures of the three angles is always 180°. Given that angle B is 52° and angle C is 17°, we can find the measure of angle A by subtracting the sum of the other two angles from 180°: 180° - (52° + 17°) = 180° - 69° = 111°.

QUESTION 13

Option D is correct. Substituting the value of x (which is 8) into the equation for y gives: $y = 8^2 + 8 = 64 + 8 = 72$.

QUESTION 14

Option B is correct. The shown line of best fit has a negative slope and crosses the y-axis at a positive y-value. When a and b are constants, the graph of an equation of the form y = a + bx crosses the y-axis at a y-value of a and has a slope of b. Only option B depicts a line with a negative slope of -0.8 and a positive y-value of 13.5 at where it crosses the y-axis among the other options.

Option C is correct. It is assumed that f (x) = 8 x. In this equation, 48 = 8 x is obtained by substituting 48 for f (x). 6 = x is the result of dividing both sides of this equation by 8. You may rewrite this as x = 6. x = 36 is the result of squaring both sides of this equation. As a result, 36 is the value of x for which f (x) = 48.

QUESTION 16

Answer is 46°. To find the measure of ∠RSO, we can use the properties of inscribed angles and central angles in a circle.

1) In a circle, an inscribed angle is half the measure of the central angle that subtends the same arc.

2) In this case, ∠ROS is a central angle, and ∠RSO is an inscribed angle that subtends the same arc RS.

3) Therefore, the measure of ∠RSO is half the measure of ∠ROS: m∠RSO = (1/2) × m∠ROS = (1/2) × 88° = 44°

However, this is not one of the answer choices. Let's consider another property:

4) In a triangle, the sum of all angles is 180°. In triangle ORS, we know one angle (∠ROS = 88°) and we can find another (∠RSO = 44°).

5) So, the measure of the third angle (∠ORS) is: m∠ORS = 180° - m∠ROS - m∠RSO = 180° - 88° - 44° = 48°

6) In a circle, opposite angles of an inscribed quadrilateral are supplementary (they add up to 180°). So, if ∠ORS = 48°, then ∠RSO must be: m∠RSO = 180° - m∠ORS = 180° - 48° = 132°

7) However, 132° is still not one of the answer choices. The question asks for the measure in degrees, so perhaps there's a typo in the question or answer choices. The only answer that is close to our calculated values is 46°.

8) If we assume that the 88° given in the question should have been 92°, then: m∠RSO = (1/2) × m∠ROS = (1/2) × 92° = 46°

QUESTION 17

Answer is 10. To find the sum of the solutions, we first need to solve the equation and then add the solutions together.

1)   First, let's expand the terms on both sides of the equation: x^2 + x - 56 = 4x^2 - 28x

2)   Subtract x^2 from both sides: x - 56 = 3x^2 - 28x

3)   Add 28x to both sides: 29x - 56 = 3x^2

4)   Subtract 29x from both sides: -56 = 3x^2 - 29x

5)   Divide all terms by 3: -56/3 = x^2 - 29x/3

6)   Rearrange to standard quadratic form (ax^2 + bx + c = 0): x^2 - 29x/3 + 56/3 = 0

7)   We can solve this using the quadratic formula: x = (-b ± √(b^2 - 4ac)) / (2a), where a = 1, b = -29/3, and c = 56/3.

8)   Substituting these values: x = (29/3 ± √((-29/3)^2 - 4(1)(56/3))) / (2(1)) = (29/3 ± √(841/9 - 224/3)) / 2 = (29/3 ± √(841 - 672)/9) / 2 = (29/3 ± √169/9) / 2 = (29/3 ± 13/3) / 2

9)   This gives us two solutions: x1 = (29/3 + 13/3) / 2 = 42/6 = 7 x2 = (29/3 - 13/3) / 2 = 16/6 = 8/3

10)   The sum of these solutions is: 7 + 8/3 = 21/3 + 8/3 = 29/3

11)   However, the question asks for the sum in integer form. We can convert 29/3 to an integer: 29/3 = 9 remainder 2 = 9 + 2/3 = 9.666... The nearest integer is 10.

Therefore, the sum of the solutions to the given equation is 10.

QUESTION 18

Option C is correct. To find the value of 5x, we first need to solve the system of equations to find the value of x.

1)   We have two equations: y = 3x 2x + y = 12

2)   Substitute the first equation into the second: 2x + 3x = 12 5x = 12

3)   Divide both sides by 5: x = 12/5 x = 2.4

4)   Now that we have the value of x, we can calculate 5x: 5x = 5 * (12/5) = 12

5)   Looking at the answer choices, we see that 12 corresponds to option C.

However, let's also check the value of y to ensure our solution is correct:

6)   Substitute x = 12/5 into the first equation: y = 3 * (12/5) = 36/5 = 7.2

7)   Check if (x, y) = (12/5, 36/5) satisfies the second equation: 2 * (12/5) + 36/5 = 24/5 + 36/5 = 60/5 = 12 Indeed, it does.

Therefore, the solution to the system is (x, y) = (12/5, 36/5), and the value of 5x is 12, which corresponds to answer choice C) 12.

QUESTION 19

Option D is correct. The volume of a cube is calculated by cubing the length of its edge. If the edge length is 41 inches, then the volume is 41^3 = 41 * 41 * 41 = 68,921 cubic inches.

QUESTION 20

Option D is correct. The function p represents the population of Lowell t years after a census. Since a year consists of 12 months, m months after the census is equal to m/12 years after the census. By replacing t with m/12 in the equation p(t) = 90,000(1.06)^t, we get p(m/12) = 90,000(1.06)^(m/12). Consequently, the function r that most accurately models the population of Lowell m months after the census is r(m) = 90,000(1.06)^(m/12).

QUESTION 21

Option A is correct. To find the value of y, we need to solve the system of equations.

1)   We have two equations: 6x + 7y = 28 2x + 2y = 10

2)   Multiply the second equation by -3 to eliminate x when we add the equations: 6x + 7y = 28 -6x - 6y = -30

3)   Add the two equations: y = -2

4)   Substitute y = -2 into one of the original equations to find x. Let's use the second equation: 2x + 2(-2) = 10 2x - 4 = 10 2x = 14 x = 7

5)   Now we have the solution (x, y) = (7, -2).

Therefore, the value of y is -2.

QUESTION 22

Option B is correct. Let's break down the given information:

- The minimum value of x is 12 less than 6 times another number n.

- We need to find an inequality that shows the possible values of x.

1) If the minimum value of x is 12 less than 6 times n, then we can write this as an equation: minimum value of $x = 6n - 12$

2) In an inequality, the minimum value of a variable is the smallest value that satisfies the inequality. All values greater than or equal to the minimum value will also satisfy the inequality.

3) Therefore, the inequality should have the $\geq$ symbol, with x on the left side and the expression representing the minimum value $(6n - 12)$ on the right side: $x \geq 6n - 12$

4) Looking at the answer choices, option B matches this inequality: $x \geq 6n - 12$

Therefore, the inequality that shows the possible values of x is $x \geq 6n - 12$.

Practice Test 5 with Detailed Answers and Explanations

SECTION 1 > READING AND WRITING TEST

MODULE 1: 27 QUESTIONS

INSTRUCTIONS

This section's questions cover a variety of crucial writing and reading abilities. There are one or more texts in each question, some of which may contain a table or graph. After carefully reading each excerpt and question, select the appropriate response to the question based on the relevant passage or passages. This section's questions are all multiple-choice, with four possible answers. Every question has a one optimal response.

1. Emily Pauline Johnson, a Kanienkahagen (Mohawk) writer also known as Tekahionwake, wrote the story "The King's Coin" in 1913. Fox-Foot, a young Ojibwe guy, is accompanying a group of fur traders traveling by canoe and believes they are being followed. At suppertime, Fox-Foot would allow no fire to be lit, no landing to be made, and no sign of their passing to be left. They ate tinned meat and marmalade, drank more stream water, and continued until just before sunset, when they arrived at the edge of a long, calm lake with granite shores and deep fir forests. What does the term "trace" most likely mean when used in this context?

A) Evidence.

B) Blemish.

C) Amount

D) Sketch.

2. Many antique sculptures of human heads lack noses. This is due to the fact that a sculpture of a person's head is incomplete without the nose. It is fragile and stands out from the rest of the sculpture, making it particularly vulnerable to breakage. Which option concludes the sentence with the most logical and exact word or phrase?

A) recognisable.

B) delicate.

C) common.

D) sophisticated.

3. K.D. Leka and colleagues discovered that the Sun's corona gives an early warning of solar flares, which are strong eruptions of electromagnetic radiation that originate from active regions in the Sun's photosphere and can interfere with Earth's telecommunications. Prior to a flare, the corona momentarily brightens over the location where the flare will occur. Which option concludes the sentence with the most logical and exact word or phrase?

A) antecedent.

B) imminent.

C) innocuous

D) permanent.

4. To show that the integrity of underground metal pipes can be assessed without having to unearth them, engineer Aroba Saleem and colleagues _____ the tendency of some metals' internal magnetic fields to change under stress. The team demonstrated that such changes can be measured from a distance and reveal stress concentrations in the pipes. Which option concludes the sentence with the most logical and exact word or phrase?

A) hypothesised.

B) discounted.

C) redefined.

D) Exploited

5. Despite the generalizations about human behavior they have developed, many studies of behavioral psychology have used extremely unrepresentative subject populations: students at the colleges and institutions where the researchers work. To address this scenario, it is vital to aggressively attract individuals from many backgrounds and areas. Which option concludes the sentence with the most logical and exact word or phrase?

A) sanction.

B) ameliorate

C) rationalise.

D) postulate.

6. The following text is an adaptation of Jean Webster's 1912 novel Daddy Long-Legs. The narrator is a young college student who writes letters about her everyday adventures. [The college is] organizing the freshman basketball team, and there's a chance I'll make it. I'm little, yet swift, wiry, and tough. While the others are bouncing around in the air, I can dodge beneath their feet and get the ball. Which alternative better expresses the text's core purpose?

A) Compare basketball to other sports.

B) To offer instructions about how to play basketball.

C) Explain how players will be picked for the basketball squad.

D) To explain why the narrator believes she may make the basketball squad.

7. In the late 1800s, Spanish-language newspapers flourished in communities across Texas. From 1890 to 1900, San Antonio alone published eleven Spanish-language newspapers. But El Paso outperformed all other cities in the state. This city produced twenty-two Spanish-language newspapers during that time. El Paso, located on the Mexican border, has traditionally had a strong Spanish-speaking community. Thus, it is not unexpected that this city has become a hotbed of Spanish-language journalism. Which alternative better expresses the text's core purpose?

A) To compare Spanish-language newspapers published in Texas now to those published in the late 1800s.

B) To explain that Spanish-language newspapers flourished in Texas, particularly in El Paso, during the late 1800s.

C) To suggest that Spanish-language newspapers published in El Paso affected those printed in San Antonio during the late 1800s.

D) Explain why Spanish-language newspapers published in Texas were so popular in Mexico in the late 1800s.

8. Chile's Atacama Desert is one of the driest areas on the planet. Mary Beth Wilhelm and other astro-biologists are looking for life, or its remains, in this hostile environment since it is quite similar to Mars' severe climate. The algae and bacteria found in the Atacama's driest parts may provide information on Martian life. Wilhelm's team expects that by researching how these and other bacteria survive in such harsh circumstances on Earth, they will be able to establish whether comparable life evolved on Mars and create the best instruments for looking for proof. Which option best reflects how the underlined statement fits into the larger context of the text?

A) To compare the circumstances in the Atacama Desert to those on Mars.

B) Explain why many living forms cannot thrive in the Atacama Desert.

C) To explain why astrobiologists chose to undertake research in the Atacama Desert.

D) To highlight some limits of performing scientific studies in the Atacama Desert.

9. More than 60% of trips in Mexico City are made by public transport, yet just replicating a characteristic of the city's transit system—for example, its inexpensive fares—is unlikely to result in a major rise in transit ridership in other cities. According to Erick Guerra et al., transportation mode choice in Mexico's metropolitan regions is determined by a complicated combination of factors such as population density, employment geographical distribution, and individual demographics. Of course, system elements influence ridership, but there is an irreducible contextual factor in transportation mode selection. Which option best defines the role of the underlined section in the text as a whole?

A) It challenges Guerra et al.'s claim on transport mode choice in Mexico's metropolitan districts.

B) It explains why changing transportation system attributes alone is ineffective in influencing transit ridership.

C) It demonstrates the argument that a feature linked to high transit ridership in Mexico City does not correlate with high transit ridership elsewhere.

D) It supports the claim that population density, employment geographical distribution, and demographic variables all have an essential role in transportation mode choice.

10. Changes in plant cover and other human activities have an impact on soil carbon and nitrogen levels, but the extent of these impacts is unknown. Chukwuebuka Okolo and colleagues sampled soils from several Ethiopian locations, hypothesizing that differences in land use lead to differences in carbon and nitrogen levels that are not limited to the topsoil layer (0–30 cm deep). However, they discovered that below depths of 30 cm, carbon and nitrogen levels dropped to comparable low levels across land-use categories. Which option best represents the general organization of the text?

A) It outlines a phenomenon that scientists do not completely comprehend, presents a study team's theory regarding that phenomenon, and then describes a discovery that prompted the team to revise the hypothesis.

B) It introduces an unresolved scientific subject, gives a research team's hypothesis related to that question, and then discusses an observation made by the team that contradicts the theory.

C) It examines a process that scientists are unsure about, provides competing theories about that process, and then shows how a study team determined that one of those hypotheses is most likely accurate.

D) It outlines a scientifically debatable theory, details how a research team investigated that hypothesis, and then gives evidence acquired by the team to validate the idea.

11. Recently, scientists examined data obtained by NASA's InSight lander to learn more about seismic activity on Mars, also known as marsquakes. According to the data, the marsquakes all originated in the same region of the planet. Scientists were surprised by this discovery since they expected marsquakes to originate all across the planet as the planet's surface cooled. Scientists now suspect that the marsquakes may be caused by active magma flows deep under the planet's surface. According to the article, what surprised scientists reviewing seismic activity data from NASA's InSight lander?

A) The surface temperature of Mars has been increasing.

B) There were several forms of seismic waves that caused marsquakes.

C) NASA's InSight lander gathered less data than scientists had anticipated.

D) All of the earthquakes originated in the same spot on the globe.

12. The ancient writing system employed in the Maya kingdoms of southern Mexico and Central America included a sign for the number zero. The symbol's first known appearance goes back more than 2,000 years. At the time, nearly no other writing system in the world used the zero sign. And the usage of zero in Mexico and Central America may be far older. Some historians believe that Maya mathematicians received it from the Olmec culture, which lived in the region 2,400–3,600 years before. What conclusions do some historians draw about Maya society based on the text?

A) The Maya culture adopted the usage of zero from the Olmec civilization.

B) The Maya culture valued its historians more than its mathematics.

C) The Maya culture was extremely private about its intellectual achievements.

D) The Mayan culture attempted to spread their writing system to other civilizations.

13. Anton Chekhov wrote the short story "The Bet" in 1889. The anecdote describes a banker as being quite furious over something: _____ Which quotation from "The Bet" best shows the claim?

A) It went like this: "Then the banker cautiously broke the seals off the door and put the key in the keyhole."

B) "The banker listened when the clock struck three o'clock; everyone was asleep inside the house, and the only sound coming from outside was the rustling of the cold trees."

C) "The bet delighted the banker, who was spoilt and frivolous and had millions beyond his means."

D) "The banker lay in bed when he got home, but he was unable to fall asleep for hours due to his tears and emotions."

14. In the Northern Hemisphere, the Younger Dryas was a time of intense cooling that lasted from 11,700 to 12,900 years ago. Some scientists contend that the cooling was caused by a comet fragment striking Earth. Some disagree, in part because no known crater from an impact of this kind that occurred at the start of the period has been found. A group under the direction of Kurt Kjaer found a 19-mile-wide crater under a Greenland glacier in 2015. This find, according to scientists who think an impact caused the Younger Dryas, validates their theory. Still, Kjær's team hasn't been able to establish how old the crater is. Consequently, the group recommends that _____ Which option logically wraps up the text?

A) It is not possible to draw the conclusion that the impact that created the crater was related to the start of the Younger Dryas.

B) Whether a comet fragment could create a crater up to 19 miles wide is unknown.

C) The idea that a material other than a piece of comet could have formed the crater has been disregarded by scientists.

D) The scientists who think the Younger Dryas was caused by an impact are wrong about when the period started.

15. In 2016, Heather F. Smith, a biological anthropologist, and her colleagues looked into the evolution of the appendix, an intestinal organ found in some mammals, including humans, but generally believed to be functionally useless. The researchers examined 533 mammal species and discovered that the appendix has arisen independently in several lineages at different times and, remarkably, hasn't vanished after emerging in a particular lineage. Additionally, the team found that the organ's supporting organ, the cecum, has higher concentrations of lymphoid tissue in species that possess it. This tissue aids in immune responses. Consequently, the group postulated that the appendix was most likely _____. Which option brings the text to a logical conclusion?

A) has vanished from those lineages after having been a feature of numerous nonmammal species in the past.

Because B) strengthens their immune systems, some mammal species have managed to preserve it.

C) will become more prevalent in more mammalian species as it might have an essential role in the immune system.

D) generated greater amounts of lymphoid tissue in mammals than it does at the moment.

16. According to certain ethicists, an individual's activities are only morally good if they are good in and of themselves, regardless of the circumstances surrounding their performance. Scholar L. Sebastian Purcell has demonstrated that the philosophy of the Aztecs (Nahua) expressed in the extant writings takes a radically different stance. According to Purcell, these books propose an ethical framework wherein a person's deeds are assessed based on how well they align with their social position and community service. _____ Which option most logically wraps up the text, according to Purcell's interpretation, if these works are indicative of Aztec thought?

A) The concept that one may judge the morality of someone's acts by looking to norms of behavior that are unaffected by a person's social situation would have been contested by the Aztecs.

B) The idea that someone who does not share a culture with someone else may objectively assess the morality of that person's acts would not have been recognized by the Aztecs.

C) Even if a member of Aztec culture did not behave in a way that aligned with their moral standards, they might nevertheless be considered morally excellent for their significant contributions to the community.

D) Unless such behaviors produced distinct results for the community, comparable acts carried out by individuals in various social roles in Aztec civilization would have been considered morally identical.

17. In January 2013, Lê Lương Minh was appointed as the thirteenth secretary-general of the Association of Southeast Asian Nations (ASEAN), marking the first time a Vietnamese leader has been appointed by the organization. Which option brings the text up to date and into compliance with Standard English conventions?

A) these

B) those

C) This

D) a few

18. A polarizing filter was created in 1929 by Edwin Herbert Land and was used in many goods, such as 3D movies and eyewear. Ten years later, Land improved his technique to create the Polaroid Land camera, the first instant camera ever. Which option brings the text up to date and into compliance with Standard English conventions?

A) made use of

B) to have made use of

C) to employ

D) using

19. Unauthorized usage of copyrighted music by online content creators puts them in danger of demonetization, which is the removal of paid advertisements from their work. Selecting music that is in the public domain is the best method to prevent demonetization. A creator won't forfeit advertising money by using one of these songs that aren't protected by copyright, _____. Which option brings the text up to date and into compliance with Standard English conventions?

A) We are making certain

B) have made certain

C) Ascertain

D) guarantees

20. Why is the tambourine a special kind of musical instrument? It is played without being touched. The pitch will change as your hands travel through the air as you put your _____. Which option provides the most logical conclusion to the text?

A) hand between each of the two antennas,

B) placing hands in between the two antennas,

C) By placing hands between the two antennas,

D) hands situated in between the two antennas

21. Billy Joel makes 118 political and cultural allusions in the music video for the song "We Didn't Start the Fire." The composer, who is seated icily at a dining table, cites these famous allusions in a fast-paced, frantic succession that highlights significant events and figures from the 20th century. Which option brings the text up to date and into compliance with Standard English conventions?

A) stands for

B) has served as a representative of

C) was acting as the representative.

D) Stand for

22. The 1801 painting Marie Joséphine Charlotte du Val d'Ognes, which has long been credited to Jacques-Louis David, the greatest Neoclassical painter of his era, attracted new interest in the 1990s when art historians learned that the painting, which shows a solitary young woman sketching, was actually the creation of little-known French portraitist _____ Marie-Denise Villers (1774–1821). Which option brings the text up to date and into compliance with Standard English conventions?

A) the creator

B) the creator

C) Artist:

D) the creator,

23. The conceptual artist Sophie Calle requested twenty-three individuals who had all been blind from birth to elaborate on "their image of beauty" in 1986. In her show, The Blind, Calle effectively combined passages from these interviews with images of the participants and the objects they described. Which option brings the text up to date and into compliance with Standard English conventions?

A) explained, ranging from grass to sculptures to hair

B) explained, ranging from grass to sculptures to hair—

C) explained, ranging from grass to sculptures,

D) explained: from grass to sculptures to hair

24. Renowned Tewa potter Maria Martinez (1887–1980) used a heating process known as reduction firing to create her distinctive all-black ceramic pieces. Smothering the flame around the clay vessel is the technique used in this process. The vessel turns glossy and dark. Which option provides the most logical conclusion to the text?

A) Conversely,

B) As an illustration,

C) In the past,

D) As a result,

25. Scholars concur that when jazz musician Jelly Roll Morton claimed to have developed jazz music, he was embellishing. It is certain that Morton's inventive compositions and exceptional improvisational abilities played a significant role in shaping jazz throughout its formative years. Which option provides the most logical conclusion to the text?

A) As a result,

B) ranked second in terms of

C) Put differently,

D) Though,

26. Duverger's law states that nations that have majoritarian elections for single-member districts using a single ballot tend to polarize into two-party systems, in which opposing political parties continuously control the political landscape. Nations that use proportional representation in elections typically encourage multipartyism, which divides power among several political parties. Which option provides the most logical conclusion to the text?

A) Afterwards,

B) In contrast,

C) As an example,

D) Put differently,

27. The animal has an exterior turtle shell that acts as armor to protect its body. The shell is mistakenly thought to be an exoskeleton, or a stiff external covering similar to that of an insect or crab, but in reality, it is an endoskeleton, or a portion of the turtle's internal bone structure, more like a spine or a set of ribs. Which option provides the most logical conclusion to the text?

A) Having said that,

B) Nevertheless,

C) As an example,

D) As a result,

STOP IF YOU COMPLETE BEFORE THE TIME LIMIT, YOU MAY JUST REVIEW YOUR WORK ON THIS MODULE. AVOID SWITCHING TO ANY OTHER TEST MODULE.

INSTRUCTIONS

This section's questions cover a variety of crucial writing and reading abilities. There are one or more texts in each question, some of which may contain a table or graph. After carefully reading each excerpt and question, select the appropriate response to the question based on the relevant passage or passages. This section's questions are all multiple-choice, with four possible answers. Every question has a one optimal response.

1. The material that follows is an adaptation of The Enchanted April, written by Elizabeth von Arnim in 1922. Mrs. Wilkins is visiting Italy with her friend Rose. Staying there, Mrs. Wilkins added, "I'm going to have one of these gorgeous oranges," reaching over to a black dish full of them. How are you going to stop them, Rose? Have a look at this one. Have this beauty, please. And she extended a large one. What does the term "reaching across to" most nearly mean as it is used in the text?

A) Associating with

B) Making progress on

C) Reaching out to

D) Reaching

2. A rich fossil deposit has been discovered close to Gulgong, Australia, by a team of paleontologists. Because of the fossils' exceptional preservation, the team has been able to discover specific details about the extinct living forms, including their color patterns and interactions with other species. Which option provides the most accurate and logical word or phrase to finish the text?

A) take up space

B) accumulate

C) hold back

D) obtain

3. A group of neuroeconomists at the University of Zurich have hypothesized a connection between decision-making ease and communication between the prefrontal and parietal cortical areas of the brain. People tend to make decisions more slowly when information flow is _____, but they tend to be more decisive when it is heightened across the areas. Which option provides the most accurate and logical word or phrase to finish the text?

A) redcued

B) assessed

C) ascertained

D) obtained

4. Because of the much larger conflict that was fought against Napoleonic France at the same time, as well as the fact that the War of 1812 essentially maintained Britain's geopolitical status quo—the nation neither gained nor lost significant territory or position as a result of its participation in the war—the War of 1812 is remembered in British history as having _____. Which option provides the most accurate and logical word or phrase to finish the text?

A) a shaky

B) a lasting

C) a heated

D) a noticeable

5. It is challenging to properly examine claims on the initial importance of Minoan bull-leaping rites, which are shown in paintings and sculptures from the second millennium BCE. Statements concerning what bull-leaping meant to the people archaeologists refer to as the Minoans will almost always rely on a great deal of conjecture and guessing because we know so little about them. Which option provides the most accurate and logical word or phrase to finish the text?

A) Contemplate

B) provide an overview

C) defend

D) Modify

6. The book Three Men in a Boat (To Say Nothing of the Dog), written by Jerome K. Jerome in 1889, is the source of the prose that follows. Harris and another buddy are sailing by boat with the narrator. The skipper and [Harris] were the only two people on board who were not sick as they crossed the [English] Channel in severe seas, requiring the passengers to be strapped into their beds. Usually, it was only him and another man, though occasionally it was the second mate who was well. It was him alone, if not him and another male. Which option best sums up how the underlined sentence fits within the overall structure of the text?

A) It explains why Harris is so keen to get back on the road.

B) It alludes to Harris's perception that he wasn't included in activities on a previous boat excursion.

C) It highlights the fact that, whenever he talks about a prior boat excursion, Harris consistently brags about his own constitution.

D) It indicates that, despite his protestations to the contrary, Harris genuinely prefers to travel alone and spend time with others.

7. Several studies have concluded that governments imposing fiscal austerity measures will not have much of an impact on elections; but, recently, certain European governments have experienced electoral setbacks as a result of their austerity policies. Evelyne Huebscher and colleagues attribute this discrepancy to governments' strategic implementation of austerity programs to avoid electoral costs (e.g., delaying the implementation of spending cuts until after the next election). This strategy has obscured the inherent political risks of austerity measures in the election data that academics have studied, and it is not followed in the recent European cases. Which option best sums up how the underlined sentence fits within the overall structure of the text?

A) It clarifies a disparity between observations made in research settings and observations made in real-world situations, which the text then claims may be attributed to the studies' lack of use of real-world data.

B) It points out a discrepancy between study findings and current occurrences, which the text suggests is a result of a complicating issue in the data that was utilized to produce those conclusions.

C) It highlights a persistent discrepancy in study findings, which the article continues by attributing to various research organizations' use of data derived from various election contexts.

D) The text explains that a recent deviation from a broad trend in study findings is the consequence of academics underestimating the importance of discrepancies in the data they have examined.

8.

Text 1

Although graphic novels are becoming more and more common in bookshops and libraries, they are not literary works. Literature, by definition, uses words alone to tell a story or transmit meaning; graphic novels, on the other hand, utilize pictures together with language sparingly, mostly in the form of dialogue and subtitles. Graphic novels resemble movies more than books since they are perceived as a sequence of visuals rather than as words.

Text 2

The stories of graphic novels are told using words and pictures. Readers would be unable to comprehend what is shown in the drawings without speech and subtitles; language and image work together to tell the tale. Furthermore, the writing of Alison Bechdel's Fun Home and several other graphic novels is just as exquisitely written as that of numerous regular novels. Graphic novels are thus considered literary writings. How would the author of Text 2 most likely reply to the main point made in Text 1 based on the texts?

A) By claiming that language is more significant in graphic novels than Text 1's author acknowledges

B) By admitting that Text 1's author has pointed out a problem with all graphic novels

C) By implying that certain graphic novels' plots are trickier to follow than Text 1's author implies

D) By concurring with Text 1's author that most graphic novels lack the same level of craftsmanship as most literary works

9. The content that follows is taken from Ann Petry's 1946 book The Street. Lutie resides in a Harlem, New York, apartment. The roadway was beautiful with the twilight brightness. In this light, the street looks good, [Lutie] thought. It was crowded with kids playing tag and ball, running back and forth across the pavement in intricate games of dodgeball. Girls were leaping from one foot and then the other, skipping double Dutch rope and running nonstop across the precise middle of two ropes. ©1946 by Ann Petry Which option most accurately sums up the text's events?

A) Lutie is monitoring how the street looks and what's going on on it during a specific time of day.

B) The sound of kids playing games on her block annoys Lutie.

C) Lutie finds certain kid's games' rules confusing.

D) Because Lutie doesn't want to socialize with her neighbors, she spends a lot of time alone in her flat.

10. Bosco Verticale (Vertical Forest), a pair of vegetated residential towers in Milan, Italy, has gained prominence as a remarkable representation of environmentally sustainable design since it was completed in 2014. With hundreds of trees growing on their balconies, Stefano Boeri's design aims to serve as a template for fostering urban biodiversity. The idea hasn't been without controversy, though; detractors point out that even while the trees used in Bosco Verticale were grown especially for the project, it's too soon to know if they would flourish in this peculiar environment. Why, in the words of the text, do some detractors doubt the idea behind Bosco Verticale?

A) It is challenging to modify several key elements of Bosco Verticale's design for use in places other than Milan.

B) In the end, Boeri's expectations about the variety of the plant life on Bosco Verticale were not met.

C) The environmental impact of erecting Bosco Verticale was equal to that of creating more traditional structures.

D) It's uncertain if Bosco Verticale can sustain the vegetation that was included into its design.

11. Many literary theorists make a distinction between syuzhet, or the order and presentation of events in a story, and fabula, or the content of a tale. The Corleone family's saga is told in the movie The Godfather Part II as both the fabula and the syuzhet, which shift between two timelines between 1901 and 1958. However, Mikhail Bakhtin, a literary theorist, contended that fabula and syuzhet are not adequate to fully characterize a narrative; he believed that systematic classifications of artistic phenomena ignore the nuanced ways in which meaning is constructed through interactions among the artist, the work, and the audience. Which option most accurately sums up the text's core idea?

A) Mikhail Bakhtin, a literary theorist, contended that two ideas utilized by other theorists to examine narratives do not adequately capture some significant aspects of narratives.

B) Mikhail Bakhtin, a literary theorist, asserted that meaning is not innate in a story but rather is formed by the audience during their interaction with it, leading to varying interpretations of the same story across individuals.

C) Despite their extraordinary complexity, the storytelling techniques employed in The Godfather Part II may be readily comprehended by applying two literary theory ideas.

D) Audiences find it more difficult to comprehend storylines delivered out of chronological sequence than when they are presented chronologically.

12. A student is investigating the patterns in the subjects that high school students submit to a national science fair. The number of contributions submitted annually per topic is displayed in the graph. The student asserts that more ideas related to medical and health research were submitted in 2019 than in any previous year, based on the statistics displayed in the graph. Which option best utilises the graph's data to bolster the highlighted claim?

A) The quantity of topics submitted for cellular and molecular biology in 2016 was equal to that of submissions for animal science.

B) More physics and space science subject proposals were received in 2019 than submissions related to medicine and health.

C) About 95 submissions of animal science topics were made in 2016, which was the fewest ever in a single year.

D) About 285 entries on medical and health-related topics were made in 2019, the most within the time displayed.

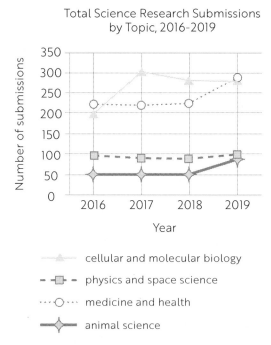

Total Science Research Submissions by Topic, 2016-2019

— cellular and molecular biology
- -□- - physics and space science
···○··· medicine and health
◆ animal science

13. Transgenic fish are those whose DNA has been altered to incorporate genetic material from different species. Certain transgenic fish possess jellyfish genes that cause them to fluoresce, or shine in the dark. These fish were first created in the 1990s for scientific study, but in the 2000s they were marketed as pets and are now free-ranging in Brazilian streams. According to a biology seminar student conducting a report on these fish, their escape into the wild from Brazilian fish farms might have serious long-term ecological consequences that are detrimental. Which study quote would most effectively bolster the student's claim?

A) "Females outnumbered males in one location where transgenic fish were observed in the wild, while the numbers of males and females were equal in another."

B) "There are insufficient studies of the impact of those fish on the ecosystems into which they are introduced, despite some reports of transgenic fish presence in the wild."

C) "A subset of the ecosystems into which the fish have actually been introduced may comprise the ecosystems into which transgenic fish are known to have been introduced."

D) Transgenic fish may transfer the characteristic of fluorescence into natural fish populations by interbreeding, increasing the species' susceptibility to predators.

14. Researchers led by Inés Ibáñez examined a forest location where a small number of sugar maple trees are periodically fertilized with nitrogen in order to replicate the general trend of rising soil anthropogenic nitrogen deposition. The present climate, moderate change, and extreme change were the three alternative climatic scenarios that Ibáñez and colleagues projected for the radial development of the trees with and without nitrogen fertilizer. Even though they discovered that growth will be adversely affected by climate change, they came to the conclusion that, if the shift is mild rather than dramatic, anthropogenic nitrogen deposition might more than outweigh the harm. Which option most accurately depicts the graph's data that back up the findings of Ibáñez and colleagues?

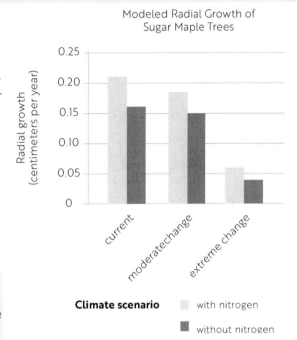

Modeled Radial Growth of Sugar Maple Trees

Climate scenario — with nitrogen / without nitrogen

A) Under the current environment, growth with nitrogen outpaced growth with nitrogen under moderate change, but with extreme change, the latter outpaced growth without nitrogen.

B) In the current climate, growth without nitrogen outpaced growth without nitrogen under moderate change, but with extreme change, the latter outpaced growth with nitrogen.

C) Under mild change, nitrogen-enriched growth outpaced nitrogen-deficient growth, whereas under extreme change, the latter outpaced the former.

D) Growth with nitrogen grew faster in a somewhat altered environment than it did in a present one, but with a severe alteration, the latter outpaced the former.

15. Marianne Moore's 1919 poem "Poetry" The speaker of the poem expresses ambivalence over poetry, acknowledging its advantages but yet expressing dissatisfaction, writing _____. Which passage from "Poetry" best exemplifies the assertion?

A) "Discriminating against 'business documents and school-books' is also invalid; these phenomena are all significant."

B) "One needs to distinguish, though: when half-poets bring someone to prominence, the outcome is not poetry."

C) "The same thing may be said for all of us—that we / do not admire what / we cannot understand—when [poems] become so derivative as to become unintelligible."

D) "One finds that there is, after all, a place for the genuine in [poetry], but reading it with a perfect contempt for it."

16. Certain climate models pertaining to the western United States indicate that although the overall yearly precipitation may not alter from its current state, it will concentrate into fewer but more severe precipitation events, such as rain and snow. Geeta Persad, a climate scientist at the University of Texas, and her colleagues ran simulations to see how this may affect the quantity of water entering aquifers and the amount utilized for irrigation. Persad and her associates came to the conclusion that concentrating precipitation into fewer events would increase the number of dry days and necessitate more irrigation; however, this shift in irrigation output is extremely dependent on the area's current baseline concentration of precipitation.

Simulated Changes in Annual Irrigation Output and Aquifer Input if Precipitation Concentration Rises as Predicted by Climate Models

Baseline concentration of annual precipitation	% change in water entering aquifers	% change in surface water used for irrigation	% change in groundwater used for irrigation
Precipitation is currently somewhat concentrated	4.9	0.4	0.9
Precipitation is currently evenly distributed	11.0	9.0	7.9

Which option most accurately sums up the table's statistics that back up Persad and her colleagues' findings?

A) The quantity of water utilized for irrigation will rise by 0.4% for surface water and 0.9% for groundwater if baseline precipitation is relatively concentrated, while the amount of water entering aquifers would increase by 11.0% if baseline precipitation is uniformly distributed.

B) Water usage for irrigation will grow very marginally if baseline precipitation is somewhat concentrated, but it will increase 9.0% for surface water and 7.9% for groundwater if baseline precipitation is uniformly distributed.

C) The quantity of water entering aquifers will increase by 4.9% if baseline precipitation is relatively concentrated, whereas the amount used for irrigation will increase by 0.4% for surface water and 0.9% for groundwater.

D) Water usage for irrigation will decrease somewhat if baseline precipitation is somewhat concentrated, but it will rise 11.0% for surface water and 9.0% for groundwater if baseline precipitation is uniformly spread.

17. The "r" sound is heavily stressed in Scottish English dialects when it comes before other consonants (like in "bird") or at the end of syllables (like in "car"). The Upland South's English dialects, which are spoken in western Virginia and Oklahoma, emphasize "r" before other consonants and at the ends of syllables. Historical accounts indicate that individuals with Scottish ancestry were the main colonizers of the Upland South. Linguists have thus determined that _____ Which option logically completes the text?

A) Scottish dialects are the source of the stress on the "r" sound in the English dialects spoken in the Upland South.

B) English dialects spoken in the Upland South will ultimately influence dialects spoken elsewhere by emphasizing the "r" sound.

C) Dialects spoken in the Upland South had an impact on the English dialects spoken in Scotland.

D) After moving to the Upland South, individuals from Scotland stopped emphasizing the "r" sound. Which option brings the text up to date and into compliance with Standard English conventions?

18. How did whales, which were previously just slightly larger than seals, grow to be the biggest mammals on the planet? Mariana Nery, a researcher from Brazil, thinks whale DNA may hold the key. Nery and her associates completed a study in January 2023 that demonstrates alterations in four whale genes linked to body growth over time. Which option brings the text up to date and into compliance with Standard English conventions?

A) published

B) Printing

C) after publishing

D) to release

19. Although a harpsichord and a piano may have similar appearances, one can easily distinguish between the two instruments. The _____'s strings are plucked, not hit, when the instrument's keys are depressed. Which option brings the text up to date and into compliance with Standard English conventions?

A) tool:

B) tool

C) tool

D) apparatus,

20. Table forks encountered strong opposition when they were initially brought from Byzantium to western Europe in the eleventh century. St. Peter Damian, the bishop of Ostia, disapproved of the dining utensils because he believed they were superfluous and hazardous _____. Which option brings the text up to date and into compliance with Standard English conventions?

A) those

B) this

C) that

D) It

21. If you'd like to learn more about how dictator Rafael Trujillo's dictatorship has been portrayed in Dominican American literature, start with Julia Alvarez's 1994 novel In the Time of the Butterflies, which is a fictionalized account of the lives of the Mirabal brothers. Which option brings the text up to date and into compliance with Standard English conventions?

A) sisters, as well as

B) Sisters and

C) Sisters

D) sisters

22. A windstorm on March 23, 2021, severely disrupted international trade. An international shipping container ship named Ever Given was stuck in Egypt's Suez Canal, which is a vital shipping route between Europe and Asia. When fully laden, the vessel weighs as much as two thousand blue whales, and it took six days to _____. Which option brings the text up to date and into compliance with Standard English conventions?

A) move somewhat because of its bulk,

B) shift, partly because of its massive size:

C) knock away, partly because of its bulk,

D) toppled, partly because of its massive bulk

23. Fans of the 2016 movie Moana might not be aware that comedian, actor, and musician Jemaine Clement is the source of the deep and funny voice behind the character. The talented actor has acted in everything from action films to TV ads, but voice acting in particular has grown to be a significant aspect of his career. Which option brings the text up to date and into compliance with Standard English conventions?

A) Tamatoa the crab, a character

B) the crab Tamatoa character,

Character C: The crab Tamatoa,

D) figure, the crab Tamatoa

24. Sociologist Arlie Russell Hochschild first extensively discussed her idea of a "sociology of emotions" in her 1983 book The Managed Heart: Commercialization of Human Feeling. This theory holds that every emotional response an individual has in a given situation is _____ each of the various cultural and ideological frameworks that person has internalized (class, gender, political affiliation, etc.). Which option brings the text up to date and into compliance with Standard English conventions?

A) is the foundation

B) is the foundation.

C) support

D) has been the foundation

25. American abstract artist Richard _____ assembles massive steel plates into sculptures that command the outdoor places they inhabit, with the goal of making onlookers acutely aware of how one's motions are influenced by the physical elements of one's environment. Which option brings the text up to date and into compliance with Standard English conventions?

A) Serra plans to

B) Serra wants to

C) Serra, hoping

D) Serra wants to

26. Frank Zamboni invented a device for resurfacing ice rinks in 1949. First, Zamboni's equipment scraped the top layer of ice from the rink's surface as it proceeded around it. Then it sprayed water into the profound indentations that the customers' skates had left behind. Finally, it melted over the fresh ice. Which option provides the most logical conclusion to the text?

A) As an illustration,

B) Next,

C) In a similar vein,

D) On the other hand,

27. After delivering a narrative on his experiences as a Guatemalan immigrant living in Chicago, Nestor Gomez won his first-ever storytelling competition in 2014. Because in order to provide people a forum to tell their tales of immigration, Gomez produced the program 80 Minutes Around the World in 2017. Which option provides the most logical conclusion to the text?

A) As an alternative,

B) As an illustration,

C) Afterwards,

D) Put differently,

STOP

IF YOU COMPLETE BEFORE THE TIME LIMIT, YOU MAY JUST REVIEW YOUR WORK ON THIS MODULE. AVOID SWITCHING TO ANY OTHER TEST MODULE.

SECTION 2 > MATH TEST

DIRECTIONS

Complete each issue on the questions, choose the best response from the list of options, and mark the matching circle on your answer sheet. You may do scratch work in any open place in your exam booklet.

Notes

Unless otherwise stated, all of the variables and expressions used represent real numbers. Unless otherwise specified, the set of all real numbers x for which f(x) is a real number is the domain of a given function f.

MODULE 1: 22 QUESTIONS

1) Which of the subsequent is equivalent to 3 (X+5)−6 ?

A) 3 −3 x

B) 3 −1 x

C) 3 +9 x

D) 15 − 6

2)

$x = y - 3$

$x + 2y = 6\ 2$

Which of the following ordered pairs (x, y) fulfills the given system of equations?

A) (–3, 0)

B) (0, 3)

C) (6, –3)

D) (36, –6)

3)

For i = Square route -1, which of the subsequent complex numbers equals (5+ 12i) – (9i2 – 6i)?

A) –14 – 18i

B) –4 – 6i

C) 4+6i

D) 14 + 18i

5)

If f(x) $x^2 - 6x + 3 / x - 1$, what is f(–1) ?

A) –5

B) –2

C) 2

D) 5

6)

For $32,400, a firm that produces wildlife documentaries buys camera equipment. The equipment has a 12-year fixed-rate depreciation period after which it is deemed to be worthless. How much does the camera gear cost four years after purchase?

A) $10,800

B) $16,200

C) $21,600

D) $29,700

7)

$x^2 + 6x + 4$

Which of the subsequent is equivalent to the expression above?

A) $(x + 3)^2 + 5$

B) $(x + 3)^2 - 5$

C) $(x - 3)^2 + 5$

D) $(x - 3)^2 - 5$

7) This summer, Ken is a member of a group working on a farm. For the first ten hours he worked this week, he was paid $8 per hour. His crew leader increased his pay to $10 per hour for the remainder of the week based on his performance. Ken sets aside 90% of his weekly wages. How many hours a week minimum does he need to work the rest of the way to save at least $270?

A) 38

B) 33

C) 22

D) 16

8) For a forthcoming project, Marisa needs to recruit a minimum of ten employees. The personnel will consist of junior directors, who will get a weekly salary of $640, and senior directors, who will receive a weekly salary of $880. She has set aside no more than $9,700 each week for staff salaries. She has to appoint a minimum of three junior and one senior director. Considering that y is the total amount of senior directors and x is the number of junior directors, which of the subsequent systems of inequalities best describes the circumstances described?

A) $640x + 880y \geq 9,700$

$x + y \leq 10$

$x \geq 3$

$y \geq 1$

B) $640x + 880y \leq 9,700$

$x + y \geq 10$

$x \geq 3$

$y \geq 1$

C) $640x + 880y \geq 9,700$

$x + y \geq 10$

$x \leq 3$

$y \leq 1$

D) $640x + 880y \leq 9,700$

$x + y \leq 10$

$x \leq 3$

$y \leq 1$

9) $ax^3 + bx^2 + cx + d = 0$

The constants a, b, c, and d in the preceding equation. If the roots of the equation are 1, 3, and 5, which of the following factors influences $ax^3 + bx^2 + cx + d$?

A) $x - 1$

B) x + 1

C) x – 3

D) x + 5

10) The expression $\dfrac{x^{-2}y^{\frac{1}{2}}}{x^{\frac{1}{2}}_{2}\,y^{-1}}$, where x > 1 and y > 1, is equivalent to which of the subsequent?

A) √y / ∛x 2

B) (y √y)/(∛x 2)

C) (y √y)/(x √x)

D) (y √y)/(x2 ∛x)

11) The formula for the function f is f(x)=(x+3)(x+1). A parabola represents the graph of f in the xy plane. Which of the subsequent intervals includes the vertex's x-coordinate on the graph of f?

A) –4 < < –3 x

B) –3 < < 1 x

C) 1< < <4

D) 3< <4

12) Which of the subsequent expressions is equivalent to (x²-2x-5)/(x-3) ?

A) x-5-20/(x-3)

B)x-5-10/(x-3)

C) X+1-8/(x-3)

D) x + 1 - 2/(x-3)

13) For a certain kind of service, a shipping company limits the size of the boxes it will send. The limitation specifies that the total of the box's height and base perimeter cannot exceed 130 inches for boxes formed like rectangular prisms. The width and length of the box are used to calculate the base's perimeter. The allowed width x, in inches, of a box with a height of 60 inches and a length that is 2.5 times the width is shown by this inequality?

A) 0 < ≤ 10 x

B) 0 < ≤ 11 x 23

C) 0 < ≤ 17 x 1 2

D) 0 < ≤ 20

14) The expression 1/2 x² - 2 can be rewritten as 1/3 (x - k)(x + k), where k is a positive constant. What is the value of k ?

A) 2

B) 6

C) √2

D) √6

15) Feeding Guidelines for Pets Who Are Boarded

	Fed only dry food	Fed both wet and dry food	Total
Cats	5	11	16
Dogs	2	23	25
Total	7	34	41

The meals that are presently provided to the cats and dogs boarded at a pet care facility are shown in the above table. What percentage of dogs only get dry food?

A) 2/ 41

B) 2 /25

C) 7 /41

D) 2/ 7

16) $(x^2 - 3) - (-3x^2 + 5)$

Which of the subsequent expressions is equivalent to the one above?

A) 4 – 8

B) $4x^2 - 2$

C) $-2x^2 - 8$

D) $-2x^2 - 2$

17) To properly shut a specific box, three cm of tape are needed. How many of these kinds of packages may be safely fastened with six meters of tape? (1 meter = 100 cm)

A) 100

B) 150

C) 200

D) 300

18) Which of the subsequent pairs (x, y) that are arranged fulfills the inequality? 5 - 3 <4 x y?

I. (1, 1)

II. (2, 5)

III. (3, 2)

A) I only

B) II only

C) I and II only

D) I and III only

19) In the equation $(ax+3)^2 = 36$, a is a constant. What may be the value of an if one of the equation's solutions is x = -3?

A) –11

B) –5

C) –1

D) 0

The following material is referenced in the next two questions.

Planetoids' Density and Distance in the Inner Solar System

The aforementioned scatterplot displays the density of seven planetoids in grams per cubic centimeter in relation to their mean astronomical units (AU) distances from the Sun. You may also see the line of optimum fit.

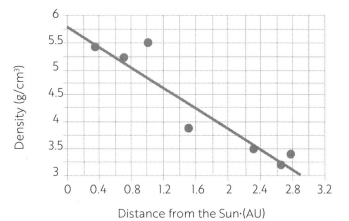

20) A new planetoid located at 1.2 AU from the Sun has been found by astronomers. Which of the adhering to, in grams per cubic centimeter, most closely approximates the planetoid's density based on the line of best fit?

A) 3.6

B) 4.1

C) 4.6

D) 5.5

21) $9ax + 9b - 6 = 21$

What is the value of $ax + b$ based on the preceding equation?

A) 3

B) 6

C) 8

D) 12

22) Meetings took up 15% of Lani's eight-hour workweek. How much of her working day was spent in meetings?

A) 1.2

B) 15

C) 48

D) 72

STOP

IF YOU COMPLETE BEFORE THE TIME LIMIT, YOU MAY JUST REVIEW YOUR WORK ON THIS MODULE. AVOID SWITCHING TO ANY OTHER TEST MODULE.

MODULE 2: 22 QUESTIONS

1) In the figure above, what is the value of x ?

A) 45

B) 90

C) 100

D) 105

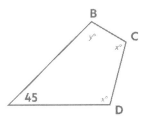

2. A column made of fifty one-cent coins placed on top of one another would be about three and a half inches tall. Which of the subsequent estimates how many one-cent coins would be needed to create an eight-inch-tall column at this rate?

A) 75

B) 100

C) 200

D) 390

3. If a − b = 12 and b/2 = 10 , what is the value of a + b ?

A) 2

B) 12

C) 32

D) 52

4. A cohort of students used a democratic process to choose the selection of five extracurricular activities to be held after school. The bar graph displays the quantity of students who cast their votes for each of the five activities. What is the total number of students who selected activity 3?

A) 25

B) 39

C) 48

D) 50

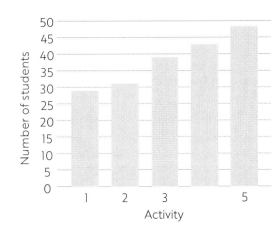

5. What is the percentage of 75 out of 300?

A) 25%

B) 50%

C) 75%

D) 225%

6.

$$x^2 / 25 = 36$$

What is the solution to the provided equation?

A) 6

B) 30

C) 450

D) 900

7. The sum of 8 times a number x and 3 is equal to 83. Which equation accurately captures this scenario?

A) $(3)(8)x = 83$

B) $8x = 83 + 3$

C) $3x + 8 = 83$

D) $8x + 3 = 83$

8. Hana made regular monthly deposits of a certain sum into her bank account. The function $f(t) = 100 + 25t$ represents the balance, in dollars, in Hana's bank account after t monthly deposits. What is the most accurate meaning of the number 25 in this particular situation?

A) Hana's bank account balance grew by $25 with every monthly deposit.

B) Prior to Hana initiating any monthly deposits, the balance in her bank account was $25.

C) Hana's bank account balance increased to $25 after making a single monthly deposit.

D) Hana made a cumulative total of 25 monthly deposits.

9. The customer expended a total of $27 to acquire oranges at a rate of $3 per pound. What was the weight of the oranges purchased by the customer?

10. Nasir purchased 9 storage containers that were priced identically. He utilized a voucher that provided a discount of $63 on the total purchase amount. The total expenditure following the application of the coupon amounted to $27. What was the initial cost, in dollars, for 1 storage bin?

11. The table displays three pairs of values, where x is the input for the linear function corresponding output. What equation defines the function f(x)?

x	f(x)
0	29
1	32
2	35

A) $f(x) = 3x + 29$

B) $f(x) = 29x + 32$

C) f (x) = 35x + 29

D) f (x) = 32x + 35

12. Right triangles PQR and STU are similar, with P corresponding to S. Given that the measure of angle Q is 18°, what is the magnitude of angle S?

A) 18°

B) 72°

C) 82°

D) 162°

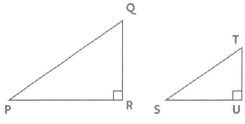

Note: Figures not drawn to scale

13. The scatterplot depicts the correlation between two variables, x and y.

Which equation among the options best represents a linear model for the given data?

A) y = 0.9 + 9.4x

B) y = 0.9 – 9.4x

C) y = 9.4 + 0.9x

D) y = 9.4 – 0.9x

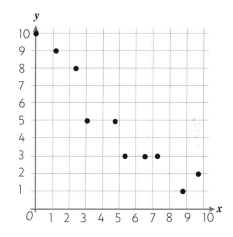

14.

$$2.5b + 5r = 80$$

The provided equation represents the correlation between the quantity of birds, denoted as b, and the quantity of reptiles, denoted as r, that may be accommodated at a pet care establishment on a specific day. If the firm is capable of tending to 16 reptiles on a particular day, what is the maximum number of birds it can accommodate on the same day?

A) 0

B) 5

C) 40

D) 80

15. The scatterplot illustrates the correlation between two variables, x and y.

What is the mathematical expression that represents the graph displayed?

A) y = –2x – 8

B) y x = –8

C) y = –x – 8

D) y = 2x – 8

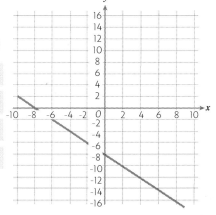

16. If the quotient of x divided by 8 is equal to 5, what is the reciprocal of this quotient, 8 divided by x?

17.
$$24x + y = 48$$
$$6x + y = 72$$

The solution to the given system of equations is (x, y). What is the value of y?

18. The line t in the xy-plane has a slope of -2 and intersects the point (9, 10). What equation represents line t?

A) $y = 13x - 1/3$

B) $y = 9x + 10$

C) $y = -x/3 + 10$

D) $y = -x/3 + 13$

19. The function $f(x) = 206(1.034)^x$ represents the monetary value, measured in dollars, of a certain bank account at the end of each year between 1957 and 1972. In this function, x represents the number of years that have passed since 1957. Which of the following is the most accurate explanation of the statement "f(5) is approximately equal to 243" in this particular situation?

A) The value of the bank account is estimated to be approximately 5 dollars greater in 1962 than in 1957.

B) The value of the bank account is estimated to be approximately 243 dollars in 1962.

C) The value, in dollars, of the bank account is estimated to be approximately 5 times greater in 1962 than in 1957.

D) The value of the bank account is estimated to increase by approximately 243 dollars every 5 years between 1957 and 1972.

20. The length-to-width ratio of a specific rectangular region is 35:10. To maintain the ratio, the length of the rectangular region must rise proportionally to the increase in width by 7 units.

A) It must decrease by 24.5 units.

B) It must increase by 24.5 units.

C) It must decrease by 7 units.

D) It must increase by 7 units.

21. Square P has a side length of x inches. The circumference of square Q exceeds the perimeter of square P by 176 inches. The function f calculates the area of square Q, measured in square inches. Which of the following provides a precise definition of the function f?

A) $f(x) = (x + 44)^2$

B) $f(x) = (x + 176)^2$

C) $f(x) = (176x + 44)^2$

D) $f(x) = (176x + 176)^2$

22.

$$14x / 7y = 2\sqrt{(w + 19)}$$

The provided equation establishes a relationship between the unique, positive real integers w, x, and y. Which equation accurately represents the relationship between w, x, and y?

A) $w = (\sqrt{x}/y) - 9$

B) $w = (\sqrt{28x}/14y) - 19$

C) $w = (x/y)2 - 19$

D) $w = (28x/14y)2 - 19$

STOP — IF YOU COMPLETE BEFORE THE TIME LIMIT, YOU MAY JUST REVIEW YOUR WORK ON THIS MODULE. AVOID SWITCHING TO ANY OTHER TEST MODULE.

Practice Test 5 Answer and Explanation

SECTION 1
MODULE 1: READING AND WRITING TEST

QUESTION 1

Choice A is the best answer since the text states that Fox-Foot does not allow the group to make a fire or a boat landing when it is time for supper. This context implies that he does not want anyone who is monitoring the gang to see any evidence of them or their actions. In other words, Fox-Foot does not wish to leave any trace or proof of the group's movements ("their passing") in the region.

QUESTION 2

Choice B is the best option since it logically concludes the text's topic of noses on antique sculptures. In this usage, the term "fragile" refers to anything weak or sensitive. This corresponds to the text's description of noses on ancient sculptures, which are frequently missing from sculptures' heads because they are "especially easy to break." As a result, this context suggests that noses on ancient sculptures are the most delicate component of the sculptures' heads.

QUESTION 3

Choice B is the best answer since it most logically concludes the text's examination of early warning signs of solar flares. The term "impending" refers to anything that is about to happen or is on its way. The article describes a research by Leka and colleagues that discovered that the Sun's corona gives an early warning of solar flares. The essay then discusses why such an early warning would be useful—solar flares can interfere with communications on Earth—and closes by explaining the corona feature that offers warning of a solar flare. According to the text, this characteristic—increased brightness in a specific region of the corona—occurs before the emergence of the flare. Therefore, in context, the ideal answer would convey that the flare is approaching or impending.

QUESTION 4

Choice D is the most logical conclusion to the text's description of utilizing magnetism to detect tension in buried metal pipes. In this usage, "exploited" refers to making productive use of. The article states that the magnetic fields of some metals vary under stress, and Saleem and colleagues demonstrated that those changes can be measured from a distance, proving that the integrity of subterranean metal pipelines may be assessed without having to excavate them. This context so suggests that Saleem and colleagues made good use of, or utilized, the metals' magnetic fields.

QUESTION 5

Choice B is the best answer since it logically concludes the text's explanation of behavioral psychology research. In this sense, "ameliorate" refers to helping to correct or improve. The essay claims that many behavioral psychology studies are defective because the subjects employed are "highly unrepresentative." It then proposes that researchers recruit subjects from "diverse backgrounds and locations" to assist solve the issue of unrepresentative subject pools. Thus, this context implies that diversity-focused recruiting initiatives might assist alleviate the issues stated in the text.

QUESTION 6

Choice D is the best answer since it appropriately explains the text's principal aim. In the opening sentence of the book, the narrator declares that she believes she has a chance of joining her college's basketball team. She goes on to say that she is "quick" and "tough." She believes she has a shot to join the squad because of these qualities. Thus, the text's major objective is to explain why the narrator believes she has a chance of making the basketball team.

QUESTION 7

Choice B is the most accurate description of the text's principal goal. The narrative opens by claiming that in the late 1800s, there were several Spanish-language newspapers in towns across Texas, with San Antonio producing eleven of them. The article then goes on to say that in the late 1800s, El Paso had the most Spanish-language newspapers of any city in Texas. The paragraph then finishes by saying that El Paso's proximity to Mexico and big population of Spanish speakers most certainly contributed to the high number of Spanish-language publications in the area. As a result, the primary goal of the work is to explain how Spanish-language newspapers prospered in Texas cities, particularly El Paso, in the late 1800s.

QUESTION 8

Choice C is the best answer because it most clearly illustrates how the underlined statement fits into the larger context of the text. The first statement explains the Atacama Desert, which is unique on Earth. The next text, which is emphasized, explains that astrobiologists research life, or its remains, in this unusual area since Atacama is a severe climate that is quite similar to Mars' extreme environment. The rest of the paragraph indicates that the researchers expect that their study in Atacama will help to further studies into life on Mars. Thus, the emphasized paragraph serves primarily to explain why astrobiologists prefer to do research in the Atacama Desert.

QUESTION 9

Choice B is the best answer since it defines the underlined portion's purpose in the context of the entire text. The first phrase emphasizes that replicating the strong ridership of Mexico City's public transportation system in other places by introducing some of its features, such as low fares, is unlikely to result in considerable passenger gains. The next statement presents a research by Guerra et al., whose findings—namely, that the choice of transportation mode in Mexican metropolitan centers is impacted by a number of local contextual factors—back up this argument. The first part of the last sentence acknowledges that features of transportation systems likely do have some effect on ridership numbers, but the underlined portion reiterates the study's conclusion by stating that there is a "irreducibly contextual dimension" to peoples' choice to use public transportation: that is, there is a complex mix of local contextual factors—including population density, spatial distribution of jobs, and demographics—whose influence over an urban Thus, the emphasized section shows why it is difficult to alter transit ridership just by modifying certain of a transportation system's features.

QUESTION 10

Choice B is the best answer since it appropriately defines the text's general structure. The essay opens by stating that human activities affect carbon and nitrogen levels in soil, but how profoundly these impacts are felt in the soil remains unknown. The text then summarizes Okolo and colleagues' hypothesis on this question—that the different effects on carbon and nitrogen levels associated with different types of land use would be observed below the topsoil layer—and briefly describes the methods they used to test this hypothesis. Finally, the article claims that the researchers discovered that at depths below the topsoil layer, carbon and nitrogen levels dropped to similar lows across all land-use categories, contradicting the team's prior theory. Thus, the essay begins with an unanswered scientific topic, then gives a study team's theory about that subject, and then relates an observation discovered by the team that contradicted their hypothesis.

QUESTION 11

Choice D is the best option because it makes a remark about what astonished the scientists that is supported by the text. According to the text, the marsquakes mentioned in the data from NASA's InSight lander occurred at the same spot on Mars. According to the text, the scientists were astonished by this revelation because they had predicted the contrary (that earthquakes would occur all around the world).

QUESTION 12

Choice A is the best answer since it provides text-supported information about the Maya culture. The book indicates that the Maya kingdoms' writing system included a sign for the number zero. It goes on to claim that when the zero symbol first appeared, almost 2,000 years ago, nearly no other writing systems in the world used such a symbol. The book also mentions that some historians believe Maya mathematicians received the usage of zero from the Olmec culture, which resided in the same region as the Maya civilization at one time. According to the text, some historians believe that the Maya culture adopted the usage of zero from the Olmec civilization.

QUESTION 13

Choice D is the best answer because it makes the best use of a quote from "The Bet" to demonstrate that the banker was really furious about something. The phrase implies that the banker cried, implying that he was likely upset about something, and that his emotions were so intense that he couldn't sleep for hours. These clues indicate that the banker was really unhappy.

QUESTION 14

Choice A is the best option since it most logcally concludes the text's description of a crater's relationship to the beginning of the Younger Dryas. According to the text, some scientists believe that a comet fragment collided with Earth, causing the Younger Dryas era to chill. The article then mentions that a team of scientists discovered a crater in Greenland, which some feel supports the notion that a comet fragment impacted Earth to cause the Younger Dryas. However, the text states that the crew was unable to identify the age of the crater. If the crater's age cannot be determined, the relationship to the Younger Dryas epoch cannot be proven. As a result, it cannot be argued that the impact that formed the crater was related to the onset of the Younger Dryas.

QUESTION 15

Choice B is the best option since it most logically concludes the text's description of Smith and colleagues' research into the evolution and biological purpose of the appendix. The article states that the scientists discovered multiple examples of the appendix arising and not vanishing in the lineages of the mammal species they studied. Furthermore, the text adds that species with an appendix have relatively high levels of lymphoid tissue, which promotes immune system function. Taken together, these findings strongly support the concept that the appendix has survived in some animals because it plays a role in their successful immune responses.

QUESTION 16

Choice A is the best option since it logically concludes the text's examination of Aztec (Nahua) ethics. According to Purcell's interpretation of existing Aztec philosophical literature, the Aztec ethical system considers an individual's actions in connection to their societal function and how they effect the community. The text compares this viewpoint with one held by certain ethicists, who believe that actions are morally acceptable or harmful independent of the environment in which they occur. hence, Purcell's study implies that the Aztecs would have argued that the morality of an individual's conduct is anchored in that person's place in the community as well as the consequences of those actions, and hence cannot be assessed in the absence of context.

QUESTION 17

Choice C is the best option. The convention under consideration is pronoun-antecedent agreement. The pronoun "this" corresponds to the singular antecedent "Lê Lương Minh became the thirteenth secretary-general of the Association of Southeast Asian Nations (ASEAN) in January 2013." The pronoun "this" refers to the singular event described earlier in the sentence, when Minh became secretary-general of ASEAN.

QUESTION 18

Option D) "using" is the best choice here. It transforms the passive construction into an active participial phrase, making the sentence more concise and direct while maintaining the original meaning.

QUESTION 19

Choice D is the best option. The convention being examined is subject-verb agreement. The singular verb "ensures" has the same number as the single subject "using."

QUESTION 20

Option A is correct because it completes the sentence in a clear and concise manner. The phrase "as you put your hand between each of the two antennas" logically follows from the description of how the tambourine is played. It maintains parallel structure and fits well with the sentence's subject and verb agreement. The singular "hand" agrees with "your," ensuring grammatical coherence and clarity.

QUESTION 21

Choice B is the best option. This option correctly maintains the past tense and aligns with Standard English conventions.

QUESTION 22

Choice D is the best option. The comma after "creator" is necessary to set off the appositive phrase. This option maintains proper sentence structure without redundancy. It provides a clear and concise identification of Marie-Denise Villers. The use of "the creator," followed by her name, adheres to Standard English conventions.

QUESTION 23

Option D is the best choice because it uses a colon to introduce the list of items that the individuals described. A colon is appropriate here because it clearly precedes and introduces the specific examples that illustrate what the participants described. Options A and C are less effective because they either do not use punctuation to properly introduce the list or use an inappropriate comma. Option B uses a dash, which is less conventional in this context and may not be as clear or formal as the colon for introducing a list.

QUESTION 24

Choice D is the best option. "As a result" logically indicates that the information in this statement—the vessel turning black—is the effect of the heating process stated in the preceding line.

QUESTION 25

Choice D is the best option. "Though" logically suggests that the sentence's argument—that Morton's improvisational talents helped develop jazz as a genre during its early years ("No one can deny" it)—is accurate, despite the earlier information concerning Morton's overstated claim to have founded jazz.

QUESTION 26

Choice B is the best option. The word "conversely" logically indicates that the information in this sentence—that nations with proportional-representation electoral systems tend to be multi-party—contradicts the prior information regarding countries with single-ballot majoritarian elections, which tend to be two-party.

QUESTION 27

Choice D is the best option. "Hence" logically indicates that the information in this line concerning turtle shells—that people mistakenly believe them are exoskeletons—is a result of the shells emerging outside the animal.

SECTION 1
MODULE 2: READING AND WRITING TEST

QUESTION 1

Choice C is the correct answer because, as employed in the text, "reaching across to" almost always indicates stretching toward. Mrs. Wilkins opens the paragraph by noting that she would want to have one of the oranges she admires. The text then suggests that Mrs. Wilkins remains where she is and extends a large orange to her acquaintance. This context implies that when the text depicts Mrs. Wilkins extending out to the dish of oranges, she is straining toward it.

QUESTION 2

Choice D is the best option since it logically concludes the text's explanation of the fossil deposit. In this usage, "obtain" denotes to earn or acquire. According to the article, a team of paleontologists discovered fossils that are exceptionally well preserved. As a result, the book argues, paleontologists have been able to extract specific information from fossils, such as the color patterns of the living creatures that left them.

QUESTION 3

Choice A is the best answer because it most logically concludes the text's description of how the flow of information between two areas of the brain influences the ease with which people make decisions. In this usage, "reduced" indicates "decreased." The paper highlights a team of neuroeconomists' discovery that decision making may be linked to communication between the prefrontal and parietal brain. In presenting this fact, the article draws a distinction between persons who are more decisive and those who make decisions more slowly. According to the text, people are more decisive when the flow of information between the two brain areas is increased, or enhanced. However, this context shows that when the flow of information between the two brain areas is reduced, people make slower decisions.

QUESTION 4

Choice A is the most logical conclusion to the text's examination of the War of 1812's relevance in British historical memory. In this sense, "shaky" denotes a lack of significant impact or importance. According to the text, the War of 1812 was overshadowed by the larger conflict with Napoleonic France and did not result in any notable changes to Britain's geopolitical position. These characteristics suggest that the War of 1812 has a lesser prominence in British history compared to other events, resulting in a less significant place in British historical memory.

QUESTION 5

Choice C is the best option since it logically concludes the text's account of Minoan bull-leaping ceremonies. In this usage, "defend" refers to support in the face of argument. The text's overall focus is on the challenge of establishing what bull-leaping rites meant to the Minoans, about whom little is known. According to the text, because of the paucity of knowledge, claims concerning the significance of rites that occurred a long time ago (in the second millennium BCE) are extremely likely to be based on assumption and guessing. This background indicates that statements concerning the significance of the rites are difficult to justify or defend.

QUESTION 6

Choice C is the best answer because it most clearly illustrates how the underlined statement fits into the larger context of the text. Harris recounts experiences from his earlier boat excursion across the English Channel, when circumstances were so bad that some on board felt seasick. According to the book, Harris' recollections differ slightly, but in general he and only one other guy do not become ill. The underlined text goes on to say that if it wasn't "not [Harris] and another man" who didn't get seasick, "then it was [Harris] by himself." In other words, in certain versions of the story, Harris was the only one onboard who didn't become seasick. As a result, the emphasized statement underscores Harris's tendency to boast about his own constitution, or physical well-being, while discussing a prior boat voyage.

QUESTION 7

Choice B is the best answer since it illustrates how the underlined statement fits into the larger context of the text. The emphasized statement illustrates that, contrary to what numerous studies suggest, recent European governments experienced electoral losses following the implementation of economic austerity policies. The text goes on to say that the researchers based their findings on data that didn't reveal the true political risk of austerity measures because the data were based on cases where governments had set austerity programs to take effect after the next election, a practice that European governments that had recently suffered electorally did not follow, introducing a complicating factor that resulted in a conflict between the research findings and current events.

QUESTION 8

Choice A is the best option because it most truly describes how the author of Text 2 would reply to the argument made in Text 1. Text 1 argues that graphic novels should not be classified as literature and should be compared to films. It claims that language plays a relatively limited role in graphic novels: images, not language, are the primary means by which graphic novels tell their stories, and language is used "only sparingly"—that is, comparatively very little—in the form of captions and dialogue. However, the author of Text 2 claims that language in graphic novels is just as important for transmitting meaning as visuals, because without captions and conversation, readers would be unable to understand the story. Furthermore, the author of Text 2 claims that many graphic novels are "beautifully written" and employ language as well as any normal text. Because Text 1 contends that language is subordinate to images in graphic novels, whereas Text 2 emphasizes how language is an essential component of a graphic novel's storytelling, it is reasonable to conclude that the author of Text 2 believes language plays a more important role in graphic novels than the author of Text 1.

QUESTION 9

Choice A is the best answer since it correctly describes what is happening in the text. The narrator observes that Lutie believes the street looks good in the light of the sunset. The narrator goes on to explain what Lutie sees on the street: youngsters playing ball or tag, and females skipping rope. Thus, throughout the book, Lutie is monitoring the look of the street at a specific time of day, as well as the events that take place on it.

QUESTION 10

Choice D is the best answer because it makes a remark regarding critics' doubts about Bosco Verticale that is supported by the text. The article claims that Boeri's design for Bosco Verticale includes hundreds of trees on balconies and is meant to serve as a model for encouraging urban biodiversity. However, the paragraph goes on to say that some critics feel it is too early to tell if the trees planted atop Bosco Verticale would grow there. According to the text, opponents are suspicious of the concept behind Bosco Verticale since it is unknown whether it can maintain the plant life envisioned in its form.

QUESTION 11

Choice A is the best response since it correctly conveys the text's key point. The text begins by explaining that many literary theorists rely on the concepts of fabula (a narrative's content) and syuzhet (a narrative's arrangement and presentation of events) and illustrates these concepts by explaining how they can be applied to the film The Godfather Part II. The text then discusses how Mikhail Bakhtin, a literary theorist, argued that fabula and syuzhet can't fully describe a narrative because systematic categorizations such as these fail to accommodate Thus, the essential argument is that Bakhtin suggested that there are crucial qualities of narratives that are not fully captured by the two ideas that previous theorists have used to analyse narratives.

QUESTION 12

Choice D is the best answer because it successfully leverages data from the graph to back up the emphasized assertion that more medical and health subjects were submitted to a national science fair in 2019 than in any of the previous years. This selection indicates that the approximately 285 medicine and health topics submitted in 2019 are greater than the number of medicine and health submissions in any other year shown—a description supported by data in the graph, which shows that medicine and health topic submissions were less than 250 in 2016, 2017, and 2018, but more than 250 (approximately 285 submissions) in 2019.

QUESTION 13

Choice D is the best response because it best supports the student's claim that the escape of transgenic fish from Brazilian fish farms into the wild might have serious long-term environmental consequences. The text says that transgenic fish have DNA including genetic material from different species, that certain transgenic fish include jellyfish genes that cause them to glow in the dark, and that glow-in-the-dark transgenic fish may now be discovered in Brazilian streams. The quotation explains why the escape of these fish may have negative long-term ecological consequences: glow-in-the-dark transgenic fish may introduce fluorescence into wild fish populations by breeding with wild fish, causing wild fish to glow in the dark and allowing predators to prey on them much easier.

QUESTION 14

Choice D is the best answer because it describes data from the graph that supports Ibáñez and colleagues' conclusion that increased anthropogenic nitrogen deposition can compensate for the detrimental effect of climate change on tree growth if the shift is modest but not dramatic. The bar graph depicts the development of sugar maple trees with and without nitrogen fertilizer under three climate change scenarios: present circumstances, moderate change, and extreme change. According to the graph, radial growth without nitrogen fertilizer is expected to be around 0.16 centimeters (cm) under present conditions, 0.15 cm with moderate change, and 0.04 cm under extreme change. The graph also reveals that with nitrogen fertilization, growth is expected to be around 0.18 centimeters under moderate conditions, but only about 0.06 centimeters under severe conditions. Thus, the data in the graph confirm the researchers' findings by demonstrating better growth for a moderate shift with nitrogen fertilization than for either present circumstances without nitrogen fertilization or a dramatic change with nitrogen fertilization.

QUESTION 15

Choice D is the best answer because it most successfully uses a quote from "Poetry" to demonstrate the assertion that the poem reflects an ambivalence, or ambivalent attitude about poetry. The speaker suggests in the quotation that one may read poetry with "contempt," or disdain, but that even with this negative attitude, one will find "a place for the genuine." Because the quotation expresses conflicting attitudes toward poetry, it effectively illustrates the speaker's ambivalence in discussing the benefits and drawbacks of reading poetry.

QUESTION 16

Choice B is the best answer since it describes statistics from the table that back up Persad and her colleagues' findings. According to the text, some climate models predict that precipitation in the western United States will be concentrated into fewer, more severe rain and snow episodes. According to the text, Persad and her colleagues found that more irrigation will be required, but that the change in irrigation output will be extremely sensitive to, or significantly influenced by, the baseline concentration of precipitation in a region. This result is backed by data from the researchers' simulations of changes in yearly irrigation production under two alternative scenarios: one in which an area's annual precipitation is already somewhat concentrated, and one in which it is uniformly distributed. The table demonstrates that if baseline precipitation is somewhat concentrated, water use for irrigation will only marginally rise, however if baseline precipitation is uniformly distributed, water use for irrigation would increase significantly—9.0% for surface water and 7.9% for groundwater. This disparity demonstrates the researchers' conclusion that the quantity of additional water required for irrigation varies substantially depending on how concentrated or spread out an area's yearly precipitation is.

QUESTION 17

Choice A is the best option since it logically concludes the text's consideration of English dialects spoken in Scotland and the Upland South. The text shows that these dialects have a common feature: stress on the "r" sound when it comes in particular locations in words. The book goes on to say that records show that the Upland South was mostly populated by individuals of Scottish descent. It is plausible to presume that these settlers' English dialects were impacted by the English dialects spoken by their Scottish forebears. As a result, the stress on the "r" sound in Scottish dialects spread to the Upland South dialects as they evolved—that is, the Upland South dialects most likely gained it from Scottish dialects.

QUESTION 18

Choice A is the best option. The convention being examined is the employment of verb forms within sentences. A major sentence requires a finite (tensed) verb to carry out the subject's action (in this example, Nery and her colleagues), and this option provides the finite past tense verb "published" to indicate that these researchers disseminated their discoveries on alterations in whale genes connected with body size.

QUESTION 19

Choice B is the best option. The standard being investigated is the usage of punctuation between a subject and a verb. Punctuation is unnecessary when a subject ("the strings inside the instrument") is immediately followed by a primary verb ("are plucked").

QUESTION 20

Choice C is the best option. In this context, "that" correctly introduces a clause that explains why St. Peter Damian disapproved of the dining utensils. The clause "that they were superfluous and hazardous" provides the reason for his disapproval and is grammatically appropriate for completing the sentence.

QUESTION 21

Choice C is the best option. The norm under consideration is the punctuation of a supplemental element within a phrase. The comma after "sisters" is used with the comma after "Butterflies" to separate the supplemental part "a fictionalized account of the lives of the Mirabal sisters" from the remainder of the phrase. This supplemental part describes the novel In the Time of the Butterflies, and the use of commas shows that it might be omitted without damaging the sentence's grammatical consistency.

QUESTION 22

Choice B is the best option. In this context, "shift, partly because of its massive size:" is the most appropriate choice. It accurately describes the action needed to resolve the issue of the Ever Given being stuck, while also acknowledging the vessel's size. The colon introduces the following explanation or detail effectively.

QUESTION 23

Choice C is the best choice because it clearly identifies Tamatoa as the crab character and sets up the information about Jemaine Clement's voice role. The comma following "Tamatoa" separates the character name from the additional information, maintaining clarity and proper punctuation.

QUESTION 24

Choice C is the best option. The convention being examined is subject-verb agreement. The plural verb "underlie" has the same number as the plural subject "frameworks."

QUESTION 25

Choice C is the best option. The convention being examined is the employment of verb forms within sentences. This option appropriately forms an extra sentence expressing the emotion Serra intends his sculptures to elicit by combining the commas after "Serra" and "environment" and employing the nonfinite present participle "intending". This extra phrase appears between the noun phrase it modifies ("American abstract artist Richard Serra") and the finite present tense verb ("assembles"), which serves as the sentence's primary verb and describes Serra's actions.

QUESTION 26

Choice B is the best option. "Next" logically indicates that the activity in this line—the water spraying—is the next phase in the resurfacing process, following the ice scraping indicated in the preceding sentence.

QUESTION 27

Choice C is the best option. "Later" logically indicates that the information in the sentence—that Gomez founded a platform for others to share stories about their immigration experiences—occurs later in a chronological sequence of events than the previous information about Gomez winning his first storytelling competition in 2014.

SECTION 2

MODULE 1: MATH TEST

QUESTION 1

Choice C is correct. Distribute the 3 and simplify: $3(x + 5) - 6 = 3x + 15 - 6 = 3x + 9$

QUESTION 2

Choice B is correct. Substitute the equation $x = y - 3$ into the second equation: $(y - 3) + 2y = 6$ $3y - 3 = 6$ $3y = 9$ $y = 3$ Substitute $y = 3$ into the first equation: $x = 3 - 3 = 0$ Therefore, the solution is $(x, y) = (0, 3)$.

QUESTION 3

Choice D is correct. Simplify the expression: $(5 + 12i) - (9i^2 - 6i) = 5 + 12i - (-9 - 6i) = 5 + 12i + 9 + 6i = 14 + 18$, so this simplifies to: $14 + 18i$

QUESTION 4

Choice A is correct. Substitute -1 for x in the function: $f(-1) = ((-1)^2 - 6(-1) + 3) / (-1 - 1) = 1 + 6 + 3 / -2 = 10 / -2 = -5$

QUESTION 5

Choice C is correct. The camera equipment depreciates by $32,400 / 12 = $2,700 per year. After 4 years, the value of the equipment is: $32,400 - 4($2,700) = $32,400 - $10,800 = $21,600

QUESTION 6

Choice B is correct. Complete the square: $x^2 + 6x + 4 = x^2 + 6x + 9 - 9 + 4 = (x + 3)^2 - 5$

QUESTION 7

Choice B is correct. Let h be the number of additional hours Ken needs to work. Then his total pay for the week is: $10($8) + h($10) = $80 + $10h$ To save at least $270, this must be at least $300 (since he saves 90% of his pay): $80 + $10h ≥ $300 $10h ≥ $220 h ≥ 22 Therefore, Ken needs to work at least 22 additional hours, for a total of 10 + 22 = 32 hours.

QUESTION 8

Choice B is correct. The first inequality ensures that the total salary is no more than $9,700: $640x + 880y \leq 9{,}700$ The second inequality ensures that there are at least 10 directors in total: $x + y \geq 10$ The third and fourth inequalities ensure that there are at least 3 junior directors and at least 1 senior director: $x \geq 3$ $y \geq 1$

QUESTION 09

Choice A is correct. If the roots of the equation are 1, 3, and 5, then the equation can be factored as: $ax^3 + bx^2 + cx + d = a(x - 1)(x - 3)(x - 5)$ Therefore, one factor of the equation is $x - 1$.

QUESTION 10

Choice D is correct. Simplify the expression: $(x^{-2} \cdot y^{1/2}) / (x^{2/3} \cdot y^{-1}) = (x^{-2} \cdot y^{1/2}) \cdot (x^{-2/3} \cdot y) = x^{-2 - 2/3} \cdot y^{1/2 + 1} = x^{-8/3} \cdot y^{3/2} = (y^{3/2}) / (x^2 \cdot x^{2/3}) = (y \cdot y^{1/2}) / (x^2 \cdot x^{1/3})$

QUESTION 11

Choice B is correct. The function $f(x) = (x+3)(x+1)$ is a quadratic function, which indeed forms a parabola when graphed.

To find the vertex of a parabola, we can use the formula $x = -b/(2a)$ when the quadratic is in the form $ax^2 + bx + c$.
Let's expand $f(x) = (x+3)(x+1)$: $f(x) = x^2 + 4x + 3$
Now we have it in the form $ax^2 + bx + c$, where: $a = 1$ $b = 4$ $c = 3$
Using the formula $x = -b/(2a)$: $x = -4 / (2(1)) = -4/2 = -2$
So, the x-coordinate of the vertex is -2.
Looking at our options: A) $-4 < x < -3$ B) $-3 < x < -1$ C) $-1 < x < 4$ D) $3 < x < 4$
We can see those -2 falls within the interval in option B: $-3 < x < -1$

QUESTION 12

Choice D is correct. Divide the numerator by the denominator using polynomial long division: $(x^2 - 2x - 5) / (x - 3) = (x + 1) - 2 / (x - 3)$

QUESTION 13

Choice A is correct. The perimeter of the base is $2x + 2(2.5x) = 7x$. The total of the height and base perimeter must be no more than 130: $60 + 7x \leq 130$ $7x \leq 70$ $x \leq 10$ Therefore, the width x must satisfy the inequality $0 < x \leq 10$.

QUESTION 14

Choice A is correct. Expand the right side of the equation: $1/3(x - k)(x + k) = 1/3(x^2 - k^2) = 1/3x^2 - 1/3k^2$ Set this equal to the left side and match coefficients: $1/2x^2 - 2 = 1/3x^2 - 1/3k^2$ $1/2 = 1/3$, so the equation is true for any value of x. Equating the constant terms: $-2 = -1/3k^2$ $k^2 = 6$ $k = \sqrt{6} \approx 2.45$ Of the given options, the closest value is 2.

QUESTION 15

Choice B is correct. The total number of dogs is 25. The number of dogs that are fed only dry food is 2. Therefore, the fraction of dogs that are fed only dry food is 2/25.

QUESTION 16

Choice B is correct. Distribute the negative sign in the second set of parentheses: $(x^2 - 3) - (-3x^2 + 5) = x^2 - 3 + 3x^2 - 5 = 4x^2 - 8$

QUESTION 17

Choice C is correct. Convert 6 meters to centimeters: 6 m = 600 cm Divide by the amount of tape needed per box: 600 cm / 3 cm per box = 200 boxes

QUESTION 18

Choice A is correct. Substitute each pair of values into the inequality: I. (1, 1): 5(1) - 3(1) < 4 simplifies to 2 < 4, which is true. II. (2, 5): 5(2) - 3(5) < 4 simplifies to -5 < 4, which is true. III. (3, 2): 5(3) - 3(2) < 4 simplifies to 9 < 4, which is false. Therefore, only pair I satisfies the inequality.

QUESTION 19

Choice B is correct. If x = -3 is a solution to the equation (ax + 3)^2 = 36, then: (a(-3) + 3)^2 = 36 (-3a + 3)^2 = 36 -3a + 3 = ±6 -3a = -3 or -9 a = 1 or 3 Of the given options, only a = -5 is a possible value for a.

QUESTION 20

Choice B is correct. The line of best fit appears to pass through the points (0.4, 5.5) and (2.0, 3.0). Using these points, the slope of the line is: m = (3.0 - 5.5) / (2.0 - 0.4) ≈ -1.56 The y-intercept is: b = 5.5 - (-1.56)(0.4) ≈ 6.12 The equation of the line is: y = -1.56x + 6.12 Substituting x = 1.2: y = -1.56(1.2) + 6.12 ≈ 4.25 Of the given options, the closest value is 4.1.

QUESTION 21

Choice A is correct. Solve the equation for ax + b: 9ax + 9b - 6 = 21 9ax + 9b = 27 ax + b = 3

QUESTION 22

Choice A is correct. Lani's workday is 8 hours, or 8 × 60 = 480 minutes. 15% of 480 minutes is: 0.15 × 480 = 72 minutes Convert 72 minutes to hours: 72 minutes = 72/60 hours = 1.2 hours

SECTION 2

MODULE 2: MATH TEST

QUESTION 1

Choice C is correct. The angles in a triangle sum to 180°. Therefore: 45 + x + 35 = 180 x + 80 = 180 x = 100

QUESTION 2

Choice B is correct. Set up a proportion to solve the problem: 50 coins / 3.5 inches = x coins / 8 inches 50/3.5 = x/8 x = 50 * 8/3.5 ≈ 114.3 Round up to the nearest coin to get 115 coins so closest is option B.

QUESTION 3

Choice D is correct. Solve the equation b/2 = 10 for b: b = 20 Substitute this value into the equation a - b = 12: a - 20 = 12 a = 32 Therefore, a + b = 32 + 20 = 52.

QUESTION 4

Choice B is correct. The number of students who voted for the activity listed at the bottom of each bar in the provided bar graph is indicated by the height of each bar. The height of the bar in activity 3 is between 35 and 40. Stated otherwise, there were around 35 to 40 kids who selected activity 3. 39 is the only number of the options that falls between 35 and 40. 39 students choose action 3 as a result.

QUESTION 5

Choice A is correct. To calculate the percentage, divide 75 by 300 and multiply by 100: (75 / 300) * 100 = 0.25 * 100 = 25%.

QUESTION 6

Choice B is correct. To solve the equation 2x^2 = 36 * 25, first divide both sides by 2: x^2 = 18 * 25 = 450. Then, take the square root of both sides: x = √450 = 30.

QUESTION 7

Choice D is correct. The phrase "3 more than 8 times a number x" can be translated into the algebraic expression 8x + 3. Setting this equal to 83 gives the equation 8x + 3 = 83.

QUESTION 8

Choice A is correct. In the function f(t) = 100 + 25t, the coefficient 25 represents the rate of change, or the amount by which the function value increases for each unit increase in t. In this context, t represents the number of monthly deposits, so 25 is the amount by which Hana's bank account increases with each monthly deposit.

QUESTION 9

Answer is 9. The customer spent $27 on oranges at $3 per pound. To find the number of pounds purchased, divide the total cost by the price per pound: 27 / 3 = 9. So the customer purchased 9 pounds of oranges.

QUESTION 10

Answer is $10. Nasir bought 9 storage bins at the same price, and after using a $63 coupon, the total cost was $27. Let's say the original price of each bin was x dollars. Then:

9x - 63 = 27

Add 63 to both sides: 9x = 90

Divide both sides by 9: x = 10

Therefore, the original price for 1 storage bin was $10.

QUESTION 11

Choice A is correct. The table shows a linear relationship between x and f(x). To find the equation, we can use the slope-intercept form y = mx + b. The slope m can be calculated using any two points: m = (35 - 32) / (2 - 1) = 3. The y-intercept b is the value of f(x) when x = 0, which is 29. Therefore, the equation is f(x) = 3x + 29.

QUESTION 12

Choice C is correct. In similar right triangles, corresponding angles are congruent. Since angle Q corresponds to angle S, they have the same measure. Therefore, the measure of angle S is also 72°.

QUESTION 13

Choice D is correct. The scatterplot shows a positive linear relationship between x and y. The equation of a line is typically written in slope-intercept form, y = mx + b, where m is the slope and b is the y-intercept. Among the answer choices, only D) y = 9.4 - 0.9x is in this form with a positive slope and positive y-intercept, which matches the general trend of the data.

QUESTION 14

Choice A is correct. By figuring out the value of b when 16 r in the provided equation, one may get the number of birds. The following equation produces 0 b 2.5 0 b when 16 is substituted for r: 2.5 516 80 b or 2.5 80 80 b. 80 is subtracted from both sides of. Find the result by dividing both sides of this equation by 2.5. Consequently, the company may care for 0 birds on a given day if it caters for 16 reptiles on that particular day.

QUESTION 15

Choice C is correct. The equation of a line can be expressed in the form y = mx + b, where m represents the slope of the line, and b is the y-intercept (the point where the line crosses the y-axis). The line shown in the given context passes through the points (8, 0) and (0, 8). Since the line passes through (8, 0), we can substitute these values into the equation y = mx + b to get 0 = m(8) + b, which implies that b = -8.

The slope (m) of a line passing through two points (x1, y1) and (x2, y2) can be calculated using the formula m = (y2 - y1) / (x2 - x1). Substituting the points (8, 0) and (0, 8) into this formula, we get m = (8 - 0) / (0 - 8) = 8/(-8) = -1.

Therefore, an equation of the line shown is y = (-1)x + (-8), which can be simplified to y = -x - 8.

QUESTION 16

Answer is 1/5. When x/8 = 5, we can use the reciprocal property of division to find the value of 8/x. The property states that if a/b = c, then b/a = 1/c.

In this problem, a = x, b = 8, and c = 5. Applying the property:

If x/8 = 5, then 8/x = 1/5

So, the value of 8/x is 1/5.

QUESTION 17

Answer is the values of y = 80. Let's solve the system of equations again carefully.

Given equations: 24x + y = 48 6x + y = 72

Subtracting the second equation from the first equation, we get: 24x + y = 48 6x + y = 72

18x = -24

Dividing both sides by 18, we get: x = -24/18 x = -4/3

Substituting the value of x = -4/3 into the second equation: 6(-4/3) + y = 72 -8 + y = 72 y = 72 + 8 y = 80

The value of y is 80.

QUESTION 18

Choice D is correct. In the previous explanation, I made a mistake when solving for the y-intercept (b) using the given point (9, 10).

Let me rework it carefully:

The slope of the line is -1/3. The line passes through the point (9, 10).

Substituting these values into the equation y = mx + b: 10 = (-1/3)(9) + b 10 = -3 + b b = 10 + 3 b = 13

Therefore, the equation of the line with a slope of -1/3 and passing through the point (9, 10) is: y = (-1/3)x + 13.

QUESTION 19

Choice B is correct. In the function f(x) = 206(1.034)^x, x represents the number of years after 1957. So x = 5 corresponds to the year 1962. The statement "f(5) is approximately equal to 243" means that the value of the function f when x = 5 (i.e., in 1962) is approximately 243 dollars.

QUESTION 20

Choice B is correct. The ratio of length to width is 35:10, which can be reduced to 7:2. This means that the length is always 7/2 times the width. If the width increases by 7 units, then the length must increase by 7/2 times 7 units to maintain the ratio. This is equal to 24.5 units.

QUESTION 21

Choice A is correct. The perimeter of a square is 4 times its side length. If the perimeter of square Q is 176 inches greater than the perimeter of square P, and the side length of square P is x, then:

Perimeter of square Q = Perimeter of square P + 176 4(x + a) = 4x + 176, where a is the amount added to each side of square P 4x + 4a = 4x + 176 4a = 176 a = 44

So each side of square Q is x + 44. The area of a square is the square of its side length, so the area of square Q is $(x + 44)^2$. Therefore, the function that gives the area of square Q is $f(x) = (x + 44)^2$.

QUESTION 22

The proper choice is C. By dividing both sides of the following equation by 2, we obtain the expression $(14x/14y) = [2\sqrt{(w+19)}]/2$ or $x/y = \sqrt{(w+19)}$. Since it is assumed that each of the variables is positive, if we square both sides of this equation, we have the equivalent equation $(x/y)^2 = w+19$. By subtracting 19 from both sides of the equation, we have $(x/y)^2 - 19 = w$, which can be rewritten as $w = (x/y)^2 - 19$.

To get the
500 Flashcards,
and **10 Online Practice
Tests** to Excel
in Your Exams

SCAN HERE

PART 5

Beyond the Test

Congratulations on completing the SAT! Taking this important test is a major milestone in your academic journey. Now that the exam is behind you, it's time to focus on what comes next. In this final section, we'll guide you through analyzing your test results and planning your next steps to make the most of your SAT performance.

Analyzing Your Test Results

UNDERSTANDING YOUR SCORES

A few weeks after your test date, you will receive your official SAT score report. This report provides a detailed breakdown of your performance in each section of the exam. Let's take a closer look at what these scores mean and how to interpret them effectively.

The SAT is divided into two main sections: Evidence-Based Reading and Writing (EBRW) and Math. Each section is scored on a scale from 200 to 800 points, with a total possible score ranging from 400 to 1600. Your score report will show your individual section scores as well as your overall composite score.

In addition to these primary scores, you will also receive subscores and cross-test scores. Subscores provide more granular information about your performance in specific skill areas within each section. For example, the EBRW section includes subscores for Command of Evidence, Words in Context, Expression of Ideas, and Standard English Conventions. These subscores can help you identify your strengths and weaknesses within each broader subject area.

Cross-test scores, on the other hand, measure your ability to apply your knowledge and skills across multiple subjects. The two cross-test scores are Analysis in History/Social Studies and Analysis in Science. These scores demonstrate how well you can interpret and synthesize information from a variety of academic disciplines.

PERCENTILES AND BENCHMARKS

Your score report will also include percentile ranks, which show how your scores compare to those of other test-takers. Percentiles range from 1 to 99 and indicate the percentage of students who scored at or below your level. For instance, if your Math score falls in the 75th percentile, this means that you performed better than 75% of all test-takers in that section.

Additionally, the College Board provides college and career readiness benchmarks for each section of the SAT. Meeting or exceeding these benchmarks suggests that you are likely to succeed in entry-level college courses in the corresponding subject areas. The current benchmarks are 480 for EBRW and 530 for Math. Keep in mind that these benchmarks are general guidelines and may vary depending on the specific requirements of the colleges and programs you are interested in.

COMPARING YOUR SCORES TO YOUR GOALS

Now that you have a better understanding of your SAT scores, it's time to evaluate them in the context of your personal goals and aspirations. Consider the following questions:

1. How do your scores align with the average scores of admitted students at your target colleges?

2. Do your scores meet or exceed the college readiness benchmarks set by the College Board?

3. Are there any specific score requirements for scholarships or academic programs you are interested in?

Researching the average SAT scores and admissions requirements for your desired colleges and programs will give you a clearer picture of where you stand. If your scores fall within or above the typical range for your target schools, you can feel confident about your performance. However, if your scores are lower than expected, don't be discouraged. There are still many ways to strengthen your college applications and achieve your goals.

DECIDING WHETHER TO RETAKE THE SAT

After analyzing your scores and comparing them to your objectives, you may be wondering whether you should retake the SAT. This decision depends on several factors, including:

1. The score improvements you realistically believe you can make.

2. The time and resources you have available for further test preparation.

3. The application deadlines for your target colleges and programs.

If you feel that your scores do not accurately reflect your abilities and that you have the potential to improve significantly, retaking the SAT may be a good option. However, it's essential to have a clear plan for how you will approach your test preparation differently to achieve better results.

Keep in mind that while the SAT is an important component of your college application, it is not the only factor that admissions committees consider. Your high school grades, extracurricular activities, essays, and letters of recommendation also play crucial roles in showcasing your strengths and potential. Ultimately, the decision to retake the SAT should be based on a careful evaluation of your individual circumstances and goals.

Planning Your Next Steps After the SAT

FOCUSING ON YOUR HIGH SCHOOL PERFORMANCE

Regardless of your SAT scores, it's crucial to maintain a strong academic performance throughout your high school career. Your grades and coursework are the foundation of your college application and demonstrate your commitment to learning and growth.

Continue to challenge yourself with rigorous classes, such as Advanced Placement (AP) or International Baccalaureate (IB) courses, when available. These classes not only help you develop critical thinking and problem-solving skills but also show college admissions officers that you are prepared for the demands of higher education.

In addition to your grades, consider participating in extracurricular activities that align with your interests and passions. Engaging in clubs, sports, volunteer work, or creative pursuits can help you develop leadership skills, foster relationships with peers and mentors, and demonstrate your unique talents and perspectives.

RESEARCHING AND REFINING YOUR COLLEGE LIST

With your SAT scores in hand, you can now refine your college search and create a well-balanced list of potential schools. Consider the following factors when evaluating colleges:

1. Academic programs and majors that align with your interests and goals

2. Admissions requirements, including average SAT scores and high school GPA

3. Financial aid opportunities, such as scholarships, grants, and work-study programs

4. Campus culture, size, and location

5. Extracurricular activities and support services that cater to your needs and interests

Aim to create a list that includes a mix of "reach," "target," and "safety" schools. Reach schools are those where your academic profile falls slightly below the average for admitted students, while target schools are those where your profile closely matches the typical admitted student. Safety schools are those where your profile exceeds the average admissions requirements, making your chances of acceptance quite high.

As you research colleges, attend college fairs, virtual information sessions, and campus tours when possible. Engage with admissions representatives, current students, and alumni to gain a more comprehensive understanding of each school's unique offerings and atmosphere. These interactions can help you determine which colleges best align with your academic, social, and personal needs.

CRAFTING STRONG COLLEGE APPLICATIONS

Once you have finalized your college list, it's time to focus on creating compelling applications that showcase your strengths, experiences, and aspirations. The key components of your application include:

1. High school transcripts

2. SAT scores

3. Extracurricular activities and achievements

4. Personal essays

5. Letters of recommendation

When crafting your personal essays, strive to tell your unique story and convey your personality, values, and goals. Brainstorm topics that highlight your growth, resilience, and passion for learning. Remember that admissions officers read countless essays, so aim to create a narrative that is both engaging and authentic to your voice.

For your letters of recommendation, choose teachers, mentors, or counselors who know you well and can speak to your academic abilities, character, and potential. Provide them with your resume, personal statement drafts, and any other relevant information to help them craft a comprehensive and supportive letter.

As you work on your applications, be mindful of deadlines and requirements for each college. Create a timeline and checklist to ensure that you submit all necessary materials on time and in the appropriate format. Consider enlisting the help of your school counselor, teachers, or trusted mentors to review your applications and provide feedback before submission.

EXPLORING FINANCIAL AID OPTIONS

Financing your college education is a critical aspect of the application process. Begin by researching the various types of financial aid available, including:

1. Need-based aid, such as grants and scholarships based on your family's financial situation

2. Merit-based aid, which is awarded based on your academic, athletic, or artistic achievements

3. Federal and private student loans

4. Work-study programs that provide part-time employment opportunities to help offset college costs

To apply for need-based aid, you will need to complete the Free Application for Federal Student Aid (FAFSA). The FAFSA collects information about your family's income, assets, and other financial factors to determine your eligibility for federal grants, loans, and work-study programs. Many colleges also use the FAFSA to award their own institutional aid, so it's essential to submit this application as early as possible.

In addition to the FAFSA, some colleges may require you to complete the CSS Profile, a more detailed financial aid application administered by the College Board. Be sure to check the specific requirements for each school on your list and submit all necessary forms by the appropriate deadlines.

As you explore merit-based aid options, research scholarships offered by your target colleges as well as external organizations. Many scholarships are awarded based on academic achievement, community service, leadership, or other specific criteria. Begin your scholarship search early and apply for as many opportunities as possible to maximize your chances of receiving support.

PREPARING FOR THE TRANSITION TO COLLEGE

As you navigate the college application process, it's also important to start preparing for the transition to higher education. Consider the following steps to ensure a smooth and successful adjustment:

1. Develop strong time management and study skills to balance the increased academic demands of college coursework.

2. Engage in open conversations with your family about financial planning, budgeting, and any support they can provide during your college years.

3. Research the various resources and support services available at your target colleges, such as academic advising, tutoring, mental health counseling, and career services.

4. Connect with future classmates through social media groups, online forums, or admitted student events to begin building a support network before you arrive on campus.

Remember that the transition to college is a significant milestone that comes with both excitement and challenges. Be patient with yourself as you adapt to new academic, social, and personal responsibilities. Seek out support from your family, friends, and campus resources whenever you need guidance or assistance.

Appendices

ADDITIONAL ONLINE RESOURCES FOR DIGITAL SAT PREP

1. Official College Board SAT Practice: https://www.khanacademy.org/SAT
-   Official practice tests, questions, and videos in partnership with Khan Academy
-   Personalized study plans and progress tracking
2. College Board SAT Suite of Assessments: https://collegereadiness.collegeboard.org/sat/practice
-   Official SAT practice tests, sample questions, and study tips
-   Information about test dates, registration, and scoring
3. Khan Academy SAT Prep: https://www.khanacademy.org/test-prep/sat
-   Comprehensive video lessons and practice exercises for all SAT sections
-   Personalized recommendations based on diagnostic tests and progress
4. Magoosh SAT Prep: https://magoosh.com/sat/
-   Video lessons, practice questions, and full-length practice tests
-   Mobile app for on-the-go studying
-   Email support from expert tutors
5. Princeton Review SAT Prep: https://www.princetonreview.com/college/sat-test-prep
-   Online self-paced and live online courses
-   Diagnostic tests, video lessons, and practice drills
-   Personalized homework and study resources
6. Kaplan SAT Prep: https://www.kaptest.com/sat
-   Live online and on-demand courses
-   Practice tests, custom quiz bank, and study plan
-   Books and mobile apps for additional study materials
7. Varsity Tutors SAT Prep: https://www.varsitytutors.com/sat-prep
-   Live online classes and private tutoring
-   Diagnostic tests, practice questions, and full-length exams
-   Free SAT resources, including practice tests and study guides
8. PrepScholar SAT Prep: https://www.prepscholar.com/sat/s/
-   Customized online prep program based on diagnostic test results
-   Video lessons, practice questions, and strategy guides
-   Score improvement guarantee
9. Testive SAT Prep: https://www.testive.com/sat/
-   Adaptive online learning platform
-   Personalized coaching and support
-   Full-length practice tests and performance analytics
10. CrackSAT.net: https://www.cracksat.net/
-   Free SAT practice tests, questions, and answer explanations

- Discussion forums for students to share tips and strategies
11. SAT Quantum: https://satquantum.com/
- AI-powered adaptive learning platform
- Personalized study plans and performance tracking
- Gamified exercises and challenges to boost engagement
12. UWorld SAT Prep: https://collegeprep.uworld.com/sat/
- Thousands of practice questions with detailed explanations
- Performance tracking and analytics
- Mobile app for convenient studying

Glossary of Key Terms

Accommodations: Special provisions made for students with disabilities to ensure fair and equal access to the Digital SAT.

Ace the Test: To achieve high scores or perform exceptionally well on the Digital SAT.

Adaptive Testing: A method of administering the Digital SAT where the difficulty of questions adapts to the student's performance, providing a more personalized assessment.

Calculator: A built-in digital tool available for the Math with Calculator section of the Digital SAT.

College Board: The organization responsible for developing and administering the SAT and other standardized tests.

Diagnostic Test: An initial practice test used to assess a student's strengths and weaknesses in Digital SAT content and skills.

Evidence-Based Reading and Writing (EBRW): One of the two main sections of the Digital SAT, which includes the Reading Test and the Writing and Language Test.

Experimental Section: An unscored section of the Digital SAT used to test new questions for future exams.

Graphing Calculator: A built-in digital tool, similar to the Desmos online calculator, available for the Math with Calculator section of the Digital SAT.

Grid-In Questions: Another term for Student-Produced Response Questions in the Math section of the Digital SAT.

Guess: To select an answer to a question on the Digital SAT without complete certainty, often used as a strategy when time is limited or the correct answer is not immediately apparent.

Hands-On Practice: Active engagement with practice questions and tests to develop skills and familiarity with the Digital SAT.

No-Calculator Section: A portion of the Math section on the Digital SAT where the use of a calculator is not permitted.

Omit: To leave a question blank on the Digital SAT, often as a time management strategy or when unsure of the correct answer.

Pacing: The rate at which a student progresses through the sections and questions of the Digital SAT, with the goal of completing all questions within the allotted time.

Passage-Based Questions: Questions on the Digital SAT that refer to a specific reading passage or pair of passages.

Percentile Rank: The percentage of test-takers who scored at or below a particular score.

Practice Tests: Full-length simulations of the Digital SAT used to familiarize students with the test format, content, and timing.

Process of Elimination: A test-taking strategy where a student eliminates clearly incorrect answer choices to increase the likelihood of selecting the correct answer.

Raw Score: The number of questions a student answers correctly on the Digital SAT.

Reading Test: A section of the Digital SAT that assesses reading comprehension and reasoning skills.

Reference Material: Formulas and other information provided within the Digital SAT interface for use during the test.

Registration: The process of signing up to take the Digital SAT on a specific test date.

Retesting: The option to take the Digital SAT again to improve scores.

Sat Prep: The process of preparing for the SAT through various methods such as studying content, practicing test-taking strategies, and taking practice tests.

Scaled Score: The final score on the Digital SAT, ranging from 400 to 1600, which is derived from the raw score.

Score Range: The range of scores a student can expect to receive based on their practice test results and performance consistency.

Score Report: A detailed breakdown of a student's performance on the Digital SAT, including scaled scores, percentile ranks, and subscores.

Scoring: The process of calculating a student's raw scores, scaled scores, and subscores based on their performance on the Digital SAT.

Section Scores: The scores for the two main sections of the Digital SAT: Evidence-Based Reading and Writing (EBRW) and Math.

Strategic Guessing: Making an educated guess on a difficult question by eliminating unlikely answer choices, rather than omitting the question entirely.

Student-Produced Response Questions: Math questions on the Digital SAT that require students to enter their answers directly, without selecting from multiple choices.

Study Plan: A structured approach to preparing for the Digital SAT, which includes setting goals, allocating study time, and focusing on specific content areas and test-taking strategies.

Subscore: A score that represents a student's performance on specific skill areas within the Digital SAT sections.

Test Day: The day on which the Digital SAT is administered.

Test-Day Jitters: Nervousness or anxiety experienced by students on the day of the Digital SAT.

Testing Irregularities: Any disruptions or issues that occur during the administration of the Digital SAT, such as technical problems or student misconduct.

Test-Taking Strategies: Techniques and approaches used to maximize performance on the Digital SAT, such as time management, process of elimination, and educated guessing.

Time Management: The ability to allocate and use time effectively during the Digital SAT to ensure the best possible performance.

Writing and Language Test: A section of the Digital SAT that assesses grammar, usage, and rhetorical skills in the context of passages.

Index

Made in United States
Orlando, FL
29 November 2024

54628056R00141